LONDON IN FLAMES

The Capital's History Through its Fires

Or the Impact and Impetus of London's Fires

ANNA MILF

Saw the fire grow...in a horrid, malicious, bloody flame,
not like the fine flame of an ordinary fire.

Samuel Pepys 3rd Sept. 1666

One of The London Pride Collection

Comerford & Miller

London in Flames first published in 1998 by
Comerford & Miller 36 Grosvenor Road, West Wickham, Kent, BR4 9PY
under their *London Pride Collection* Imprint.

UK Distributors. Central Books, 99 Wallis Road,London E11 5LN

Cover design: Ad Lib Design, London, N19 / (0171) 263-1531
Cover pictures Front: Chartered Insurance Institute. Back: London Fire and Civil Defence Authority.
Typeset: Simon Burgess Design, 6 Cook Road, Crawley, Sussex, RH10 5DJ
Printed and bound in Malaya.

A catalogue record for this book is available from the British Library.

IBSN 1 871204 12 7 hb
IBSN 1 871204 13 5 pb

Acknowledgements

A number of individuals and organisations, ranging from the Household Cavalry and Royal Armouries to Thames Water and the TUC, have been of great assistance in the preparation of this book. Several have provided unique information, invaluable illustrations or permitted photography on their premises. My grateful thanks are extended to them all, and in particular to:

Gordon White, David Williamson, Colin Easton and Barbara Hyde—LFCDA press office; Judy Seaborne, Graham de Core—LFCDA Library; John Rodwell, Roy Still—Fire Brigade Museum; Fire Service College; Kent Fire Brigade; Mick Wortley—Westerham Fire Brigade; Peter Woodman—Croydon Fire Brigade; Kent Fire Brigade; Northumberland Fire & Rescue Service; Andy Gilchrist—Fire Brigades Union; James Heaney—Insurance Institute of London; A P D Lancaster—Gan Insurance; Stewart Kidd—Fire Protection Association. Ged Ellis—Company of Firefighters; Robin Bawtree—Company of Carmen; Colin Middlemiss—Company of Watermen & Lightermen; Bob Coombs—Dennis Fire, Guildford; Fred Deakin—Morris Merryweather; Fred Redding—Selfridges Archive; Mrs J Faraday—John Lewis Partnership Archivist; Arding & Hobbs; Chartered Insurance Institute; Port of London Authority.

Sir David Burnett in connection with the Tooley St Fire; Rosemary Nicholson, Dr C Thacker—Museum of Garden History; Roger Appleby—Curator City of London Police Museum; Martin Cruwys—Group Archivist Royal & Sun Alliance; Margaret Saunders—Information Centre Manager, Commercial Union; Sheree Leeds—Norwich Union Museum; Nicholas Redman—Company Archivist Whitbread; Richard Nelson—Thorn Security.

Corporation of London; Guildhall Library; Oona Wills—London Museum picture library; London Library; Bernadette Haffner—Westerham Library; Daniel Maye—Librarian New York Fire Dept.

And finally, infinite gratitude to my husband, Alfred, for enduring my Luddite attachment to WordPerfect which only he could reconcile by disk, fax and e-mail with the publisher's state of the art computer technology.

In a book covering many centuries, historical facts can be elusive, vague or contradictory. Once in print, if only 1% can definitely be proven wrong, such errors will be pointed out soon enough. Having done all the historical research, picture research, photography and writing myself, any such errors are acknowledged in advance as my own, and apologies offered.

The Author

ANNA MILFORD's London in Flames is her third book about London, and her fourth of historic research. A qualified City of London guide and lecturer, she was born within the sound of Bow Bells, Past occupations include cruise boat cook, milliner's apprentice, solicitor's clerk and audience researcher for BBC/ITV. She has also survived the Black Chair as a TV 'Mastermind' contender on her chosen special subject the English Civil War.

She and her husband, a retired consulting civil engineer and active computer enthusiast, live in Kent near Chartwell and their twin sons are in banking and travel.

Anna is currently working on *A fired by Villainy, the incendiary history of arson*, and has returned to a long-deferred study of Ladies' Firsts, the first women in the professions. Shoehorned into any spare time is gardening, tennis, photography, speaking engagements and travel.

By the Same Author

Eye and Ear Witnesses – 350th Anniversary English Civil War
Lord Mayors Of London – 800 Years, Published by Comerford & Miller
Ring The Bells Of London Town
Slay Us A Dragon (for children)

LONDON IN FLAMES

Foreword

Foreword

Fire, variously described as man's oldest friend yet his greatest enemy, remains as much an enigma today as it was in Roman times when the first recorded firefighters, the vigiles, patrolled the encampments of early London.

The metropolis has been the scene of many great conflagrations, many of them well-documented by contemporary diarists who, without exception, marvelled at the all-consuming ferocity and hunger of this most spectacular of elements.

Even as we approach the Millennium, with all the benefits that the rapid growth in technological development has brought to modern society, fire remains an ally to most of us yet a deadly foe for the unfortunate few.

Anna Milford sub-titles her book 'the impact and impetus of London's fires' which could, in effect, be the modus operandi of any Chief Officer of the London Fire Brigade, charged as we are with the responsibility of protecting those who live and work in our great city or come as visitors.

We can never expect to tame fire but we can lessen its impact with the considerable benefit of hindsight and, this is my confirmed belief, by placing great importance on the assessment (and, thereby, the potential elimination) of risks. It is by looking at the risks themselves, planning to reduce the likelihood of those risks by becoming a reality and, finally, by training our firefighters to deal with those incidents that do occur in a safe and competent way that we will move progressively towards our concept of a 'safer city'.

It is more than a hope – perhaps belief would be a more appropriate word – that if a social history of the effects of fire on London is written a century from now observers will look back to the Millennium as the dawning of an age when, if you will excuse the pun, it could be said that fire, if not meeting its master, at least met its match.

Brian Robinson CBE, OStJ(OB), QFSM, FIFireE,
Chief Fire Officer and Chief Executive,
London Fire and Civil Defence Authority.

INTRODUCTION

Preventing the Mischiefe of Fire by Negligence, Treason or Otherwise

The world's great cities have always burned, but London has gone up in flames more frequently, and more spectacularly, than most.

The devastation of the Great Fire is less astonishing than the fact that it had not happened many times before. That 1666 claims centre stage as the *only* significant London fire until the 1940 Blitz is due to contemporary diarists, citizens, clerics, bigots and a schoolboy whose accounts overshadow all other fires throughout its history. Urban conflagrations were actually so commonplace that only the most notable were even recorded until the 18th Century. Victorian inventories show scores of deaths and millions of pounds worth of fire damage annually, many in warehouses, garment factories, mills and docks. Iron ships were as vulnerable as wooden ones, with scuttling often the only way to extinguish burning hold cargoes.

Four times the blazing destruction of London has been deliberate. Boadicea's tribesmen swept down on Londinium in 61AD, reducing it to ashes. Vengeful peasants in revolt against the 1381 poll tax fired Southwark, butchered the Archbishop of Canterbury and made a bonfire of the vanities of the Palace of the Savoy. In 1780, London was terrorised by the anti-Catholic frenzy whipped up by Lord George Gordon when drunken rioters burned suspected papists' property, fired Newgate, released the felons and attacked the Bank of England. The Blitz was the last, and longest, ordeal by fire.

Fires destroyed much that was irreplaceable but also a great deal ripe for oblivion. No ordinances forbidding timber and thatch had the impact on Tudor and Stuart London of the building regulations imposed, and obeyed, after the Great Fire. Nor could any Edwardian town planning scheme have levelled such swathes of the capital as the Blitz.

London glows in the light of its fiery past. Gog and Magog stand guard in Guildhall; the City's survival and renewal symbolised by the phoenix depicted on Magog's shield. Another phoenix features as the crest of the Blacksmiths, while salamanders support the arms of the Ironmongers, both Companies adept with fire and iron. The Chartered Insurance Institute displays another of these mythical fire dwellers as does the Company of Firefighters.

William the Conqueror ordered the curfew and in 1189 London's first mayor ordered party walls of stone but as late as the Great Fire, most houses were still of wood and many thatched. Carelessness, then as now, caused most fires: candles, lamps, embers, chimneys and craftsmen's furnaces and braziers, forerunners of errant blowtorches. Lightning struck more than once and, when St Paul's tower burned in 1561, argument raged over the impiety of quelling the fire of God's wrath. The cry of the night bellman, *Take care of your Fire and Candle—be charitable to the Poor—pray for the Dead,* fell mainly on deaf ears on all counts. The City Fathers continually imposed rules, regulations and fines to mitigate fire danger but Londoners opted to live over a powder keg rather than obey laws passed for their own good. Fiercely independent citizens were prepared to see their shops robbed or burned down rather than submit to any interfering, arbitrary force for the protection of the community.

Not that the capital lacked fire precautions, only effective ones. Every parish kept buckets, fire hooks and ladders in the church porch, and later a wooden fire engine with a list of *stout men* to operate it but with no central control or liaison between parishes these were useless in a real emergency. Nonetheless they remained in force until mid-19th century.

Trade powered London's expansion and prosperity. Merchant Adventurers were well established by Tudor times, soon followed by the Muscovy Company (furs), Turkey Company, Royal Africa Company and Guinea Company (gold, ivory, cocoa, slaves) and Merchants of Virginia (tobacco). Founded in 1600 was the greatest of all, the East India Company, and yet to come were the Hudson's Bay Company (furs) and South Seas Company (financial bubbles). Most of these specialised in the import and export of highly combustible commodities.

A 1600 list records *25 cities and 641 great townes* in the kingdom of which only Bristol, Norwich and York reached 30,000 inhabitants. The maps of Wyngaerde (1550) and Hollar (1647) show a century's tentacle growth of London, by the latter date crammed with 300,000 citizens and rivalled only by Paris and Constantinople. The capital did enjoy a primitive water supply but was served by no fire brigade, no police force and no insurance company.

During the Civil War, the Lord Mayor published *Seasonable Advice for preventing the Mischiefe of Fire by Negligence, Treason or Otherwise,* advising citizens to dowse household fires with *milk, urine, sand, earth or dirt.* A glimmer of communal responsibility shone in the command that each *Parish to have a Great Squirt on wheels* and be ready to lend assistance in neighbouring areas. Some of these inadequate extinguishers were exported to New England, already plagued by urban fires of its own.

If trade followed the flag, fire followed trade. Everything linked to shipping was inflammable: timber planking, masts, hemp, ropes, rigging, sails, tar and turpentine, with swinging oil lamps between decks and braziers or open fires for working iron or heating tools. Loaded ships were moored in mid-stream or double and tripled berthed alongside wharves with goods stacked from cellar to attic in towering lines of warehouses. Increasing quantities and variety of cargoes flowed up the Thames, bringing in increasing customs revenues little of which was spent to minimise, let alone prevent, outbreaks of fire in the docks.

The 19th Century was little better overseas although fire brigades and insurance companies were now pooling their knowledge and experience. Destructive fires ravaged Spanish Town Trinidad (1808), Moscow (1812), Washington (1814), Quebec (1815 and1865), Constantinople (1826) and (1865), New York (1835), Hamburg (1842), Montreal (1852), Manila (1865), Chicago (1871), Boston (1872). American prairie fires and Australian bush fires caused recurrent disasters.

One beneficial outcome of the Great Fire was the fledgling fire offices—forerunners of the mighty Commercial Union, Eagle Star, Guardian Royal Exchange, Norwich Union, Royal & Sun Alliance. Employing Thames watermen as firefighters, these independent insurance brigades were finally amalgamated into the London Fire Engine Establishment in 1833. In 1861 their Chief Officer James Braidwood, killed in the Tooley St fire, was succeeded by Captain Eyre Massey Shaw and the LFEE become the Metropolitan Fire Brigade in 1866, exactly two centuries after the Great Fire.

Nothing, except a riot, brought Londoners into the streets like a spectacular fire. Its allure is pagan, an elemental force feeding off its own destruction, consuming the very air in a roaring, stifling inferno. Even when dowsed in a sullen hiss of steam, the flames are only thwarted, not defeated, and will spring up again elsewhere—and so will the *multitude of idle gazers*. The records are a dismal catalogue of bystanders burned, scalded, engulfed, choked, suffocated, crushed and trampled. Equally constant are complaints of crowds hampering and distracting the firefighters, blocking access to burning buildings, and causing chaos and confusion in the streets. In 1834 Turner and fellow Royal Academicians hired a boat for a better view of the blazing Houses of Parliament. Looters salvaging casks of rum were swamped by molten tallow from the Tooley Street warehouses.

When Prince of Wales, Edward VII loved *being in at a good fire* and kept his own uniform and silver helmet in a West End fire station. Queen Victoria was unamused and put a stop to her heir's hobby after he was nearly killed during the 1882 Alhambra theatre fire.

Mounting financial losses and death tolls failed to stop Londoners firing muskets up burning chimneys and drying gunpowder over braziers while employers flouted safety regulations and falsified insurance claims. Fire risks from overcrowding, jerry-building and social unrest were later fuelled by commercial and domestic usage of gas, electricity and petrol: hazards multiplied in the 20th Century by toxic chemicals and nuclear waste.

Saving of life was secondary to saving property, but gradually wheeled ladders and escape chutes became standard equipment, along with breathing apparatus. Matched greys from Tilling's of Peckham 'horsed' the LFEE and the capital's public transport into the 20th Century. Though steam was the wonder of the Victorian age, the first motorised appliance appeared in 1903. Merryweather of Manchester and Dennis Fire of Guildford are firms still providing appliances to the London Fire Brigade.

After inspecting the Pudding Lane outbreak, Lord Mayor Bludworth reckoned that *a woman could piss it out.* Almost three centuries later G V Blackstone, author of the *British Fire Service* and a chief fire officer, concluded that *firemen see so much of useless waste and tragedy that they look forward to the time when scientific advances and a more ready recognition of fire hazards by every inhabitant of the land will make their brigades redundant and things of the past.*

Bludworth and Blackstone were over-optimistic. Far from yielding to scientific advances fire thrives on them, as the explosions and blazes at Flixborough Chemical works (1974), King's Cross underground (1987), Piper Alpha oil rig (1988), Windsor Castle (1992) and in the Channel Tunnel (1996) demonstrated.

Television's 'London's Burning' dramatises the role of modern firefighters and emphasises the dangers of fire. A more sombre example of the perils is the Memorial Wall in Highgate Cemetery commemorating LFB officers killed on duty.

The capital is always at risk. Today it is better protected than ever by the London Fire and Civil Defence Authority (LFCDA), with around 6,000 operational firefighters and 500 vehicles. Their job is to tackle the blaze once alerted; that of the citizen is to: *Get out! Get the Brigade out! Stay Out!*

CHAPTER I

DARK AGES LIT BY FIRE

Vigiles, Aquarius, Siphonarius and all That

Julius Caesar did not come, see and conquer—*veni, vedi, vici*—in 55BC. Having questioned captured Gauls he came across the Channel, did not like what he saw of Britannia and went away again. His dismissive verdict was of somewhere *nobody except traders journeyed without good cause, and even they know only of the seacoast.*

Not until the Emperor Claudius invaded with elephants in 43AD did the Romans conquer Britain, laying out army camps, garrison towns, defensive walls, paved roads and triumphal arches. Since other cities of the Empire had fire fighters based on the *Vigiles* of Rome it is unlikely that London, Lincoln, York and Colchester were without similar protection, although no records exist.

The original *familia publica* were under the direction of a magistrate, but they were neither enthusiastic nor efficient. Being slaves they owned nothing themselves so lacked any incentive to notify the authorities of suspicious smoke and flames, or risk their lives saving a citizen's or patrician's house and chattels.

After a third of Rome was damaged by fire in 6AD, Emperor Augustus scrapped the *familia publica* and set the city's firefighters on a military footing, as the French *Sapeurs Pompiers* still are.

One cohort of *Vigiles*, 1000 men, were allocated to each of Rome's seven districts, an estimated 7000 firefighters for a city of around a million inhabitants. *Aquarius* was the officer in charge of water supplies; *siphonarius* responsible for the hoses; *unicinarius* for the fire hooks. The word *siphos* was in common use, referring in this context to one of the pneumatic and mechanical inventions of a 1ᵃ Century Greek mathematician, Hero of Alexandria. Equipment consisted of carts piled with fine-sounding *scalae, perticae, dolebrae, centones* and *formiones*, with *spongiae and secures* for mopping up afterwards, (ladders, poles, pickaxes, wet blankets and dampened wicker mats plus sponges and brooms). The corps' barracks, *excubitoria*, were also on army lines with gymnasia, baths and flush sanitation. As their reputation grew, *Vigiles* considered themselves the equal of legionnaires, and any freed man earned full citizenship after six years.

Like modern firefighters they spent only a small proportion of their time extinguishing fires. Training and servicing of equipment was important; officers and men were expected to follow a rota of night fire watching on the city walls. *Vigiles* were empowered to enter houses to check on likely fires and, if an owner's negligence caused a fire that damaged adjoining properties, the officer in charge could have him flogged. They were also responsible for pursuing absconding slaves and minding the clothes of those patronising the civic bath houses, *laconum*, but not rescuing *felix in arbor* (a cat up a tree).

The Romans chose the well-watered north bank of the Thames for Londinium, building a forum and basilica, the largest North of the Alps. All was enclosed within a square mile of wall around 200AD under Septimius Severus. Impregnable and fireproof, the wall was of masonry interspersed with mortared brick courses, and contained over a million cubic feet of stone, transported along the Medway and Thames from quarries near Maidstone.

Many of Britain's busiest roads still follow the lines of their Roman predecessors. Ermine Street lead to Lincoln, York and the Wall; Watling Street to St Albans, Chester and Anglesey and the Fosse Way to Aqua Sulis, modern Bath, and to Exeter. Plutarch describes them running *in a straight line, paved with hewn stone or laid with sand deposits, well stamped down. Where mountain torrents or ravines cut through the countryside viaducts were built and as both banks were made parallel the whole construction had a symmetrical and harmonious appearance.* These were military roads for marching legions not cavalry, carts or commerce, since their steep camber and smooth surface were rendered doubly hazardous by Britain's relentless rain.

Along the river were wharves and warehouses piled high with imported goods and native products ready for export. The Romans missed the sunshine and sophistication of their native land, so trade was brisk in wine, oil, glassware, jewellery, pottery, Samian ware and weapons. Shipped out were coal, cattle, hunting dogs, silver, tin, hides and particularly fair-haired, blue-eyed slaves. Roman technical knowledge extended to central heating by underfloor and wall ducts of hot air fed by exterior wood-fuelled furnaces, a frequent cause for calling out the *Vigiles*. Bathrooms had hot water, latrines being multi-seated and water-flushed. All these home improvements, so desirable in a damp, cold land, disappeared for fifteen hundred years when the Empire fell.

Tacitus referred to *Londinium, which though undistinguished by the name of a colony, was much frequented by merchants and trading vessels and was a great centre of commerce.* If by *copia negotiatorum et commeatuum maxime celebre negotiatorum* he meant dealers or middlemen, rather than simple buyers and sellers, it validates London's claim as a centre for international trade.

Less than twenty years after Claudius' invasion, Londinium and the south of England were pacified and co-existing with the invaders. Elsewhere the tribes were still hostile, notably in East Anglia where the dying king had bequeathed the Iceni lands to Emperor Nero. An uprising led by his flame-haired widow was savagely put down and, according to Tacitus, the queen was flogged and her daughters raped. Within months a vengeful Boadicea advanced on the centre of alien power and its collaborationist populace, devastating the garrison town of Colchester en route.

The Roman commander heeded *neither the tears nor the entreaties of the stricken citizens* and withdrew, leaving them to be *massacred, hanged, burnt and crucified.* Laden with plunder, the Iceni then burned St Albans, increasing their alleged toll of slaughter to 70,000. But they were ambushed and massacred by the legions on the way home and, choosing death rather than capture, Boadicea took poison. Three years later, Nero's Rome went up in spectacular pyrotechnics to an imperial, musical accompaniment.

That Londinium rose again with speed and splendour from the ashes was mainly due to a new governor's insistence on reconciliation, rather than revenge. During Hadrian's reign, in 100AD, a second fire destroyed the new city of quarried stone, brick, tile and imported marble, interspersed with the wattle and daub huts of the natives. Twenty feet below the streets two distinct layers of blackened rubble and ash mixed with crushed red brick and mortar show the scale of these Boadicean and Hadriatic fires.

Mid-3rd Century Londinium, by now called 'Augusta', boasted the forum and basilica in Leadenhall, the governor's palace by Cannon Street, public baths on Huggin Hill, as well as the Temple of Diana on Ludgate Hill, an underground Temple of Mithras and an amphitheatre discovered in 1985, adjacent to Guildhall.

All this glory was doomed when Alaric the Visigoth, an Arian Christian, advanced on the gates of Rome in 410. The legions were hastily withdrawn from Britain, the Romano-Britons left to their fate despite the desperate plea that:

The barbarians drive us into the sea,
and the sea drives us back to the barbarians.

Picts and Scots surged over Hadrian's wall, and Germanic hordes devastated East Anglia and Kent by fire and sword. London was then cut off not only from the sea but its vital hinterland, driving the inhabitants to the brink of starvation, and flight. The city may well have been abandoned for five or six generations, with all vestige of civic practices, customs, street plan, religion and personal names being lost. The *Anglo Saxon Chronicle* makes no mention of London, despite relating events in York, Chester, Gloucester and Bath. Nor is there much archaeological 'dark earth' to mark this mysterious period.

But how dark were the Dark Ages, peopled as they were by Angles, Saxons, Jutes, Vortigern, King Arthur, Hengist and Horsa? London must have recovered quickly, since Pope Gregory sent missionaries to *reconvert* the islanders as early as 597. Another pope appointed Mellitus as Bishop of London in 680. In his Northumberland monestry, Bede, the meticulous Geordie historian, penned his *Ecclesiastical History of the English People* in the 8th Century, saying that in 604 *King Ethelbert built a church dedicated to the holy apostle Paul*, the same Saxon church that St Erkenwald rebuilt after it burned down.

Vikings swept across the country in mid-9th Century, overrunning the North, East Anglia, Mercia and Kent. London did not escape fire and pillage then, nor when the Norsemen returned with a great fleet a century later. Buying them off with Danegeld led to both repeated attacks and further extortion; English silver coins of this era still turn up in Scandinavian digs.

A century later England was a prosperous, united kingdom, with relative peace on the borders of Wales and the North. London was a walled city of merchants' houses, thriving wharves, markets and many churches, including St Paul's and the stone-built Abbey of St Peter on Thorney Island. It had its own limited self-government headed by the Bishop and Port-Reeve and a folkmoot of citizens was held thrice-yearly at Paul's Cross. It was ripe for the Norman Conquest in 1066.

Though the *Vigiles* were not even a distant memory, London had to wait exactly eight hundred years for the formation of the Metropolitan Fire Brigade in 1866.

CHAPTER 2

MEDIEVAL LONDON

The holy church of St Paul, the episcopal see of London, burnt down.

Unlike his Norse ancestors, the Conqueror aimed to take over the capital as a going concern, not a blazing ruin, so he came to terms with its rulers.

His charter of 1067 in the Guildhall archives states: *I, William the King, greet William the Bishop, and Godfrey the Portreeve, and all the burgesses within London, French and English friendly. I acquaint you, that I will that ye be all the laws worthy that were in King Edward's day. And I will that every child be his father's heir, and after his father's day. And I will not suffer that any man to do you any wrong. God preserve you.*

During his coronation in the Abbey, nervous guards mistook acclaim from those inside as the signal to those outside to attack. After slashing into the sullen crowd, they set fire to the nearest houses, almost destroying the city William had been at such pains to inherit intact. Alarmed, and as a warning against any hint of rebellion, William constructed a moated fortress on the riverside, giving rise to the warning that the *Tower is to the Wall as the padlock to the chain.*

Fire was an ever-present danger in medieval Europe—regrettable, but inevitable, so only the most devastating conflagrations rated a mention in civic records. This lack of identifiable outbreaks is no proof that one community was better protected against the flames than another.

The City wall was impervious to fire or flood, massive Norman masonry rising from indestructible Roman foundations. The old gates remained, Aldgate leading to the fields of Essex, breadbasket of the City. The Walbrook flowed from Finsbury marshes beneath the postern of Moorgate, and Ludgate gave access to the Fleet and the burial grounds without the wall. Of any Roman gridiron street pattern few traces remained, except the road running from Leadenhall through Cheapside to St Paul's, and continuing Eastwards as Newgate Street and Holborn to distant Tyburn.

The Normans ended the dedication of churches to Saxon or Norse saints, so there were no more Erkenwalds or Osyths. Among those surviving, though rebuilt or repaired after fires and Blitz damage, are St Olave Hart Street, St Magnus the Martyr, three St Botolphs, St Edmund the King and the IRA-bombed St Ethelburga.

New to England was the 'ordeal by fire'. Long before Chaucer's Pardoner with his pigs bones, relics had acquired a bad name; the ordeal involved placing the saint's fingernail, knuckle or hair in a fire for a specified time. If the fragments burned they were fraudulent, if not the relics were piously replaced in the church. Most went up in flames!

So too did the cathedral, for the third time. *The holy church of St Paul, the episcopal see of London, was burnt down, as well as many other churches and the largest and fairest part of the whole city.* The rebuilding took decades and incorporated many alterations, with the spire of lead-sheathed timber heightened to 489' in 1315.

Wharves stretched below London Bridge towards Billingsgate and the Tower and westward, accessible through the drawbridge, from Dowgate and Queenhithe to beyond Westminster. A wharf ran parallel to the river while a hithe was a small dock set at right angles with a barrier to close it off for security—hence Rotherhithe, and Queenhithe whose dues funded the consort's pin money.

In 1212 a fire in Southwark spread to the wooden houses on London Bridge. It is the first account of Londoners flocking to a fire and, after crowding onto the Bridge for a better view, being trapped by the flames. Many were burned, suffocated or trampled and the arrival of rescue boats led to more deaths when *multitude so unadvisedly rushed, that the ships being drowned, they all perished.* Though the death toll was high, if hardly the thousands repeated by Stow, it did nothing to deter sightseers at subsequent fires.

Upkeep of the Bridge and the double row of houses on it came mainly from donations, added to later by bequests of money and property: *to God and the Bridge, an orchard in Dowgate* or *three tenements by Stocks Market.* The Bridge House Estates today maintains Blackfriars, Southwark, London and Tower Bridges from the rates and rents derived from modern buildings on these valuable sites.

The chapel on London Bridge, was dedicated to St Thomas, the *holy blissful martyr of Canterbury.* It contained the bones of its founder, William de Colechurch. A long campaign to have home-grown Thomas Becket made patron saint of the City, in place of St Paul, was thwarted by Rome.

London Bridge was not unique. Its contemporary over the Rhone also had houses, 22 arches and a chapel, housing the remains of its builder, Bénézet. Floods washed away most of it in 1669, making it impossible thereafter to dance *sur le pont d'Avignon.*

Henry Fitzailwyn, goldsmith, the first recorded Mayor, initiated London's first building regulations in 1189 by ordering that all new houses should have foundations and party walls of brick or stone. Some complied, most did not, and party walls of wood and plaster remained a major cause of the spread of fires for centuries.

Old street names show how trades huddled together in very small areas: Wood Street, Milk Street, Ironmonger Lane, Budge Row (furriers), Cloak Lane, Distaff

Lane and Shoe Lane. A serious fire in one area could ruin a high proportion of a single trade or craft. The Saxon 'chepe' continued in the two open markets of East Cheap and Cheapside.

Land was scarce and expensive, but ingenious builders almost doubled the floor space between ground and top storeys by 'jettying', projecting each additional storey out over the one below. The result was the picturesque, top-heavy, gabled street scenes familiar in London up to the Great Fire. Lovers could touch hands across the gaps, neighbour gossip to neighbour or hang out washing. However, the overhangs darkened the street below and created a wind funnel effect to fan the flames.

The poor huddled in dank, filthy back-to-back hovels with neither light, heat nor water, many adjacent to overflowing graveyards. These shacks were knocked up from flimsy weatherboard, nailed to a framework of rotten posts and daubed with pitch, rendering them barely waterproof but guaranteed fire prone. Derelict mansions of citizens who had moved up in the world were crammed from attics to cellars with thousands of families. These tenements were a scandal even then, with one modest building in Vintry ward holding fifteen single persons and eleven couples. Fires were frequent but houses were swiftly rebuilt or patched up from the stores of timber kept at designated sites for just such common occurrences.

The tallage, a tax imposed on municipalities by the crown, assessed London at a thousand marks annually, far in excess of Northampton's 300, York's 200, Winchester's and Lincoln's 150 and Canterbury's 100 marks. Large or small, every town and city was vulnerable to the flames, so only those causing great damage were recorded.

Seaborne trade was expanding and with it the dangers. By 1260 London had a *Brotherhood of Shipwrights*, who shortly expanded their yards downstream to Wapping and Ratcliffe. A Navigation Act of Richard II ordered all English goods to be carried in *English bottoms*, a source of friction with foreign commercial rivals for centuries to come. William Fitzstephen, Becket's friend, had marvelled at the wealth of goods to be seen along the wharves: *Arabia's gold, spices and incense, Scythia's keen weapons, oil of palm from Babylon, Nile's precious gems' China's bright shining silks and Gallic wines, Norway's warm peltry and the Russian sables.* Fitzstephen is a delightful, if unreliable, witness for whom contemporary London, around 1200, was far superior to anywhere else. He expressed his admiration for its elected Sheriffs and magistrates, God-fearing citizens and hospitality to strangers, as well as its water supply, sewers, licensed brothels and decorous funerals. He also believed accounts that proved *London is far older than Rome.*

Everything connected with shipping was a fire hazard. Yards were stacked with seasoned timber planking, masts, hemp, ropes, rigging, sails, tar and turpentine. Warehouses were timber framed and, if not thatched, were often roofed with wooden shingles. Swinging oil lamps hung between draughty decks and any heating of tools or materials was done over open fires or charcoal braziers. The permanent, secular, gain of the Crusades was the opening up of new routes to the Guinea Coast, India, China and Java. Religious goods included wax for candles, wine and oil for consecration, relics and souvenirs, despite the ordeal by fire. Amber from the Baltic and incense from Yemen found their way to Rome and throughout Christendom, the former being used for rosaries. Weekly fast days, and Lent, meant a demand for fresh fish caught locally, and salt fish imported in vast quantities from Scandinavia and Holland which led to the development of Billingsgate.

Every ship's master tried to find return cargoes to maximise profits. Precious metals, coral, pearls, silks, cloth, furs, grain, horses, slaves, incense, spices were all part of a two way trade. Baltic fleets traded amber and timber in return for French sea salt to cure herring. Cornish tin was in demand in one market, Milanese armour in another. Iceland traded fleeces, hides, pelts, fish, whale oil, falcons and brimstone to the Mediterranean. Pottery amphorae and wooden casks were sold on after consumption of their wine, beer or butter. Before abandoning ship due to fire or wreck, emergency lifebelts could be fashioned by emptying leather wine skins of their contents and inflating them with air.

Fleets of Venetian galleys put into Sandwich before dispersing on to London and the Netherlands. Catering to the English sweet tooth they carried sugar comfits, molasses and candied fruits, as well as buttons, beads, Maltese cotton and saltpetre. The men of Sandwich harried their rivals and burned the port of Honfleur before silting up of the Sussex harbour grounded their boats. The Venetians then moved to Southampton where the old galley house is now the maritime museum, with many mementoes of 'Titanic' among the historic exhibits.

Many ships earlier never made it home either. Tempests, shipwreck, pack ice, drownings and fire at sea all claimed their victims so that mariners, fishermen and watermen accounted nationwide for a significant number of male deaths.

London's foreign merchants lived in designated areas, most notably the Hanseatic Baltic merchants in the Thames-side Steelyard. This *guildhall of the men of Cologne* took its name from the steelyard, a ubiquitous weighing device, although the merchants were known as Easterlings. The Hansa towns stretched from Bremen, Hamburg and Lubeck to Danzig, Rostock and Tallin. Together they represented the most powerful, monopolistic trading group of the Middle Ages, bringing into England amber, precious metals, wax, pitch, hemp and plate armour.

Fitzstephen says that the spire of Old St Paul's dominated *thirteen churches belonging to convents, besides 126 lesser parish churches* in London. As one of

Europe's greatest gothic churches, it had a nave half as long again as Wren's replacement. Over the centuries it degenerated from a sacred place of worship to a profane centre of business; dubious business at that, with clergy complaining that merchants regarded services as tiresome interruption of commerce. Usury, money-lending, and simony were rife in the midst of *bargains, meetings, brawlings, murders and conspiracies*. Lawyers consulted their clients, masterless men sought employment, lovers kept assignations, idlers passed the time in gossip until *the noyse in it is like that of Bees. A land of roar and loud whisper.*

In February 1444, the *steple was set on Fier with Lightenings on Candilmas Even, but swiftly quenched*. How this remarkable feat of firefighting was achieved is unclear but it took twenty years to repair the damage.

The cathedral was also a short cut for *porters and carriers of ale, beer, bread, fish, flesh and mules, horses and other beasts*. In the cloisters and chantry chapels various merchants like booksellers, vintners, carpenters and trunkmakers set up shop, filling the vaults beneath with timber, rubble and rubbish. As a place of entertainment it offered such opportunities as climbing the tower to throw coins on loiterers below, lottery draws and displays of rope-walking between the buttresses.

Southwark gave access to London Bridge and was a law unto itself. By St Mary Overie stood the Bishop of Winchester's palace, surrounded by taverns, alehouses and brothels. Outside the jurisdiction of the City Fathers, though with an alderman for Bridge Without, Bankside attracted travellers, revellers, foreigners, *rogues, bawds and vagabonds*. An unruly mix, then as now.

The high mortality of the mid-14th Century Black Death indirectly caused the second major firing of London. Shortage of agricultural workers lead to greater mobility of the remaining labour force and the break-up of feudal serfdom, but not fast enough. Grievances against the poll tax exploded into the Peasants' Revolt of 1381, when armed mobs swarmed into London to terrorise it by fire and murder in a manner unknown since Boadicea's attack of 61AD. Prisoners released from the Clink and the Marshalsea swelled the ranks in Southwark. Having pleasured themselves with the trugging house whores and beaten up the whoremasters, the rioters fired the area and moved on.

Brothel inmates were known as Joan Jollibodies or Winchester Geese, since the Bishop owned the freeholds, and the Bell, Swan, Castle, Crane and Cardinal's Hat advertised themselves on their Thames-side walls. Attempts were made to regulate this irregular trade by commanding stew-holders to charge no more than fourteen pence rent weekly, hold no single woman that would leave her sin nor accept any nun or wife. Whores, it was suggested, should lie with a man all night before receiving payment. Mayor Walworth, who quelled the revolt by killing Wat Tyler at Smithfield, was rumoured to enjoy an undisclosed income, if not personal satisfaction, as a stakeholder in several of the burned brothels.

Once across the Bridge the mob attacked the Tower and hacked off the heads of Archbishop Sudbury and Lord Treasurer Hales, instigators of the poll tax. Next target was the Savoy, home of the last of the hated trio, young Richard II's wicked uncle, John of Gaunt, Duke of Lancaster. Thwarted by his absence, the peasants cast all the fabulous, Lancastrian treasures onto a bonfire. As looting was forbidden, and a man caught with a silver chalice under his jerkin was hurled with it into the flames. Many drunk themselves into a stupor and were left to perish in the cellars when the buildings collapsed on them. They were heard *calling and crying for seven days, but none came to help them,* nor attempted to quench the flames.

The Savoy Hotel stands on the part of old site, but all that remains of *time-honoured Lancaster's* five star palace is the Queen's Chapel of the Savoy.

Medieval European trade was inextricably linked with religion and the guilds were as powerful in Germany as in England. These exclusive companies combined godly observance, trading standards, apprenticeships in their 'mystery' or mastery, social welfare and a tightly closed shop. Exclusive they may have been, in the literal sense of keeping people out rather than letting them in: however, they were essential to London's development as a trading centre.

The Weavers (1155) and Saddlers (1272) are the oldest companies according to their charters but the twelve Great Companies given arbitrary precedence in 1515 are the Mercers, Grocers, Drapers, Fishmongers, Goldsmiths, Skinners, Merchant Taylors, Haberdashers, Ironmongers, Salters, Vintners, Clothworkers. Two of these dealt in metals, four in foodstuffs or wine and the other six were concerned with some form of cloth, fur or other wearing apparel.

Equally vital in feeding the capital were the Brewers, Bakers, Butchers and Poulterers. Wax Chandlers supplied the candles for churches and fine houses, and Tallow Chandlers the foul-smelling animal fat dips that lit the homes of the poor. The latter also regulated the trade in cooking oils and soap, flammable ingredients that led to frequent household fires.

The discoveries of Columbus, Vasco da Gama, Cabot and Magellan had a far reaching impact on London's trade with an influx of new goods from the East and the Americas. Surprisingly, tobacco, potatoes and sugar never merited separate livery companies for their exploitation neither later did tea, coffee and chocolate. Nor were there companies of grain dealers, coal importers or timber merchants, essential suppliers of raw materials and fuel to Bakers, Cutlers, Carpenters, Coopers, Turners, Armourers & Brasiers, Blacksmiths, Farriers and Wheelwrights.

The distribution of fuel was divided acrimoniously between the Carmen and the Woodmongers, the latter taking over coal supplies. In 1528, the Carmen were given authority over the wood wharves, leading to more disputes in which the Woodmongers temporarily gained supremacy. Arguments and fights continued until the City Fathers appointed Christ's Hospital as licenser of all carts, the fees devoted to the abandoned children in their care. After an uneasy alliance between 1605 and 1668 the companies separated again over disputed carrooms, precious parking spaces handed down from father to son, one or two of which remain extant. The Carmen, having finally seen off the Woodmongers, still have their carts licensed annually at Guildhall.

Liverymen continue to attend Common Hall to elect the Sheriffs and Lord Mayor, their companies administering charitable trusts. A few ancient companies remain actively involved in their namesake concerns—the Bakers, Brewers, Butchers, Fishmongers, Gunsmiths, Vintners.

Not for many centuries was there to be a company of fire fighters.

CHAPTER 3

PARISH PUMPS & MERCHANT ADVENTURERS

Marvellous giant fiery lightning, a spear pointed flame of fire . . .
the fall of the cross and eagle fired the south aisle

Henry VIII's passion for that sloe-eyed witch, Anne Boleyn, did more than ignite a divorce and split with Rome. It lead to the establishment of the Church of England, a secular civil service and a spate of speculative building founded on the Dissolution of the Monasteries.

Abbeys, priories and convents were given to court favourites, sold to the highest bidder or demolished and their materials used for new buildings. London's irreparable loss was their gardens, orchards, bowling greens and fishponds, most of which vanished in the boom of shoddy, high-density housing. Tall, timber-framed buildings jettying out over the street were no improvement on the old medieval fire traps, only larger and more numerous.

No longer was Britain an offshore island on the fringes of Europe, but a vital trading centre between the Old World and the New. Larger vessels led to construction of wharves downstream from the Pool towards Greenwich and a flare in rivalry between London and Bristol for dominance of the Atlantic. New routes to Africa, India and China caused even die-hards to reconsider the size and shape of the Earth.

The Merchant Adventurers were already experienced international traders; they were followed by the Muscovy, Turkey, Royal African and Guinea Companies and the Merchants of Virginia. In 1600 came the greatest of all, the East India Company and, in 1670, Hudson's Bay Company.

Wheeled traffic in the capital shared in the boom, initiating problems yet to be solved. Congestion was a constant source of complaints to the impotent authorities so even if there had been horsed fire engines, they could never have reached an outbreak with any urgency.

The cobbled streets had no pavements, leaving citizens to dodge the filth and excrement between wheelbarrows and handcarts, wagons and brewers' drays. For quicker journeys they 'took oars', and like timber, coal, cannon or newly-cast bells travelled the great highway that was London's lifeblood—the Thames.

Aping the court, merchants acquired their own carriages that required additional stabling and accommodation for coachmen and grooms. More wood, leather, hay and straw, along with the equally flammable stock in trade of coach and harnessmakers and wheelwrights, fuelled the dangers of fire. By 1625 there were over twenty coaches for public hire, around 50 by 1640, 100 during the Commonwealth, 700 by 1700 and more than 800 by George I's accession in 1714. Known as Hackney coaches, with hackney horses, they waited for custom at major inns, provoking fights and demarcation disputes with the aggressive Carmen. Around St Paul's was the place to shop for silks, satins, lace and velvets and to browse among the booksellers and printers. So that *by reason of the nobility and gentry in their coaches, often the street was so stopped up, that there was no room for foot passengers.*

Stage, and later mail, coaches were based on the same inns as hackneys. Henry VIII's Master of the Posts had organised a Royal Mail service, which was greatly improved by Charles I's Royal Post Master. Cromwell's Ordinance of 1654 *touched upon the Postage of Letters, inland and foreign* under the guidance of the Postmaster General. For two centuries the White Hart at Charing Cross, the Crown at Temple Bar, the Belle Sauvage at Ludgate, the Marygold in Fleet Street and the Saracen's Head at Westminster also served as letter offices.

The Thames was brackish and dirty and suitable only for watering horses and filling fire buckets. It was marginally less foul than the sewage swilling down the Walbrook, Holborn, Fleet, Colne and Westbourne but with no sanitation, scant personal hygiene and infrequent laundering, demand was fortunately slight. Water-sellers, weighed down by casks of *pure, spring water*, peddled the unwholesome liquid from door to door.

Gradually, wooden or lead pipes were laid along main streets, conveying water from springs north of London into City through conduits into troughs and by 'quills' into private homes. Until Peter Morice set up the wheels of his London Bridge Waterworks to force piped water uphill, all distribution depended on gravity.

The poor now had the choice of huddling in derelict monastic buildings or in hovels tarred with pitch and supported by rotten posts, still with neither light, hearth nor water. The hovels caught fire frequently and were shored up again equally frequently with rough timber taken from supplies available at set points in the City.

Furnaces and fires of braziers, armourers, blacksmiths, farriers, dyers, brewers, soap-boilers and lime-burners added to the smoke and grime of every domestic fire in the capital, and multiplied the danger. Wood was scarce, with the finest standing timber reserved for the Royal Navy, as it would be for centuries—indeed, during the Napoleonic Wars the Royal Navy was reckoned to float on 1.5m trees. Though improved mining techniques led to more sea-coal being shipped from Newcastle although expensive kindling was still needed. Across the Atlantic, New England winters were bitter, but the hardy settlers enjoyed huge fires, marvelling at the plentiful fuel that was sold far cheaper than wooden billets and faggots in London.

The list of tradesmen active in London around 1600 is the stuff of any fire insurance assessor's nightmares: clothworkers, weavers, hatters, skinners, coopers, distillers, vintners, gunmakers, weavers, carpenters, joiners, turners, bakers, basketmakers, stationers, glaziers, leathersellers, saddlers, fanmakers and wax and tallow chandlers.

As ever, home was more deadly than the street or workshop, with *burned in his bed* appearing frequently in the *Bills of Mortality*. Coal fires burned beneath wooden chimneys, candles guttered in unstable holders and bed curtains or covers caught alight from a sleeper's fallen taper.

Orders were repeatedly issued throughout the kingdom for supplies of fire engines, hooks, buckets and squirts to be kept in the churches of every parish, regularly inspected and accounted for annually at parish meetings.

An engine was itself nothing more than a wooden cask or two attached to a hand-cart, sometimes a sledge. Squirts and spouts were hand held, small ones by a single man and larger ones needing a team of three. In appearance they were like gun barrels with a handle on either side, filled by immersing in a trough or pond. When tackling a blaze, two men would hold the loaded squirt while the third worked the piston which propelled no more than a gallon or two of water at the flames at a time.

Iron-tipped fire hooks were slotted through rings under the eaves of houses and churches. Fire buckets were of leather, or sometime wood. Most were traditional in shape, but some tapered inwards making it easier to direct the flung water at the flames.

Certain English towns enforced their fire regulations with greater success than the authorities in the capital. The University of Oxford, commanding both Gown and Town, ordered *two Proctors of this University and two of the constables of the ward where fire shall so happen, shall in all haste repair to the place...taking to them both scholars and other inhabitants meetest for that purpose, labour to quench and stay the fire*. Next day the Vice Chancellor and the Mayor were to proclaim in the market place that *every person which hath in his custody any of the said {fire fighting} instruments not being his own shall forthwith bring the same to the Crier, to be delivered by him to the owner, or Churchwardens*.

At the end of the year the churchwardens had to account for these instruments, along with all the other items on the church inventory, and if necessary deliver them over in good order to their successors in office. Inadequate though the equipment now appears, it was worth stealing since any not returned promptly after a fire, and discovered by the constables, led to defaulters being fined *double value of the said instruments and punished further at the discretion of a competent Judge*.

St Paul's continued serving the capital as a place of worship, business, and entertainment. One crowd-pleaser was a mounted man ascending to the roof, an achievement which encouraged this Mr Bankes and his silver-shod horse to repeat the event at Notre Dame in Paris. According to an ìunreliableî, witness the pair were arrested by the Inquisition and burned at the stake for witchcraft.

Fires great and small bedeviled Elizabethan London as they had the early Tudor capital. Few are mentioned in any detail except the Act of God of 1561 related in the *True Report of the Burnying of the Steple and Churche of Poules (Paul's) in London*. Accompanied by a hideous crack of thunder a *marvellous giant fiery lightning, a spear pointed flame of fire* pierced the steeple, causing flames and smoke to break forth like a garland and a rush of stones to fall. Being sent for, the Lord Mayor, Bishop of London, the Lord Treasurer and the Keeper of the Great Seal gathered below, debating how best to save the rest of the cathedral. While these worthies argued, they were besieged on all sides by self-appointed experts and the first mentioned 'idle gazers', offering instant solutions: *some, pretending experience in wars, counselled the remnant of the steeple be shot down with cannon which counsell was not liked, as most perilous for the dispersing in fire. Others thought best with axes to hew down a space of the roof to stay the fire, but before the ladders could be brought, the labourers also being troubled with the multitude of idle gazers, the most part of the church was on fire. The fall of the cross and eagle fired the south aisle, and brands fell so that the steeple was burned down to the battlements.*

By now an Admiralty official had appeared and, ignoring the blazing cathedral, diverted all efforts and manpower to the saving the Bishop's palace believing that once that large building was ablaze whole streets would be in danger. *Whereupon the ladders and buckets were commanded thither, and by great labour a piece of roof of the north aisle was cut out and the fire so stayed and by much water, that part quenched and the Bishop's house preserved.* By evening the fierceness of the fire was quenched, partly due to the five hundred people who had hauled water and carried buckets but also largely to the energy and overall command of the single, unnamed Admiralty official—a lesson lost on the City Fathers.

Worthy of note were *substantial citizens [who] took pains as if they had been labourers, so did sundry gentlemen.* Though social distinctions were sharp, money making was an honourable profession and a London merchant thought himself as good as the next man in an age free of future Regency disdain for 'cits' and Victorian snobbery against trade.

A Market takes place anywhere, anytime—the street, church porch, dockside, coffee house or office—and now by telephone, fax and internet. An Exchange *is a building where at fixed times buyers and seller meet to transact business.* Paul's Walk within the cathedral served this purpose until the Tudor merchant prince, Thomas Gresham, financed a secular one based on the Antwerp Bourse. It stood at the centre of the old Roman City and was to burn down twice in sensational fashion.

750 merchants and householders funded the site and the slate-roofed, fully glazed building stood three storeys tall with four arcaded around an open court-yard. Gresham, deploring inflation and debased coinage, pronounced his famous law that bad money drives out good and insisted on his Exchange rents in gold coin. During Queen Elizabeth's visit in 1571 she allegedly found it *so marvellous, rich and strange, that let it for ever be called the Royal Exchange.*

An earthquake struck London on 6 April 1580. Tiles fell, windows rattled, houses caught fire and stones dislodged from a church tower killed one of the congregation in Christ Church, Newgate. Many prophesied the 'End was Nigh'.

Too late to help those burned out was a new fire engine extolled in a pamphlet by a lawyer, Cyprian Lucar. It showed a complicated device combining a cylinder, funnel, hose and nozzle which he claimed held a *hoggeshed of water made to squirt out water with great violence upon the fire that it be quenched*

In July 1588 a chain of beacons warned that the Spanish Armada had been sighted off the Lizard. Fire gave the alert, and it was fire which was to wreck King Philip's Enterprise of England although his galleons swept up the Channel to moor in Calais Roads, ready to swoop next day on Dover. By daybreak the Armada was in a desperate plight, clawing off a lee shore after an attack by unmanned craft *spurting fire and ordnance shooting, a horror to see in the night.* Captains cast their vessels adrift to avoid them in the crowded anchorage, irreparably damaging each other's rigging, steering and morale. Witnesses claimed later that the fireships all ran aground without setting a single galleon alight, but their fiery presence and threat in the darkness had been enough.

Londoners accepted the first Stuartís accession in 1603 with resignation, if not enthusiasm. Catholic extremists planned a murderous conflagration for 5 November 1605 to re-instate a monarch faithful to Rome, and to *blow Scotchmen back into Scotland.* But on the day when *the Parliament House should have been blown up,* the Plot was betrayed and London's most memorable fire delayed for sixty years.

James I wished to be remembered for finding London and its suburbs built *of sticks and leaving them of bricks.* However, while his Whitehall Banqueting House and Queen's House at Greenwich were constructed of austere Portland stone, his subjects preferred to build or rebuild their homes in ornate Jacobean grafted onto sturdy Tudor—timber-framed with exterior carving, jettying storeys and gabled roofs.

With over 2000 lighters serving the busy wharves of Billingsgate and Queenhithe above the Bridge, Maritime trade was increasing. Fortunes were made in tobacco, with London, claiming a monopoly over Bristol in 1639, importing the Virginia crop and shipping it out again, principally to Hamburg, with no home sales.

There was an insatiable demand for news, the more sensational the better, with pamphleteers and printers being the forerunners of the later tabloid press. Many operated around St Paul's and Paternoster Row, thumbing their noses at the authorities at Stationers Hall who were responsible for licensing all printed material and prosecuting offenders. Condemning printers in the stocks or pillory with the offending papers round their necks only incited them to further libellous excesses.

Fires anywhere in the country made splendid copy full of *heauge griefe, lamentable suffering, mortall remaines* and *losse without recoverie*. In 1586 little was left both of the Suffolk town of Beccles and of Bury St Edmunds. Marlborough burned in 1653 and Tiverton in Devon in 1598. A worse Tiverton fire in 1612 was caused by a dyer's apprentice in the absence of his master, *the boy having more mind on play and be sooner among his companions, hastened his fire exceedingly, the quicker to make it [the dye vat] boyle*. The boiler exploded, the subsequent fire destroying half the town as graphically illustrated in *Woeful Newes from the West of England*.

The collection of Thomason Tracts in the British Museum represents only a fraction of those spewing from the presses. Printers held stock woodcuts of churches, castles, bridges, burning houses, fleeing crowds, runaway coaches and accused witches, doctoring them to suit specific news items. What is clear is the inadequacy of any fire fighting equipment depicted, even the German engine detailed in Forcible Movements of 1615. The author insists his instructions are easily understood since of the two suckers one was *below to open when the handle is lifted up and to shut when it is put down, and another to open to let out the water*. Manhandled buckets remained the first line of defence, but even the wealthy Skinners' Company economised one year by having 31 old leather ones repaired.

Succeeding his father in 1625, Charles I was faced with mounting political and financial problems, but found time to consult with the Lord Mayor on *Provisions of Engins in London for Accidents of Fier*. After compliments over *new Engins for spowting of water* that had quelled a fire at Arundel House he urged that parishes should buy more of these excellent contrivances. Aware of the sharp eye kept on expenditure he added, tactfully for Charles, that the *lesser parishes may join together in providing of an Engin, but that the great parishes should provide themselves*.

In 1632 a serious fire started near Fish Street Hill, close to Pudding Lane. It spread downhill to the river and swept onto the Bridge, destroying about a third of the houses within a few hours. Idle gazers drawn to the blaze were fortunate to avoid the fate of those hundreds trapped and killed in the same place in 1212.

Inventor John Bates published a pamphlet describing how he had solved an intractable problem. Far superior to human bucket chains was siting the engine alongside a stream and forcing water up through a pipe into the barrel by leverage and suction. The probable lack of any such convenient water source where needed was ignored.

Seasonable Advice for preventing the Mischiefe of Fire in these Dangerous Times was drawn up by William Gosling, engineer, and issued by the Lord Mayor in 1643. It paints an alarming picture of the dangers in normal times, let alone wartime. Misuse of candles was a prime cause of domestic fires, from peering under the bed to placing them too close to thatch. Roundly condemned were the perilous firing of guns up chimneys to extinguish fires and the nonchalant drying of gunpowder over an open fire, as the Powder plotters had done to their painful cost when it exploded.

In America at the same time Dutch governor Stuyvesant was allocating fines levied on the burghers of New Amsterdam, later New York, towards buying improved fire engines. Householders were ordered to keep one leather fire bucket at the ready, bakers no less than three and brewers six, and all were fined for missing buckets. Tobacco was cheap, so fires caused by careless disposal of ash were frequent; it was also a crime to be caught smoking your clay pipe outdoors and endangering thatched roofs.

In 1606 the Corporation pushed a bill through Parliament to bring fresh running water into London from Hertfordshire. The powers and obligations of this New River Act were finally settled on a 'prospector' with experience of Welsh coal mining and tunnelling, Sir Hugh Myddleton MP, a Merchant Adventurer and City goldsmith. After years of disputes and financial crises, the New River was inaugurated at Islington in a lavish ceremony headed by his brother Thomas, the new Lord Mayor of London. Reference was made to *the famous Aqueduct called the New River performed at his {Hugh's} charge, not-withstanding many Natural Difficulties and the Envious Opposition he met with*. The 38 miles of new waterway, including 200 bridges, cost £18,000. James I had backed the venture financially and granted a charter. Three years later his horse threw him into the icebound river when *nothing but his boots were seen;* the rescued, bibulous monarch found the experience had *put much water into his wine*. Royal enthusiasm predictably waned as the expected returns failed to materialise and Charles I sold back the royal moiety; a costly mistake since future Myddletons, Merchant Adventurers and other canny investors reaped golden profits for over two centuries.

By 1904 time the New River Company was supplying Londoners with 41m gallons a day and providing a vital source of water for the London Fire Brigade. In that year it was taken over by the Metropolitan Water Board, which itself was absorbed by the Thames Water Authority in 1974.

CHAPTER 4

THE NOISOME PESTILENCE—PLAGUE

Less prone to casual fyrings than of yore

The Bible glowed with burning, fiery furnaces and the refining properties of fire. The Earth in flames at the Last Judgement resonated from the awesome *Dies Irae* of the proscribed Latin Mass. The *Book of Revelation* warned that all would be consumed in hail and fire mingled with blood. Despite growing religious scepticism these medieval beliefs attributing misfortunes to the Wrath of God still hampered a rational view of accidental fires.

On a less spiritual plane the capital's pollution was accepted as the price of commercial progress.

However John Evelyn, a fastidious man in a coarse age, vented his disgust after returning from court where foul-smelling, smut-laden smoke from City chimneys hung over Whitehall, besmirching everything and everyone with filth. His *Fumifugium*, on the *Inconveniencie of the Aer and Smoak of London Dissipated* appeared in 1661. Apart from the damage and disfigurement of churches and palaces, smoke *fouls our clothes and corrupts the waters so that the very rain and dews precipitate this impure vapour which with its black and tenacious spots and contaminates whatever is exposed to it.*

Apart from domestic coal and wood burning fires, there were the furnaces of swelling numbers of craftsmen including bell founders, tallow-renderers and soap-boilers. Olive oil from Castile produced the finest soap, but the making of a cheaper alternative from whale oil resulted in one of London's more pungent stinks. The fumes of all these pollutants were so bad that orchards in the Barbican and along the Strand produced only wizened, inedible fruit.

Suitably horrified by *Fumifugium*, King and Parliament resolved that something must be done. As usual, it was mostly talk with little done, or thought given, to the increasing fire risks in the overcrowded, decaying, timbered City. Several years later, Evelyn was still campaigning against the *exceedingly corrosive air of London*. It was so damaging to the classical marble statues in the gardens of Arundel House that he persuaded the Earl of Arundel to donate them to Oxford University.

If the 1657 author of *Londonopolis*, John Howell, lived to witness the Great Fire it would have undermined his assertions that the capital was less prone to *casual fyrings than of yore for besides the pitched Buckets that hung in Churches and Halls, there are divers new Engines for that purpose.* Not, he carped, that all

the orders of *the two last Kings, for building with Brick had been observed.*
Shortly after the Restoration in 1660 the limit on development was reduced to
two miles from the City centre, instead of ten. Construction and fire regulations
were strict, new building licenses had to be obtained from the authorities. All
rules were either ignored, casually adhered to or amended with a nod and a wink
after cash inducements. This effort to curb the sprawl outside the walls inadver-
tently increased the squalor, health and fire risks within. Behind the wide City
streets of Cheapside, Bishopsgate, Cannon Street and Fleet Street, were insalu-
brious lanes, alleys, courts and passages crammed with reeking hovels housing
ten times as many rats as people. The division between skilled and unskilled
labour was sharp; these were the homes of masterless men, casual workers with
no voice in civic or church affairs and offered scant protection by the Common
Law.

In 1632 fire broke out in a needlemaker's shop on London Bridge, spreading
rapidly across the congested roadway to devastate fifty houses, not all of which
were rebuilt. This fortuitous fire break would prove vital before too long.

The most sensible and comprehensive information published was probably
that contained in the *Seasonable Advice for preventing the Mischiefe of Fire, that
may come by Negligence, Treason or otherwise, especially in these dangerous
Times,* (reproduced at end of chapter) issued by the Lord Mayor in 1643. Unfortunately,
since this had emanated from the strongly Roundhead City at the time, it had
probably been withdrawn in the heady days of the Restoration rather than to be
found hanging in every man's house as recommended.

In 1662 Parliament ordered all houses with a street frontage *from such time as
it shall grow dark, until nine of the clock in the evening, upon pain to forfeit one
shilling, for every default* to hang out a lighted lantern—an additional fire hazards which could be knocked over, vandalised or blown down in a swirling wind.
Although the Act was not stringently enforced foreigners praised London as the
best lit town in Europe, a compliment that says little for street lighting overseas.

Even a small fire could ruin an individual, destroying his home, his goods and
his livelihood with nothing between his family and destitution but appeals for
neighbourly charity. Victims of major fires in country towns or large areas of a
city might eventually benefit from donations raised by means of a 'fire brief'.
Depending on the fire's severity, scale of loss and the suffering of the inhabitants,
a petition to the crown might result in the Lord Chancellor issuing a brief. This
short-dated licence was read out in churches within a specified distance of the
calamity, urging generosity to the afflicted. Large sums were often raised, but the
allocation of briefs was open to abuse and bribery, many lawful petitions were
rejected and congregations grew weary of the demands on their purses. Despite
this, fire briefs were not discontinued until 1828.

Pepys, an early sufferer from charity-fatigue, returned from St Olave Hart

Street on 30 June 1661 complaining that the *trade of briefs is come now up to so constant a course every Sunday, that we resolve to give no more to them.* Pepys's decision came after being exhorted on fourteen successive Sundays to part with his petty cash on behalf of diverse *singed citizens;* five years later he was fortunate not to be among thousands of homeless, singed citizens himself.

Though that terror was yet to come, already rats from the riverside were spreading their deadly cargo of infected fleas throughout the City.

Plague was no stranger to England. Few years in the century had been free of it, the worst outbreaks having been in 1625 and 1636. (The last case in England was in 1910). The 14th Century Black Death, killing an estimated third of Europe's people, was bubonic plague, distinguishable by glandular swellings and darkened flesh; the 17th Century scourge was pneumonic plague, affecting the lungs and intestines. Death came within hours, rather than days. Pepys first sighted a stricken house on 7 June 1665 in Drury Lane, the door smeared with a red cross and the invocation, *Lord have mercy upon us.*

The weekly *Bills of Mortality* supplied to Guildhall by the Company of Parish Clerks gave reasonably accurate figures of births (christenings) and deaths. The *Diseases and Casualties for this Week, 12th-19th September 1665* recorded the highest number of Plague deaths, 7165 out of a total of 8297 burials. Only 176 children had been christened and, of 130 parishes, only four were Plague-free.

Londoners who avoided death by Pestilence were carried off by a variety of other infirmities. *Death was the sure midwife of all children and infants passed immediately from the womb to the grave.* Along with Smallpox, Wormes, Convulsions, Consumption, Rickets and Dropsie citizens expired from Gowt, Impostumes, Scowring, Strangury, Thrush, Timpany, Tissick, Vomiting and Winde. A masterly diagnosis distinguished between 51 dying of Griping of the Guts, 11 of Rising of the Lights and 9 from Stopping of the Stomach. One man fell from the belfry of All Hallows the Great and another was *burnt in his Bed by a Candle at St Giles Cripplegate.*

Under a statute of 1603 parish vestries were reminded of their obligation to keep fire hooks, buckets and ladders in the church porch. This equipment was meant to be well maintained and if items were found damaged or missing at the annual inspection those responsible could be fined, or even dismissed. The latter was an empty threat since it was difficult enough to find individuals willing to serve on vestries in the first place. During epidemics it was the duty of each parish to appoint, and pay, special Plague officials, who were a gruesome crew:

Keepers of the City gates turned back those trying to flee without a certificate of health, or accepted bribes to let them through. Nurses needed no qualifications, were frequently drunk and robbed or starved the victims.

Watchmen were paid seven shillings a week for guarding the barred and bolted houses of the infected, inhabitants lives often depending on the good nature or roguery of these men. A few were honest and bought and delivered food, while others could be bribed to allow victims to escape while others took the cash before indulging in murder and plunder.

Common Hunt were killers of vermin. A preventive measure led to the killing of an estimated 20,000 cats and twice that number of dogs, a disastrous decision since cats kept down rats and dogs consumed the offal and filth in the streets.

Searchers of the Dead carried long white wands to warn of contagion which could be spread by entering infected houses. They certified death and notified the authorities of the cause which was entered in the *Bills of Mortality*.

Bearers of the Dead carried scarlet staves for contagion. They tied the corpsesí head and feet in shrouds, not always lifeless, and threw them in the carts when the nightly cry went up of *bring out your Dead*. When the supply of shrouds ran out, bodies were dumped naked in the Plague pits of Stepney, Wapping, Bishopsgate, Moorgate or Spitalfields. All pits were outside the walls, with Quakers and Jews having their own.

The most dreaded officials were Buryers of the Dead. These dregs of humanity tore off rings, pulled teeth, cut off hair and were rumoured to indulge in necrophilia with female corpses. Brokers of the Dead acted as bailiffs for the parish in the case of householders with no living relatives. Sale of infected household goods was sluggish but those who bought and stored furniture in the suburbs reaped huge profit in the aftermath of the Great Fire.

Charles ll and the court, justices, Lords and Commons removed to Oxford. Government had to continue, so their flight was not abject as might be thought. Among those who coped valiantly with the crisis were Lord Mayor John Lawrence, most of the aldermen and two Civil War veterans, General Monk and Lord Craven. The Archbishop of Canterbury, the Bishop of London and the Dean of Westminster shared the danger with their flocks but the Dean of St Pauls departed for Tunbridge Wells in the wake of his wealthy parishioners. Non-conformist ministers took over vacated Anglican parishes, seven dying in Cripplegate ward alone.

Samuel Pepys stayed at his desk at the Navy Office and, like John Evelyn, attended a day of public fasting to *deprecate God's displeasure against this land by pestilence and war*. Both these public servants and private diarists survived, to the benefit of posterity as well as their contemporaries. Evelyn was responsible for Dutch naval prisoners, and after sending his family out of town, *had resolved to stay at my house myself and to look after my charge, trusting in the providence and goodness of God*. Concerned with all things naval, he had watched the launch of the 'London Frigate' from the King's own pleasure-boat not long before, a most stately ship *built by the City to supply that which was burnt by accident some time since*.

In attempts to dispel the corrupted air, street bonfires were lit and people fumigated their homes. Charlatans preyed on desperate clients eager for infallible potions or magic amulets, although several physicians did remain alongside their stricken patients. The robust Dr William Boghurst ate good meals, slept well and *spent not two farthings correcting the air in my house*: he, his wife and six children all survived. Not so *Dr Burnett, my* [Pepys's] *physician, this morning dead of Plague, which is strange his servant dying of it so long ago and his house open again this month. Now himself dead, poor unfortunate man.*

Life was grim in the deserted City with *coffins exposed in the streets and shops shut up...and a pest ship for infected men.* One of the biggest bonfires burned on the steps of the Royal Exchange; many merchants left on extended journeys since trade and commerce were almost at a standstill. Traffic was so slight that grass grew between the cobblestones.

A poet bewailed the unnatural lack of activity:

> *Trade interrupted, and the Royal Burse,*
> *Quitted and Empty as the Cities Purse.*
> *While Steeples howling Day and Night do call*
> *Thousands together to one Funerall.*

In a single week Pepys reported inaccurately *Plague having a great increase this week, beyond all expectation...in the City died this week 7496 and of them 6102 of the Plague... true number nearer 10,000 from*

The *Bills of Mortality* gave a final toll of close on 70,000 dead. The true figure was probably nearer 100,000 since *the poor cannot be taken notice of through the greatness of the number, and Quakers and others that will not have any bell rung over them.* The others included nonconformists, Catholics and Jews.

Though many shops were still closed in October and *multitudes of poor pestiferous creatures begged alm,* the Plague was nevertheless subsiding and London began to come back to life. King and court returned, families were reunited, shipping revived on the Thames, street markets were busy, and the theatres and Bear Garden re-opened.

Thankful to be alive, sobered congregations packed the churches now this period of physical, rather than spiritual, danger was past. Clergy pleaded with the Almighty to chastise His humbled people no more after so many had perished in requital for the kingdom's manifold sins and wickednesses.

Never could those delivered from the Psalmist's *noisome Pestilence that walketh in darkness* have dreamed of the flaming *arrow that flieth by day* that would within months consume those very churches.

Seasonable Advice for preventing the Mischiefe of Fire, that may come by Negligence, Treason or otherwise, and is thought very necessary to hang in every man's House, especially in these dangerous Times.

'How many severall wayes, houses, Townes and Cities have been set a fire. Some hath been burnt by bad Harths, Chimnies, Ovens or by pans of fire set upon boards; some by cloaths hanged against the fire; some by leaving great fires in chimnies where the sparkes or sickles breaking fell and fired the boards, painted, Cloaths, Wainscots, Rushes, Matts, as houses were burnt in Shoreditch; some by Powder or shooting Pieces; some by Tinder or Matches; some by setting candles under shelves some by leaving candles neere their beds, some by snugges of candles, Tobacco-snuffes, burnt papers, and some by drunkards; as many houses were burnt in *Southwarke* some by warming Beds, some by looking under Beds with candles, some by sleeping at worke, leaving their Candles by them so many have been burnt of severall Trades; some by setting Candles neere the thatch of houses; some by snuffes or sparks fallen upon Gunpowder, or upon matts, rushes, chips, small-coale, and in chinkes; so *Wimbleton* was burnt; some Townes were burnt by Maultkilns; some by Candles in Stables or by foule Chimnies; some by Candles amongst hempe, flaxe, and ware-houses; some by Candles falling out of their Candlestickes; some by sticking their Candles upon potts; some by Lincks knockt at shops, stalls, sellers, windowes warehouses, dores and dangerous places; some by carrying fire from place to place where the winde hath blowne it about the streets, as it did burne *St Edmondsbury*; some by warme Sea-coale cinders put in baskets, or wooden things, as did burne *London-Bridge* And some have been burnt without either fire, or candle, as by wet hay, corne, straw, or by mills, wheeles, or such like; all which hath been by carelessnesse. And some have been fired a purpose by villainy.

Orders to be Observed that fire may not happen

Is that every house-keeper, either himselfe or one by his appointment, that should be lst up, to see to the fire and Candle, and to shut the Seller-{cellar} windowes, dores, casements, garret-windows, and to stop holes, and sinkes that fire may not come in by Treason, or otherwise. To prevent Treason that may come by wilde-fire, is to stop the wilde-fire simples, where they are soulde: Seeke to prevent fire at the beginning, and by the sight of smoake, to looke to it, for divers fires have been so prevented: Some have been prevented by smelling old wood, linnen, or woollen burne: and by hearing crackling of sticks, coales or sparkes of fire, have prevented mischiefe thereby: if you will use Candle all night, ley your Candlestick be a pot of water brim full and set it where it shall stand, and then light a Candle and sticke a great pin in the bottome of the Candle, and let is slowly into the water, and it will burne all night without danger: if the wood under the harth of a Chimnie be a fire, then take heed you doe not open it too suddenly, before you cat water upon it, for the ayre getting in, the fire will burn forth, therefore sill throw water and open it by degrees. And that the Bricklayers should look better to the foundation of harths and ovens to prevent the hurt of fire: if Chimnies be a fire, either wet hay or straw or a wet blanket or a kettle of water hung over, or bay-salt cast into the fire, or a or a Piece {gun} shot up into the chimnie, will helpe it. And that the Watch might be from day-light to day-light, at such a distance that they may see and heare from one Watch to the other; some might be upon Gates, Towers, or Churches, if need be, to give notice to the Watch below, upon any occasion, to prevent both enemy and fire.

Orders that if fire should happen, either by wilde-fire,or other wayes, to prevent the miseries thereof

Then the Bells going backward, doth give notice of fire: and that all Officers and others must keepe the streets or lanes ends, that the rude people may be kept from doing mischief, for sometimes the doe more harme that a fire: and suffer none by the workers to come neere, and all the streets from the fire to the water may have double rowes or rankes of men on each side the street, to hand emptie pales, potts, or buckets to the water, and to returne full to the fire, by the other row or ranke of people, on the same side the street so you may have divers ranks and by the order, water may be brought to quench it, or earth to choake it, and smoother it, with that speed and plenty as need requires.
All those of higher or levell ground should throw downe water, to run to the place where the fire is and there to stop it and others to sweep up the waters of kennells {central gutters} towards the fire. If water-pipes run through the streets you may open it against the house that is a fire, and set

another pipe in that upright and tow or three foot lower then the height of the head of the same water, set in some gutter, trough or pipe unto the upright pipe to convay the water to the fire, for under the foresaid height it will run itselfe from high ponds or from Sir Hugh Middletons water of Conduit-heads or from the Water-house without any other helpe, into the fire, as you will have it you may keepe great Stoopes or Squirts of wood in houses or if you will, you may have in the Parish a great Squirt or wheeles, that may do very good service.

Where milde fire is milke, urine, sand, earth or dirt will quench it, but anything else set a fire will be quenched as afore; if there be many houses standing together, and are indangered by a mightie fire before it can be quencht, or choaked with earth, then you many pull downe the next house opposite to the winde, and then earth and rubbish being cast upon the fire and round about it, will choake the violence of the fire: besides the water you may get to doe the like. Also it is necessary that every Parish should have Hookes, Ladders, Squirts, Buckets and Scoopes in a readinesse upon any occasion.

O the miseries of Cities, Townes, Villages and particular houses that have been burnt, where some could not recover their losses in their yeares after, and some never, which have been lamentable spectacles unto us, when many men, women and children have been burnt in their houses; and multitudes of people utterly undone, that saw all their wealth burned before their eyes. Besides, may have been hurt, many kild, and many burned, that came by to helpe to quench the fires. What lamentable cryes, frightings and amazement, there was to all sorts of people, some sicke, some in child-bed and great with childe, to the terrour of them all was through the miseries of fire that came by carelessnesse and wilfulnesse.

Therefore let the very sight of fire and Candle put us in minde to prevent the like miseries that have come by fire, both in London and the parts of England: for great winds may rise suddenly and enemies furies may doe mischiefe. To master the Elements is either to increase or decrease any of them, for as ayre makes fire increase, so earth will choake it and water quench it.

Preventions of fires would save the Collections of money in Churches in England, all which is for the profit and fabric of the Commonwealth. As good order and care prevent our feare of fire, so a good life prevents the wayes of sinne. And every one, mend one; then all will be mended.

The Lord commandeth us to have care of our neighbours goods, Deut. Chap 22. *For the love of our neighbour fulfilleth the Law.* Romans Chap 13

AD 1643

CHAPTER 5

THE DEVOURING ELEMENT—The Great Fire

*People in all parts distracted by the vastness of it...would have thought it
had been Doomsday and that the Heavens themselves had been on fire.*

No national event up to 1666 had ever been described so voluminously as the
Great Fire. As well as official reports, newsletters, journals and correspondence,
there was a deluge of pamphlets augmented by excruciating verses and denunci-
atory clerical tracts in Latin. Untainted by hindsight, the diary entries of Samuel
Pepys and John Evelyn are unrivalled, fairly reeking of smoke and the crackle of
flames. The most readable contemporary accounts, written up later but shudder-
ing with remembered horrors, are Thomas Vincent's *God's Terrible Voice in the
City*, Captain Bedloe's *Narratives of the Popish Plot and the Burning of London*
and Rev. William Taswell's *Autobiography and Anecdotes*.

Most writers were convinced an unappeased Jehovah had unleashed His thun-
derbolts in the wake of the Plague, even a religious, but rational, man like Evelyn.
A few dared to question His justice and judgement in ignoring the obvious target
of the dissolute and profane Court at Whitehall and striking the hardworking,
God-fearing City instead.

When Elizabeth died in 1603 there were approximately 4m people in England
and Wales and 200,000 in London. By 1666 these figures had risen to 5m and
300,000. Tudor London had been smaller but was still an immense warren of
overcrowded, combustible wooden houses, thatched hovels, narrow streets and
primitive water supplies. A few hooks, ladders and buckets were the only
weapons against fire yet, surprisingly despite this, every previous outbreak,
including the 1561 lightning strike on St Paul's, was contained without devastating loss.

Why?

Undeserved good luck? Luck which ran out in September 1666 when *this fatal
night began that deplorable Fire near Fish Street.*

A brief chronology charts the escalating catastrophe:

Sunday, 3 September: *A woman could piss it out*
In the early hours fire broke out in Farynor's bakery in Pudding Lane and soon
ignited adjoining houses and the Star Inn. It was soon taken seriously enough for
the Lord Mayor to be called out from his home in Aldersgate. Bludworth arrived
around 3am, uttered his historically, and politically, incorrect verdict and

returned to bed. To be fair to Bludworth, which is unusual, large fires were so commonplace that his reaction, if not his comment, was not as ludicrous as it now appears. Pepys, wakened by the maids, peered out of the window and, reckoning the flames a safe distance from Seething Lane, also returned to bed.

Fanned by the wind, the fire advanced down Fish Street Hill to the river and fastened greedily on wharves and warehouse. Closeness to the dockside was the first disastrous consequence of the initial fire's location. Though whole streets of dry, wooden buildings would have been utterly destroyed, they would never have generated the heat and tenacity of flames feeding on coal, timber, oil, tallow, wax, sugar, spirits, flax, hemp and cordage.

The Thames proved no barrier. Racing onto London Bridge, the fire consumed everything until checked by the open space left since the fire of 1632. Sparks alighted on Southwark and scorched, without disfiguring, the spiked traitor's heads on the gatehouse. Amazingly Nonsuch House in the centre of the Bridge, built of carved and painted timber secured by wooden dowels, escaped damage.

The actual stone Bridge was impervious to fire, but the second disastrous consequence at this early stage was that burning houses collapsed inwards onto the twelve foot wide highway. This blocked the route for those fleeing on foot and prevented help arriving from Southwark. Far worse was the destruction of the wooden waterwheels beneath the Northern arches, cutting off the piped supply that might have saved the City.

The footpath approach to the Bridge passed beneath the tower of St Magnus the Martyr, the first church to be burned. It was followed by St Laurence Pountney with its soaring spire, Fishmonger's, Watermen's and Dyer's Halls. Northwards, the fire was checked for a while by Cannon Street.

By Sunday night the situation was serious but not yet causing major concern to the authorities. Others were more alarmed, watching flames *mount up to the top of the highest houses, they descend down to the bottom of the lowest vaults and cellars...no stately building so great as to resist their fury.*

With most of the waterfront aflame, Evelyn found *the people so astonished that from the beginning, I know not by what despondency or fate, they hardly stirred to quench it, so that there was nothing heard or seen but crying and lamentation, running about like distracted creatures without at all attempting to save even their goods, such a strange consternation there was upon them.*

Pepys, who made notes throughout the Fire and wrote up his journal afterwards, watched as darkness fell and *saw the fire grow...in a horrid, malicious, bloody flame, not like the fine flame of an ordinary fire.* Back in Seething Lane, he transferred his valuables, including his journal, to the cellar and buried other things in the garden. Before dawn he had second thoughts about the safety of the cellar, piling everything into a cart which he accompanied in his night-gown to the safety of a friend's premises in Bethnal Green

Monday, 4 September: *Burning still rages, the very pavements glowing with fiery redness*

Now wharves and warehouses on both northern sides of the Bridge were engulfed from Billingsgate in the West to Queenhithe in the West, where both St Peter and St Benet's on Paul's Wharf and the College of Arms were burned. The Fire was now master of the prosperous commercial and residential areas of Eastcheap, Fenchurch Street, Cornhill and Lombard Street and across Stocks Market into Threadneedle Street. Watling Street was burning, threatening the south side of Cheapside, the wealthiest street in the capital. The Woodmongers, Vintners, Blacksmiths and Cordwainers were among many companies who lost their halls that day. In Vintry ward Whittington's almshouses in College Hill and the church where he was buried, St Michael Paternoster Royal, burned along with St James Garlickhythe and St Mary at Hill.

The greatest loss was Gresham's Royal Exchange: *the glory of the merchants is now invaded with much violence. How quickly did the fire run round the galleries filling them with flames.* All the kingly statues fell from their niches *down upon their faces and the greater part of the stone building after them, the founder's statue only remaining, and with such a noise as was dreadful and astonishing.* As well as all the fallen statues, Pepys saw a cat taken from the ruins, alive but with its fur singed off. The East India Company had leased the cellars for storage, mainly of pepper, and a heady aroma of roasted spices hung over the area for days. With most of its main warehouses outside the City walls, this was the Company's only serious loss.

Londoners took to the river in horrified fascination to witness the extent of the fire, the denunciation of latter-day prophets ringing in their ears. One minister thundered that the angry Lord would send no Flood to destroy by water, *but an arrow in a flaming point, a flaming bow...to destroy London with fire.*

Though Somerset House on the Strand was well away from the flames, already the Queen Mother, Henrietta Maria, left by river for the sanctuary of Hampton Court. At Westminster, money chests from the Exchequer were loaded into boats, ready at a moment's notice to be rowed further upstream to another royal residence.

Tuesday, 5 September: *You may stand where Cheapside is and see the Thames*

The area lost in the first two days was doubled on Tuesday. It was a day of such unchecked devastation that most like Evelyn prayed their *eyes may never behold the like again.* Out of control and spreading in all directions, the Fire blazed almost to the Tower in the East now and the Temple in the West and was only checked northwards by London Wall. St Paul's, Guildhall, St Mary le Bow and nearly forty other churches, St Paul's School, Christ's Hospital, Mercers', Grocers', Drapers' and Merchant Taylors' and most of the remaining livery halls were in the line of fire. So too were Pepys's birthplace and family's home, off Fleet Street.

A stunned Londoner saw Guildhall, seat of the City government, consumed. *A fearful spectacle which stood the whole body of it together for several hours after the fire had taken it, without the flames, (I suppose because the timber was such solid Oake) in a bright shining coal, as if it had been a Palace of Gold, or a Great Building of Burnished Brass.*

But for the scaffolding surrounding it, St Paul's might have withstood the flames, but once they took hold there was no hope. *Though so high above all buildings in the City yet within a while doth yield to the violent assault, strangely first takes fire at the top. Now the lead melts and runs down as if it had been snow before the sun and great beams and massy stones with a great nose fall on the pavement and break through into Faith's Church underneath, now great flakes of stone scale and peel off strangely from the side of the walls.*

Evelyn, taking time off from his fire post near Fetter Lane, marvelled that *the stones of Paul's flew like granados, the melting lead running down the streets in a stream and the very pavements glowing with fiery redness so as no horse nor man was able to tread on them and the demolition had stopped all the passages so that no help could be applied. Nothing but the Almighty power of God was able to stop [the flames] for vain was the help of man.*

Wednesday, 6 September:　*Neither boat, barge, cart nor coach is to be had, all the streets full of goods and the fire flaming into the very Temple.*

A few sailors had shown what they could do on Monday, but the pleas of Pepys, concerned at the danger to the Navy Office and the Tower arsenal, were not answered until almost too late. Summoned in force from the Deptford and Woolwich royal dockyards, generously supplied with gunpowder and under the King's direct orders, the sailors succeeded where the parish pumps had failed. Barrels of powder were set in each house, a long fuse set and fired so the force of successive explosions dislodged the buildings from their foundations before they collapsed into the street. The debris was then dowsed and carted speedily away.

To see the flames checked for the first time was an inspiration to those *who hitherto had stood as men intoxicated...when almost all was lost, infusing a new spirit into them that the fury of it began sensibly to abate about noon...there was yet no standing near the burning and glowing ruins by near a furlong's space.*

Clothworkers' Hall continued burning for days, as did other large buildings, *in one body of flame, it being the cellar full of oil* but the worst was over and the wreckage contained within 634 stricken acres
From All Hallows by the Tower to Temple Bar, and from the Thames to Newgate, Cripplegate, Smithfield and Bishopsgate, all was smouldering desolation.

Evelyn, fastidious as ever, recoiled from *the stench that came from some poor creatures bodies, beds and other combustible goods.* He likened the aftermath to *some great City laid waste by a cruel enemy...nor could one possibly have known where one was but by the ruines of some Church or Hall that had some remarkable tower or pinnacle remaining.* A justifiable murmur of 'I told you so' is discernible since he had warned in *Fumifugium* of infinite mischief likely if *coal and wood wharves and magazines of oil and resin* and shops selling such combustibles were permitted in the heart of the City.

A German visitor wrote of *the most destructive fire England has ever seen for five days and nights it raged with such fury that all human means of combatting it were unavailing...in an hour's walk from the Temple to the Tower where is within the wall hardly anything left standing, all is ruins.*

There were small mercies. Had the flames spread and attack'd the Conqueror's White Tower *where the magazine of powder lay, [the explosion] would not only have beaten downe and destroyed all the bridge, but sunke and torne the vessells in the river, and render'd the demolition beyond all expression for several miles about.*

Charles II and the Duke of York, exhibiting both presence and power, impressed everyone with the decisiveness of their actions. Riding around the perimeter of the fire the royal brothers dismounted to help fight it, or more often prompt some action from those standing helplessly at the mercy of an enraged fire. Their example inspired others when *handling buckets when they stood up to the ankles in water, and playing the engines for many hours together which people seeing fell to work with effect having so good fellow labourers.*

Another witness was confident that *had not the Duke forced all people to submit to his commands by this time I am confident there had not been a house standing near Whitehall. . . environed with fire, the wind high, blowed such great flakes the Duke was forced to fly for it, and had almost been stifled with the heat.* Charles' bastard son, Monmouth, also earned respect. Ironically, twenty years later when facing execution for rebellion against James II, he accused his uncle, then Duke of York, of having abetted a Catholic conspiracy to fire the City.

As military commander the Duke set up fire posts, most of them at the City gates and along the Wall under the orders of noblemen, like Lord Craven and Lord Hollis, three magistrates and the parish constable. A company of soldiers was assigned to each post to control the fleeing people and guard mounting piles of household goods dumped out of range of the fire zone. The City trained bands (militia) and the King's Whitehall Guards prevented looting, protected foreigners and only incidentally helped fight the fire which was left to civilians. Evelyn's post was in Fetter Lane, his chief concern being to save St Bartholomew's Hospital which held many of 'his' sick and wounded sailors from the fleet.

The King was lavish with praise and money, daily replenishing the purse of gold coins which he threw into the crowd to reward those battling in the heat and smoke. In contrast a City alderman rewarded thirty sailors for salvaging his goods with half a crown, while another doled out £4 to men for saving £10,000 in his money chest. One of his more liberal colleagues tossed a hatful of coins to encourage the exhausted men fighting the flames at Leadenhall, and their renewed efforts saved Whittington's stone granary and the East India Company's main warehouse. It was the first check to the Fire in two days.

Cleric, schoolmaster, soldier, Dean of Westminster and past Bishop of Rochester, John Dolben proved his mettle on the battlefield of Marston Moor and then during the Plague. Though his own school was far from the flames, on Monday he marched the Westminster boys, William Taswell among them, to St Dunstan-in-the-East near the Tower. There he drilled them into ranks of bucket fillers, bucket carriers and firefighters and with the Lord's help, and thanks to restoration work in 1633 using Portland stone, the church was As the London Bridge waterwheels were destroyed on the first day and saved. The slender steeple, identifiable in Hollar's panoramas, dominated the ruined eastern sector of the City.

The Westminster boys had been in the Abbey the day before but, when the news of the Fire spread among the congregation, Taswell slipped out. He noted in his *Anecdotes*, written when a clergyman, how at the outset the City mob *vented their rage against the Catholics and Frenchmen, imagining these incendiaries, as they thought, had thrown red hot balls into the houses.* Londoners never hesitated to attack strangers; he himself saw a blacksmith fell a Frenchman with his hammer. Out souvenir-hunting a few days later, he found the *ground so hot as almost to scorch my shoes, and the air so intensely warm I near to fainting...laid in my pockets several pieces of bell metal. Later accoutered with sword and helmet I had picked up among many others I traversed the torrid zone again.*

Pepys, for all his horror and anxiety, had been in his element, out surveying the smoking destruction on Wednesday with an alert and roving eye. *Pretty it was to see how hard the women did work in the channels sweeping of water, but then scold for a drink and be as drunk as devils.*

A no less avid spectator, Evelyn, hurried to St Paul's to view a mummified body that had tumbled from its tomb. The skull still had teeth and red hair attached and the corpse was so stiff that macabre onlookers took turns in making it stand alone on its skeleton feet. Bishop da Brabroke, deceased in 1404, was eventually to be decently reinterred in the new cathedral.

The old cathedral presented the greatest ruins of all with lead, iron work, bells and plate all melted. Destroyed too was the *exquisitely wrought Mercers Chapel, the sumptuous Exchange, the august fabric of Christ Church, all the rest of the Companies Halls, splendid buildings, arches, entries, all in dust; the fountaines dried up and ruin'd whilst the very waters remain'd boiling.*

Along the waterfront *cellars, wells and dungeons, formerly warehouses, still burning in stench and dark clouds of smoke so that in five or six miles traversing about I did not see one loade of timber unconsum'd.* Some fires smouldered for months; cellars full of oil or tallow that escaped by being covered by falling masonry generated such intense heat that when finally opened and exposed to the air they burst into flames spontaneously.

The Crown had leased part of the Hanseatic Steelyard for naval storage of flammable flax, hemp, pitch, cordage and Baltic pine masts for which Pepys frequently negotiated with the merchants. Over the years the derelict houses and landmark tower had been restored and the popular Rhenish Warehouse re-opened. Visiting Germans stayed in its guest house, and two King's Painters, Holbein and van Dyck, had lived there permanently. By Sunday night everything, save the stone tower, had gone including two pictures commissioned from Holbein, the 'Triumph of Wealth' and the 'Triumph of Poverty'. Only copy drawings remain, though his portrait of Henry VIII for the Barber-Surgeons narrowly escaped in its original home of Bart's Hospital. (It also escaped the Great Cripplegate Fire 1897).

Cannon Street station now covers the Steelyard, and by tradition the only trace of Hanseatic merchants, called the (Ea)sterlings, remains in the name of Britain's endangered pre-Euro currency.

Lord Chancellor Clarendon summed up cause and effect of the Fire: lack of water and the paucity of fire fighting equipment, he said, turned a neighbourhood misfortune into a national catastrophe.

Though the Walbrook ran with fresh, if filthy, water it too was enveloped quickly, as the London Bridge waterwheels were destroyed on the first day. The Fleet Ditch was too far away to be of any use until too late. A piped supply should have been available from the New River Company's Islington headquarters but that too failed. Stopcocks were permanent fixtures at every ward boundary controlling the flow but in the panic people dug down and hacked through the nearest hollow elm pipe, the trunk mains. Only a few buckets could be filled before the precious water then trickled uselessly into the ground.

Taswell refers to seeing several engines *all on fire, and those concerned with them escaping with great eagerness from the flames which spread instantaneous almost like wild-fire.* Buckets and handsquirts kept in the parish churches and livery halls were utilised in some instances, though such mention of engines is misleading. Illustrations of mechanical English fire-fighting appliances are mostly post-Fire; most appliances trundled into service were the old wooden casks on wheels which were not much more effective that spraying bottles of beer on the flames, or following Bludworth's advice.

Much of the parish equipment was old, broken or missing altogether. Houses were pulled down by teams of men wielding firehooks but, with no carts and often no time to remove fallen timber and thatch, the advancing flames fastened greedily onto this easy fuel. Anyone selling tools, ladders or carts in the emergency profited when supplies ran short and prices rose. Within two days the cost of a cart to remove goods from threatened homes, rose from 5s to £5 to £50.

The wind, along with lack of water and poor equipment, was a contributory factor in turning an everyday accident into a raging inferno, exacerbated by the tunnel effect of the overhanging houses. Some reports give the impression the easterly wind was gale force, yet flames ate back against it towards the Tower. Some said the wind rose and fell while others noted the stillness of the air at the outset and of later burning gusts. Intense heat causes a cycle of rising hot air and drawn-in cold air to form sudden firestorms in one area while a short distance away all is calm. As frightening as the flames was the roar of the wind as the days passed, *having the noise of a whirlwind in it* or rushing by with the clamour *as of a thousand iron chariots* with houses going *tumble, tumble, tumble from one end of the street to the other with a great crash.*

A Mr Locke of Oxford noted in his diary the curious dusky red sunset of 4th September, adding a couple of days later that the news that *London then burning, [the wind was] driven this way by an easterly wind caused this odd phenomenon.* A foreign resident's report published in Spain noted night's approach, but to onlookers *day was returning with all its light…the wind all the time fanning the flames and bringing the horror closer and keeping the remedy further away.*

The finger of blame cannot justly be pointed at any one individual, not even at Bludworth and his aldermen. One observer, who was no admirer, actually commended the City *magistrates [aldermen] who had assembled with the usual remedies of buckets, which they were provided with, but the fire was too ravenous to be extinguished with such quantities of water as those instruments could apply to it, and fastened still upon new materials before it had destroyed the old.*

Not that any contemporary had a kind word for the unfortunate Thomas Bludworth, before or after the Fire. Pepys had early on been accosted by *my Lord Mayor like a man spent with a handkerchief about his neck. To the King's message he cried like a fainting woman 'Lord, what can I do? I am spent, people will not obey me. I have been pulling down houses but the Fire overtakes us faster than we can to it.* Pepys was not alone in his criticism. Someone else *met my Lord Mayor on horseback with a few attendants looking like one frightened out of his wits* and another reckoned *if the Lord Mayor had done as much {as others} his example might have gone far towards saving the City.*

Others were obstructive rather than ineffectual. With the flames roaring along Fleet St the Duke of York ordered houses to be blown up but was accosted by a young lawyer insisting it was against the statutes to bring gunpowder into the Inns of Court. He was beaten about the head for impertinence by the Duke's Master of the Horse.

Pamphlets and news-sheets from the few working presses were snapped up by a public desperate for information. More contemplative efforts of clergy and poets appeared later, one printed by Samuel Wiseman *At the Sign of the Beaver in the Strand,* formerly at the burned *Sign of the Sun in Poultry,* was entitled *A Short and Serious Narrative of London's Fatal Fire.* It ran to 360 lines of laboured verse:

> *And now the doleful, dreadful, hideous note*
> *Of Fire, is screaméd out with a deep strained throat.*
> *Horror, and fear and sad distracted cries*
> *Chid sloth away and bid the sluggard rise.*

Sluggards were slow to rise, and when they did:

> *The Furious Fire rides on with full Career*
> *And no Repulse will its Force feel or fear,*
> *Flings down strong Structures both of Stone and Wood*
> *And proudly scorns to have its work withstood.*

Towards the end, after four days of conflagration:

> *Th' uncessant Labors and the fervent Prayers*
> *Of those two Royal Brothers, Charles and James*
> *At last effected Conquest 'bove the Flames*
> *The worthy Tears that trickle from the Eye*
> *Of his afflicted Sacred Majesty prevail'd from heaven.*

The burning of the East India Company's pepper in the Royal Exchange caught the imagination of another poet in *London's Tears mingl'd with her Ashes:*

> *Now the Imperious Element did range*
> *Without Control, kept a full Ev'ning Change.*
> *When the religious Spices for some House,*
> *Seem'd to burn Incense to the incensed Powers.'*

Pepys, having recovered his papers, wine and cheese from a hole in the garden, returned to Bethnal Green on 8 September to collect his other goods. Back home he picked up his quill, having *fetched away my journall-book to enter for five days past.*

CHAPTER 6

POST-FIRE BUSINESS (almost) AS USUAL

*...did see smoke coming out of cellars from the late great fire, now above
six months since*

In 1986, in the shadow of the Monument, the Lord Mayor Sir Allan Davies and
the Master of the Bakers' Company unveiled a plaque commemorating the disaster
of 1666, and the quincentenary of the Company's royal charter of 1486.
Master John Copeman took the opportunity to apologise that a Pudding Lane
baker, Thomas Farynor, had allegedly caused the Great Fire.

Rumours of popish plots and foreign fire raisers swept London while the City
still burned. To quell panic, the king proclaimed that the blaze had been an Act
of God and not started by enemies from abroad. He advised people to ignore false
alarms, swearing he had *strength enough to defend them from any enemy, and, by
the Grace of God, would live and die with them.*

Dark mutterings and accusing fingers were not so easily stilled:

- the Dutch were to blame: jealous of English trade and sea power and eager
  to fight fire with fire.
- the French were to blame: hand in glove with the Pope and the Jesuits and
  always ready to do a Protestant nation mischief.
- the Portuguese were to blame: a servant of the Catholic ambassador had
  been seen placing fireballs on a window ledge in Pudding Lane.
- English papists, heirs to the Gunpowder Plotters, were to blame: several
  were seen laying trails of black powder into the cellars of public buildings.
- unspecified, dastardly foreign agents were to blame: burning the waterwheels beneath London Bridge to cut off the water supply, while others
  seized the New River Company works in Islington and severed all the
  pipes.
- the Roundheads were to blame: a plot by army veterans to murder the King
  and restore the republic had been uncovered earlier but who knew what
  other conspiracies might not have festered on and burst forth on 3
  September, the very anniversary of Cromwell's death.
- any random scapegoats were to blame: a man was nearly lynched when
  found carrying a bag of fireballs, which turned out to be tennis balls. A
  woman with an apron full of fluffy chicks was similarly threatened.

John Evelyn discounted any notion that the French and Dutch, with whom we
were now in hostility, were landed, and even now entering the City, but fear of

Dutch reprisals against England for the recent defeat of Admiral de Ruyter's fleet were not altogether groundless. In August English sailors had invaded the Scheldt islands, loosing fireships against anchored merchantmen laden with Spice Island cargoes before landing to loot and torch the town.

A Hague resident wrote home shortly after the Great Fire that he had not dared go out for days and a Frenchman saw women armed with meat spits attacking anyone who did not speak English. Taswell wrote that the during the Fire itself the ignorant and deluded mob had *vented forth their rage against the Roman Catholics and Frenchmen* while his brother saw *a Frenchman almost dismembered in Moorfields*. To curb all abuse of foreigners, the King sent troops to control City refugees and keep them under guard in makeshift camps.

Amid the ruins of his business in Pudding Lane Farynor desperately tried to salvage his good name by challenging anyone to show proof that he had been negligent on 2nd September. As an experienced baker, he never failed to check his ovens and stores of faggots every night and swore that Catholic fire-raisers had targeted his bakery, and produced witnesses to back him up. In 1681 a plaque on the site of his house stated that *here by the permission of Heaven hell broke loose upon this Protestant City from the malicious hearts of barbarous Papists*. In a less bigoted age it was removed, but not without resistance.

Most people were just numbed by the scale of the catastrophe. Evelyn touring the areas of Islington and Highgate and saw *200,000 people of all ranks and degrees dispers'd and lying by heapes of what they could save from the fire, deploring their losse, and tho' ready to perish for hunger and destitution yet not asking one pennie for reliefe, which to me appeared a stranger sight than any I had yet beheld.*

The xenophobic panic subsided. Determined to remain close to their ruined homes, people built sturdier shelters of wood and canvas to withstand the worsening weather while others drifted off to stay with friends and relatives in the country and suburbs. An estimated 20,000 people, many of them small tradesmen and craftsmen never returned, an unforeseen consequences of the disaster affecting the long-term development of the post-Fire City.

Churches in the suburbs soon doubled as furniture depositories for the household effects which people had been able to drag away from their homes on carts and wheelbarrows. As well as losing their homes, Taswell's parents lost furniture worth over £40 to swindlers making off with goods they had offered to salvage, having to replace them at inflated prices. Scarcity values were brought home to Pepys when buying a second-hand copy of Hobbes's *Leviathan* which was *mightily called for, being a book the Bishops will not let be printed again*. It cost 24s, three times its pre-Fire price.

Gresham's spacious house in Broad Street, used since his death by Gresham College and later the Royal Society, was undamaged. The latter shifted temporarily to Arundel House in the Strand so that both the City Corporation and the Royal Exchange could move in to the Gresham mansion to carry on essential civic and commercial business.

The authorities were aware of the immediate needs of the huge tented towns without the walls and on 6 September the King issued a Proclamation *for the keeping of Markets to supply London with Provisions and also for the prevention of Alarms and Tumults.* Markets were set up at Smithfield, Bishopsgate and by the Tower and others opened at Ratcliffe, serving the dockside areas, and in an arc from Clerkenwell to Whitechapel. Enforcement powers granted to local justices of the peace ensured that supplies of bread and beer were sent in daily from surrounding counties. Flour was soon in short supply since the central Bridewell store had been destroyed, but fortunately not the main granary in Southwark.

If Farynor had indeed been a baking contractor to the Navy, it was ironic that the supplies of *bisket out of the Sea Stores* were released by the Victualler of the Navy. The refugees spurned this hard tack as too alien and unpalatable to replace bread. (In the Great Hunger of the 1840s Irish peasants used only to potatoes were unable, rather than unwilling, to feed themselves on grain sent as famine relief by the English government.)

Communities throughout the kingdom and beyond were quick to send financial help. York gave £398, but failed in its attempt to get the capital moved north. Marlborough sent £50 and the Italian merchants of Leghorn a generous £300. Londonderry, a creation of the City Companies who were its major landlords donated £250, which was returned next year after their own destructive fire. Receipts were issued for monies received, in one parish for *£3.6s.8 which was collected on the Fast Day towards the Relief of those Persons who have been great Sufferers by the late Sad Fire within the City of London.*

Not all donations were cash. One town offered a shipload of cheese but an offer of Irish cattle on the hoof was rejected due to bureaucratic regulation on such imports. The funds raised were entrusted for distribution to Lord Mayor Bolton, successor in October to Bludworth. Mismanagement, if not calculated fraud, led to Bolton's later conviction and disgrace for suspected *misemployment of the Collections.*

Londoners were resilient folk, having in the past twenty years endured civil war, the execution of Charles I, the Commonwealth and the Plague. Though Evelyn deplored the burning of the *best Towne in the World,* when writing to Sir Samuel Tuke in Paris he was quick to assure his friend that matters were not as serious as the exaggerated accounts in France might lead him to believe. If not business as usual, London was far from at a standstill, a verdict echoed in other reports.

Little effects of any great consequence have been lost, beside the houses, Evelyn wrote. *Our Merchants complying with foreign correspondence as if no disaster had happen'd, nor do we hear of so much as one that has fail'd. The Exchange is now at Gresham College. The rest of the City, which may consist of near a seventh part and suburbs peopl'd with new shopps, the same noise, business and commerce, not to say vanity.*

This was over-optimistic, since many long-term failures were yet to be revealed, but circumstances pertaining before the Fire should not be overlooked. Commerce had not yet recovered from the effects of the Plague, so levels of business were low. Hostilities between the British and Dutch fleets in the North Sea affected international trade and shipping in the Thames was reduced.

An improbable figure is given of 3000 merchants and bankers meeting at Gresham House, but Pepys was probably right in believing this *infinity of people [came] partly through novelty to see the new place and partly to find out and hear what is become of one man or another.* The great overseas trading companies with warehouses down river escaped lightly but many smaller commodity merchants around Mark Lane lost everything. Those immediately ruined through loss of premises and stock were many, but there were others unaffected by the Fire itself, whose businesses failed through inability to collect outstanding debts. Years after the disaster, unfortunate individuals shorn of their livelihoods languished in debtors' prisons with no means to settle their liabilities and gain release from the Fleet or the Marshalsea. There was also the knock-on effect felt throughout the country. The wool and cloth trades were particularly hard hit with producers from Whitby and York, Bristol and Coventry lamenting the destruction of unsold goods stored in the capital, much of it in Blackwell Hall.

But the gloom was not as deep as first feared. Most City merchants had been able to save account books, bonds, contracts and letters of credit and opened for business in rented premises. Silver plate and chests of coin, if they escaped looters, were recoverable beneath the rubble. Already Livery Companies which had lost their premises were planning to rebuild; the Skinners resolved first *that the foundations of the hall be dug over, and a search made for lead, iron and pewter.* It would all give welcome employment the following Spring.

Factors contributing to London's rapid recovery from the calamity included:

- The capital's unusual topography, strung out from the Tower to the Abbey along the winding course of the Thames, rather than radiating out from a compact centre. Apart from the destruction in the Blackfriars, Farringdon and Fleet Street areas, there had been little damage outside the circuit of the Roman walls.

- The divisions, administratively and geographically, between court, government, church and City: the King's residence of Whitehall Palace, the Houses of Parliament, Westminster Hall—home of the law courts— Lambeth Palace and the Abbey had never been in any danger, although the Tower arsenal came close. The Temple suffered little harm, Lincoln's Inn and Gray's Inn none at all, neither did the lawyers cease their advocacy.

The mails were disrupted, but thanks to acting Post Master James Hickes, who salvaged important packages from the creeping Fire in Dowgate, the office opened up at the Golden Lion in Cripplegate on 3rd September. Next day Hickes despatched couriers along the route to Ireland via Holyhead, advising the post masters to send letters to him at that address for conveyance to the court.

The lack of hard news affected the country more than the capital. Londoners quickly realised that the City was not mortally stricken, but the loss of the printing presses of the *London Gazette* in Blackfriars and those in the Parish Clerks' hall in Vintry meant little immediate printed material was disseminated to counteract hearsay and rumour. Yet the *London Gazette* dated from temporary premises *From Monday, Septemb.3 to Monday Septemb.10 1666* appeared within days, regretting *the ordinary course of this Paper having been interrupted by a Sad and Lamentable Accident of Fire*, a Fire, fomented by a violent easterly wind grown too big *to be mastered by any Engines*.

The *Gazette* aimed to offer His Majesty's good subjects a short, but true, account of the calamity, and so it did most graphically. The King, Duke of York, Nobility and Gentry came in for fulsome praise for their indefatigable efforts and *a thousand blessings from the poor distressed people* were heaped upon their heads. The paper was adamant that though *Diverse Strangers, Dutch and French were during the Fire apprehended upon suspicion that they contributed mischievously to it, and are all imprisoned and Informations prepared to make a severe Inquisition...[the Fire] by way of a strong wind make us conclude the whole was an effect of unhappy Chance, or the heavy hand of God upon us for our Sins*.

Householders, many of them widows, dependent on rents were ruined if tenanted houses, and their own homes, were destroyed. Though the law attempted to mediate between destitute landlords and pauperised tenants, hardship and injustice were common. Among the most flint-hearted landlords was Humphrey Henchman, Bishop of London. Displaying no sign of Christian charity to the unfortunate, he extorted every penny possible out of the ruined booksellers of church properties in Paternoster Row around St Paul's.

The pestilence which had not been totally eliminated by the end of 1665 was not burned out in 1666. Though scattered outbreaks of plague were reported in several parishes that September, there was never another major epidemic.

The King commanded Wenceslaus Hollar, protégé of the Earl of Arundel, to view the ruins from the same viewpoint as his earlier panorama. The Bohemian exile, a meticulous draughtsman, depicts a scene in his *Another Prospect of 1666* very different from the flattened desolation after the 1940 Blitz. At first sight there seems little alteration to the pre-Fire skyline beyond the loss of St Paul's roof, the lonely spire of St Dunstan's-in-the-East and breaks between some waterfront buildings. Closer inspection certainly shows most churches gutted and gaps where wooden houses had been burned to the ground, but 'within the walls' the scene was far from featureless debris and ash. Had all been razed, the aftermath would have involved only a clearance operation not large scale demolition by explosives.

Hollar also prepared a street plan of the immediate post-Fire City. Comparison with the actual rebuilding shows how large a proportion of the new City kept to the old street names and alignments. Thankful there was still a Tower to defend; the Lieutenant had already ordered 300 fire buckets, 10 ladders and 12 firehooks to be added to the complement already in place. In the light of the intense demand from all quarters, delivery of this quantity of equipment must have taken considerable time.

The rollcall of churches lost for ever has a ring as melancholy as their lost bells: from All Hallows the Less, Holy Trinity the Less, St Andrew Hubbard, St Anne Blackfriars, St Botolph Billingsgate, St Faith under St Pauls, St Gabriel Fenchurch and so on, through St John Zachary, St Lawrence Pountney, St Martin Pomeroy and St Mary Mounthaw to St Nicholas Acon, St Pancras Soper Lane and St Thomas the Apostle. Only a dank, railed patch off Cheapside marks where St Benet Sherehog once stood and not even that marks All Hallows Honey Lane or St Michael le Querne.

One eminent foreigner deplored the devastation of St Paul's, seeing only a heap of stones *cemented together by the lead with which the church was covered, this when melted fell among the ruins, which have entirely covered the relics of antiquity that were there and demolished many splendid monuments, both Catholic bishops and other men, of which scarcely any trace is to be seen.*

A Spaniard insisted that the halting of the flames before the chapel of Somerset House, where the Queen Mother worshipped, was miraculous. *The Almighty wished to rebuke the blindness of the heretics and to show in what respect he held the sovereign Sacrament of the Altar. A hundred and forty churches of the heretics including St Paul's destroyed, but at a Catholic temple the fire acknowledged itself to be conquered.* Exultantly, but inaccurately, he claims that fifty five thousand heretic homes had been burned and repeats his boast that only in the face of *our holy faith, did the flaming tempest allow itself to be subdued.* It would have taken more than a miracle to save his skin if any Londoner had heard his jubilation.

The lost taverns were mourned by those with a taste for history, as well as ale: the Bag of Nails, Shakespeare's Mermaid, Ben Jonson's Mitre, Falstaff's Boar's

Head, the Hoop, the Sugar Loaf, the Cardinal's Cap, the Eagle and the Half Moon.

Jonas Moore and Ralph Gatrix, the City surveyors, produced a preliminary report:

The Fire began upon 2nd September at one Farynor's House, baker in Pudding Lane, between the hours of one and two in the morning, and continued burning until 6th September: consuming 373 acres within the walls of the City of London and 63 acres without. There remains 75 acres yet standing within the walls unburned. 87 parish churches, besides chapels burned, house burned 13,200. 11 parishes without the walls yet standing. Rough estimates based on the destroyed houses put the number of homeless between 60-70,000.

Different criteria were used to calculate losses, so basic facts do not tally. Churches and houses destroyed waver between 84 to 89, and 12,000 to 13,200 respectively. The first overall damage estimate was made in October at £7,300,000. One issued in 1681 raised it to £9,900,000. More accurate is likely to be a third survey, published next century when all the rebuilding costs were known where losses have risen to over £10,700,000.

Taking the third survey, an average figure set the value of every house at £25 annual rent for 12 years, i.e. £300. If 13,200 houses were lost this equals £3,960,000. Added to this are 87 lost churches, valued at £8,000 each, 52 livery halls at £15,000 each, the Royal Exchange at £50,000, Custom House at £10,000, the City gates and bridges over the Walbrook and Fleet at £15,000, and various jails, including Newgate, at £23,000. Rebuilding St Paul's, largely financed by a tax on sea-coal, was estimated to cost £2m and Guildhall £40,000.

Even more difficult to quantify were private citizen's personal goods, business losses and goods stored in warehouses and wharves. A figure plucked out of the air estimated these at £3,500,000. The literary value of the books burned in Paternoster Row and St Faith's, including copies of Shakespeare's Third Folio, was inestimable. Their actual price amounted roughly to £200,000 although their antiquarian value today would run into millions.

These estimates are almost impossible to translate into modern values.

On 10 October the Dean of St Paul's, the same Dr Sancroft who had removed to Tunbridge Wells during the Plague, preached *before the King at the Solemn Fast appointed for the late Fire in London.* Lesser Protestant clergy allowed no-one else to forget their culpability for this second blast of Divine Wrath, and at their own expense kept many printers in business. Samuel Rolle, Minister of the Word, had *The Burning of London in the Year 1666,* printed at The Golden Bible on London Bridge 1667, dedicated to the *Right Honourable Algernon, Earl of Northumberland* and the *Right Honourable Edward, Earl of Manchester* (an admiral and a general who had conveniently lived down their Roundhead pasts.)

The frontispiece, folded in three, is a woodcut of the blazing City wreathed in curlicues of smoke, in itself light relief before 144 pages of fire and brimstone, linking every thunderbolt and misfortune visited upon the sinful Londoners with biblical chapter and verse. Most prints of burning London were not originals but old ones embellished with spurting flames and billowing smoke. Wise after the event, Rolle holds forth that *there is no way to save the life of a man that hath a Gangered-Limb unless you cut it off...but why was this way of blowing up Houses no sooner thought of, being so effectual, nothing could be more obvious, but God is wont to blind those whom he intends to ruin.*

Eventually he winds up beseeching the Lord to *let me live to see London rebuilt, thy People reunited, England resettled, Protestant nations reconciled to each other and this Land a Mountain of Holiness.*

Thomas Vincent suspected that the catastrophe was a sequel to the abortive Gunpowder Plot of 1605, sanctioned and blessed by His Wickedness the Pope and carried out by unscrupulous Papists. Little did they reckon that their punishment in the Hereafter would be Eternal Fire.

The Countries Sense of London's Suffering in the late most lamentable Fire was the work of a *well-wisher to the City and those who suffer with it*. This was another dense, admonitory biblical harangue in which *the godly Reader will find Instruction, Edification and Consolation, as will be some ease to his Spirit and excite him to pray for the much decaying Author, for what else can be expected at the age of Seventy Four*. Age did not deter the author from writing at length but at last he concludes, not with entire conviction, that London had been purged of its iniquities and implores that *Lord Jesus, come quickly to the streets of this new Jerusalem.*

Eventually a single foreigner was hanged as a scapegoat though any intended retribution against Catholics was nullified by the fact that Robert Hubert was a Huguenot. No-one in authority actually believed the young Frenchman guilty, although he voluntarily confessed to fire-raising and even pointed out Farynor's house amid the ruins. Since the Pudding Lane bakery was a target for sightseers this was hardly conclusive proof.

Sir Robert Vyner, already well known at court as donor of the replacement coronation regalia, was a City Sheriff at the time of the Fire. When Lord Mayor in 1674 he awarded the rare distinction of the City freedom to Charles II and James, Duke of York, for their resolute example during the sad conflagration.

Reciprocal royal honours cost nothing, as the King well knew when bestowing ducal titles on his mistresses and bastards, but he publicly recognised and knighted only one man for his conduct during the Plague and the Fire. Although Lord Mayor Bludworth had ruled himself out by his behaviour others, had laboured bravely and untiringly to save the capital and deserved recognition, but went unrewarded. The suspicion lingers that King and court were not totally dismayed by the catastrophe that had befallen the City. Memories of the Civil War were still raw, and no Stuart could forget that the City's financial aid and manpower had fuelled his father's Parliamentary opponents and armies.

Charles had a sardonic sense of humour, so perhaps it amused him to ignore a potential Sir Samuel Pepys or Sir John Evelyn in favour of an obscure Westminster lawyer. Godfrey's name rarely occurs in reports of the Fire, although as Sir Edmund Berry Godfrey he was destined to play a mysterious role later in the frenzy of the Popish Plot. In 1678 Titus Oates swore before the magistrate, Godfrey, that Papists were plotting to kill the King, crown his Catholic brother, James, and fire the City again. Shortly afterwards Godfrey was found dead on Hampstead Heath, run through by his own sword, one of the intriguing, unsolved mysteries of English history. Charles defused alarm over any plots against his life in favour of his brother with the wry comment that no-one would murder him *to put Jamie on the throne.*

Practically, as well as spiritually, these were still fearful and dangerous times with the Dutch gaining the upper hand at sea in a war over trade not territory. On 17th June 1667 flames and explosions erupted from Deptford Dockyard; rumours spread the Dutch had landed, fired the Tower and were even now murdering honest Londoners in their beds. Evelyn knew better, but was appalled at the very real attack on Chatham soon after. On 28th June he wrote in fury at seeing the Dutch fleet lying triumphantly in the Medway and beyond to the Nore. *A dreadful spectacle as ever Englishmen saw, and a dishonour never to be wiped off. Those advising his Majesty to prepare no fleete this spring deserv'd...to be hanged.*

In the river he saw the charred hulks of *the London (now the third time burnt), the Royal Oak, the James etc. yet smoking.* The ultimate dishonour was the towing away as a prize of the ship that had brought the King back from Holland to reclaim his throne in 1660. Remembering earlier confrontations with the Hollanders, older men muttered treasonably that such enemy triumphs had been unthinkable in *Oliver's day.* The loss of the warship *'Royal Charles',** which was launched in 1655 as the *'Naseby',* and had been Admiral Blake's flagship in the great victory over the Dutch at Sole Bay was a national humiliation.

Peace was finally negotiated with Holland on 24 August. Pepys, out and about as usual, heard the *bells rung but no bonfires that I hear of anywhere, partly from the dearness of firing but principally from the little content most people have in the peace.* Less than a year after the Great Fire, it occurred to no-one in authority to ban street bonfires, although the first anniversary of the outbreak would be marked by a Fast Day on 2nd September.

* Trophies from the *Royal Charles,* including the wooden taffrail with the royal arms, the white ensign and Union Jack are in the Rijksmuseum, Amsterdam.

CHAPTER 7

OUT OF THE ASHES

A golden globe placed high with artful skill,
Seems, to the distant eye, a gilded pill.
On the opening of the new Royal College of Physicians

Parliament having given the first reading to an *Act for the Rebuilding of the City* in December 1666, it received the Royal Assent on 8 February 1667.

The emphasis was on swift reconstruction on the old street plan to facilitate the full resumption of business and overseas trade before London's pre-eminence was lost to other European powers. Though his own visionary plan had been rejected, Dr Christopher Wren, appointed Surveyor General and Principal Architect, willingly accepted the daunting charge of rebuilding the *whole City, the Cathedral Church of St Paul's and all the principal churches, and other structures.*

Evelyn had been quick to submit a *Survey of the Ruines and a Plot of the new Citty* but that too was rejected. Changing tack, he approached first the Lord Chancellor and then the King to appoint his protégé, the Dutchman Kiviet, to *undertake to warfe the whole river of Thames from the Temple to the Tower, as far as the fire destroyed, with brick, without pile, both lasting and ornamental.* Unfortunately this practical scheme was not accepted either.

One of the first structures rebuilt was the Royal Exchange, re-opening in 1669 complete with Gresham's original statue and heraldic grasshoppers. The new courtyard and arcades were marked by invisible boundaries known as 'walks'. The East India merchants were located on the West, and Spanish, Virginia and Jamaica merchants on the East. Overcrowding soon led to an exodus. Specialised traders moved to nearby coffee houses which became 'exchanges' in their own right and the money dealers shifted to Change Alley.

Though the Crown revenues of the Custom House were essential to the Exchequer, the King's offer to pay for the rebuilding, linked to hint of moving it to Westminster, was treated with suspicion by the City. Wren's replacement of 1671 on the Billingsgate site cost £10,000, although who paid for it is unclear. It was destroyed by fire in 1718.

By 1671 Guildhall could again host a Lord Mayor's banquet and Newgate was slamming its iron-barred oak doors behind old lags and fresh felons. Returning parishioners worshipped in temporary tabernacles since none of Wren's churches was started until the majority of houses had been rebuilt. New livery halls, paid for by the companies, were mostly finished by then, with only three of the forty four destroyed not eventually replaced.

The Fire Court met for the first time in February 1671, Sir Matthew Hale heading the bench of 22 judges in Clifford's Inn, three of whom usually sat at any one time. Months were spent adjudicating between the rival claims of freeholders, leaseholders, landlords, home owners, business premises, single tenancies, multiple tenancies and a formidable assembly of false petitioners, all pleading lost documents or waving ingenious forgeries. The judges could only estimate valuations of destroyed properties and potential building sites until an enterprising lawyer, Stephen Primatt, published a handy price guide. His *City and Country Purchaser and Builder* was a best-seller, relied upon by all in the building business and much thumbed by those involved in the Fire Court.

Inevitably there were injustices, but the Court worked much more efficiently and quickly than had been thought possible mainly because Hale, with legal sanction, cut through age-old rights of property enshrined in Common Law. The corporation's insistence on the need to widen or extend certain main thoroughfares in the cause of fire safety and easing traffic congestion was paramount; owners receiving meagre compensation for lost frontages or curtailed ground areas. Sharp practice was not unknown, judging by the number of complaints against profiteers *making harvest* in the ruins.

The preamble to the Act referred to the multitude of variable cases to be dealt with, wherein no general rule could be prescribed. It then laid down its ground rules which were not open to argument: landlords should rebuild premises at their own expense; if landlords were unable to do so, tenants could at *their* own expense, receiving extended leases and lowered rents in return. If after three years neither party had rebuilt, the site would be sold and the proceeds passed to the landlord. Owners of freeholds rebuilding their own premises could expect a small house off a main street to cost around £200, a substantial one in the City centre to cost from £600-1,000 and a mansion in the same area between £2,500-3,500.

Wren's and Evelyn's plans, and others even more Utopian, all called for complete clearance of the rubble; this would have taken months, if not years, given how much of the City still stood. There were hundreds of tottering houses, scores of church towers, dozens of halls open to the sky, charred timber beams and flaking, stone walls. Many crypts and cellars were full of debris from collapsing floors, while others suffered only scorching and remained as solid foundations beneath the weight of roofless walls and debris, as at Guildhall.

The City Surveyors staked out new street alignments in March 1667 and in May began marking out rebuilding plots. Work then started piecemeal.

Various building acts, enforced on this occasion, led to increased use of brick, stone and tiles, although wood was still used in great quantity for frameworks, roof joists and flooring. Aiming at uniformity, these building regulations sanctioned only four types of dwellings to be erected, although attics and cellars did not count as storeys. Houses no higher than two storeys were permitted in narrow lanes, three storeys in wider streets and four storeys if fronting a main thoroughfare. The prohibition on grander houses with four storeys not fronting a street must have applied to those set back in their own grounds.

The new thoroughfares of King Street and Queen Street opened a route south from Guildhall to Thames Street (and in the 19th Century to Southwark Bridge). Other streets were widened, churches set back and the worst areas of rookeries and tenements redeveloped, causing the previous occupants to move elsewhere and create new slums. These sprouted in Whitechapel, St Giles-in-the-Fields and Seven Dials. All would become as lawless and infamous as any that flourished in pre-Fire Coldharbour, Alsatia and Blackfriars.

The poor, as always, had difficulty finding affordable accommodation, and many remained where they had found refuge, outside the Walls and in the Liberties. The nobility, whose Tudor forebears had appropriated the town houses of dispossessed bishops and abbots along the Strand, moved further West to Covent Garden, Bloomsbury and Mayfair. Rather than live above the shop as their fathers had done, wealthy merchants found it pleasanter to make their homes in the villages of Finsbury, Tottenham, Hackney or across the Bridge in Bermondsey, Deptford or Greenwich.

Of the 13,200 houses destroyed, it is estimated that 4,000 were never rebuilt. It is not entirely clear whether the shortfall in housing meant fewer citizens returned after the rebuilding, or that the lack of potential householders led to plans being curtailed. Whatever the causes, the demographic City of 1688 when Gregory King produced the first definitive English census was very different from that of 1660. King was a genealogist at the College of Arms, and his survey shows a population of 5,500,520 comprising 1,349,586 families, all meticulously assessed as to status, occupation or vagrancy.

Timber cladding and exposed beams were forbidden, the new houses having tiled roofs and sash windows. With no jutting gables or outward opening casement windows, their flat facades gave the impression of greater width, even to streets built to the same ground plans as before. These improvements and prohibitions decreased the risk of a single household fire spreading to engulf whole streets. In addition, regulations were enforceable in every parish under *An Act for Preventing and Suppressing of FIRES within the City of London and the Liberties thereof.*

The final clause reiterated the fines for infringements, appearing to be an inducement to informers. Of the Penalties and Forfeitures imposed on offenders, one half went to Christ's Hospital for the maintenance of poor children harboured and kept there, and the other to him or them that will sue for the same.

Street lighting regulations were tightened. Mr Henning, who obtained a patent on his convex lens oil lamps, soon ran into trouble with the Tallow Chandlers who saw their trade in cheap candles and tallow dips as under threat.

During the Fire, the intensity of the heat had caused molten lead to pour from St Paul's Cathedral roof, but much of the building including 240 feet of tower remained standing and services were held in part of the nave by the West door. Hopes of repairing the entire building were only abandoned when the cascades of falling stones became too dangerous and, as Wren had argued from the beginning, the whole had to be torn down. It took many barrels of gunpowder and a battering ram to reduce Old St Paul's to forty seven thousand cartloads of debris, the best of which was re-used for new churches and houses, as was the recovered lead.

Expectations by the Carmen's Company of gaining the valuable contract to remove the rubble and bring in the new stone from the wharves were not met. Instead its members lost out to a sharp contractor named Slithurst (Slyford according to the Wren Society). Appeals to the Court of Aldermen failed to break his monopoly and the Carmen were fobbed off with an order to confiscate Slithurst's carts if found carrying bricks, timber or any materials other than stone. Brawls between rival carriers enlivened the rebuilding years.

Pepys watched the cathedral's demolition with interest and nausea, persevering though finding it *strange how the very sight of the stones falling from the top of the steeple do make me sea-sick.* Earlier he had feared for his life inside the wrecked building although nothing could check his enthusiasm for anything newsworthy.

Nature was swift to claim new habitats with wind-blown wild flowers. John Aubrey noted as early as Spring 1667 a profusion of *eruca levis Neapolitana, smooth Bankcress of Naples...insomuch that they* [people] *thatch their sheds and cells with it. Before the Fire 'twas very rarely to be found...but since on the tops of the walls of St Paul's church in abundance, and never flourisht so much as in the ruins.* Another visitor remarked on *sisymbrium Irio,* known as London rocket, growing in any nook and cranny, *with little yellow heads high in the blackened tower* of Old St Paul's.

Stone for the new cathedral came from quarries on the Isle of Portland and Beer in Dorset, Burford and Headington in Oxfordshire, Reigate and Guildford in Surrey, Tadcaster in Yorkshire and Kent. Additional material was shipped from Caen in Normandy, source of stone for the Conqueror's White Tower. Wren's third design had received the royal warrant in 1675, and he lived to see the cross placed on the dome in 1710. Skilled craftsmen and rough labourers were employed for decades and distaste for labourers' clothes and habits is nothing new. Taverns were built nearby to serve the workmen and their prodigious thirst, including the Horns and Old Watling.

With no household rates or regular municipal taxes, raising revenue to run the Corporation had always been a problem, solved on an ad hoc basis by levies, imposts, customs dues and fines. Lord Mayors entertained at their own expense at home or in livery halls and, when the Mansion House was built in mid-18th Century, it was funded out of the fines of aldermen who paid handsomely to avoid the heavy expense of becoming sheriffs, and later Lord Mayor.

To finance the reconstruction of St Paul's a 'temporary' tax on sea-coal was imposed at one shilling per chaldron, a measure of capacity in which 8 gallons equal 1 bushell and 36 bushells equal 1 chaldron. The tax was raised to 3s per chaldron as the work progressed, and remained a key item of City revenue until around 1840.

As timber, stone and brick were in great demand, many investors burned their fingers in chancy schemes floated to cash in on the boom, Evelyn among them. The Dutchman Kiviet had even investigated Thames mud for its brickmaking properties and his favourable assessment may have led to Evelyn's speculation, and losses. In April 1668 he added his name to the subscription at the Royal Society for *50,000 bricks towards building a College.* On the same day he noted a printed libel by *the poor whores to Lady Castlemaine,* the King's expensive chief mistress. He was to complain again about her, and *another lady of pleasure {Mrs Nellie}, and curse of our nation.*

A view of the City from the Thames printed during the Frost Fair of 1683/84 contrasts with the pre- and post-Fire panoramas by Hollar. Houses, halls and wharves fill the north shore, but there is no St Paul's and the row of houses on London Bridge is still gap-toothed, and was never fully restored to Elizabethan glory. The main thrust of redevelopment was on domestic and commercial building, riverside wharves and warehouses. Those churches which escaped the Fire— All Hallows by the Tower, St Olave Hart Street, St Helens Bishopsgate, St Ethelburga, St Bartholomew Smithfield and St Giles Cripplegate—had congregations swollen by worshippers from ruined parishes.

Another casualty of the Fire which was never rebuilt was London's only post-Roman public latrine. It had been installed over the Walbrook by Mayor Richard Whittington in 1419, and this flush convenience reputedly had 60 seats apiece for ladies and gentlemen.

By 1666 both the Walbrook and the Langbourne were little better than sewers, though the Fleet was navigable up as far as Holborn. After the Fire a plan to beautify this waterway in the Venetian style, by lining it with handsome residences and warehouses, was blighted at source by its unregenerate neighbours upstream around Bart's. Much public good and public health would have resulted had the flames swept through the squalid areas of Newgate with its butchers' Shambles and Smithfield cattle market, sparing only St Bartholomew the Great and its attendant Hospital. (The last of the fine houses in adjacent Cloth Fair was only demolished in the 20ᵗʰ Century). The Fires of Smithfield had claimed Protestant martyrs under Mary Tudor and rather fewer Catholic ones under Elizabeth.

The most notable post-Fire speculative builder was a man whose baptismal name outdid even that of his father, Praise-God Barebones, Speaker of the Commonwealth parliament. By 1667 Barebones II's puritan past was behind him, and in place of If-Jesus-Christ-had-not-died-for-thee-thou-hadst-been-damned Barebones, he became plain Dr Nicholas Barbon and well on the way to a fortune. Having lived through the Fire, Barbon took practical steps to safeguard his new properties and was a founder partner of an insurance office situated *at the Backside of the Royal Exchange*. Realising that prevention was better than paying-out, clients were soon offered an exclusive fire service, provided by uniformed watermen who were *lusty, laborious, hazardous and dextrous in quenching sudden fire*. Should their efforts be in vain the rebuilding of clients' premises was included in the cost of the premium. Advice to quell a chimney fire by firing up it with a gun was replaced by holding a wet sheet across the hearth to keep out the air.

The Fire, as well as schemes like Barbon's, provided the impetus behind urgent improvements in English-made fire fighting equipment, as was competition from appliances imported from the continent. Manufacturers' names likes Keeling, Wharton and Strode were heard for the first time. All equipment needed to be made both more efficient and more powerful, from the leather hoses and clumsy carts to the water reservoirs and pumping mechanisms. The merits of brass or copper nozzles and gooseneck swivels rather than rigid pipes were fiercely debated and experimented with, encouraged by Charles II's appointment of Isaac Thompson as his Sworn Engine Maker. A royal command performance in 1674 saw the King at a demonstration of Sir Samuel Morland's latest engine, featuring a brass elbow acting as a universal connector to any outmoded parish engine.

The King also updated the inadequate regulations in his own palaces, one necessary clause ordered that *no person shall make use of any of his said buckets for any ordinary or private use*. Other monarchs might have taken note of this tactfully worded prohibition. The splendour of Versailles failed to mask its stinks, attributed in part to *much pissing in chimneys and corners*.

Jerry-building, shoddy construction, was rife in practice if not in name; even a century after the Fire Dr Johnson accepted as a normal hazard of London life the sudden thunderous collapse of dwellings.

Streets and squares still bear the names of those who developed areas of London both before and after the Fire—the Russell earls of Bedford, the earls of Southampton, Arundel and Albemarle, Sir Thomas Bond, Colonel Panton, Henry Jermyn, William Craven—and George Downing.

At the Restoration Charles II had exempted from general pardon only those personally involved in his father's death. The barbaric executions were halted after those of thirteen regicides whose demeanour on the scaffold won unwelcome sympathy from Londoners. In stark contrast was that of many who had sat in judgement on their erstwhile comrades-in-arms.

The most shameless turncoat was Downing, a nephew of Governor John Winthrop of Massachusetts. He had been Cromwell's Scout-Master-General in Scotland and was later appointed ambassador to Holland, a post he retained after the Restoration. So far no worse than others, Sir Matthew Hale of the Fire Court had been both a Commonwealth judge and an MP, while General Monk had turned his coat from Royalist to Roundhead before engineering the Restoration. In 1662 Downing decoyed three Roundhead colleagues to Delft, where they were arrested and returned to England. Though deploring Downing's treachery, Pepys went to see them hanged, drawn and quartered, before returning home to admire his new parlour curtains. In a phrase to make his ears burn, Downing's housing development off Whitehall was later described as *fit for persons of honour and quality*. The Prime Minister and the Chancellor of the Exchequer traditionally reside at 10 and 11 Downing Street, tenancies reversed after the 1997 Election.

Fire continued to destroy crowded cities, and not only the ramshackle tenements of the poor. In Scotland, for example, the wealthy lived, and died, in narrow, town houses, far taller than anything in London. In February 1700 *all the pride of Edinburgh, between three and four hundred families, most of the lords, lawyers and clerks were burnt beside many poor and great families.* The destruction raged unchecked, since little could be done as all the water cisterns were dry. Houses twelve and fourteen storeys high were razed to the ground and the city burned *with the greatest fervour and vehemency.* Its magnitude can be judged from an eye witness's letter commencing: *notwithstanding that I saw London burn...*

The Fire Court was wound up in 1672 and five years later the Monument was finished, designed by either Wren or, more likely, Robert Hooke. It stands at the foot of Pudding Lane, *the better to preserve the memory of this dreadful Visitation...where the Fire so unhappily began.*

An Act for Preventing and Suppressing of FIRES within the City of London and the Liberties thereof.

[edited extracts]

Item: That the wards of the City and Liberties be divided into four equal parts

East: Portsoken, Aldgate, Tower, Billingsgate, Bridge, Langbourne and Lime St.

West: Farringdon Within, Farringdon Without, Castle Baynard, Cheapside, Aldersgate

North: Cornhill, Broad St, Coleman St, Bassishaw, Bishopsgate, Cripplegate

South: Queenhithe, Bread St, Vintry, Cordwainer, Dowgate, Walbrook, Candlewick

Item: Each of the four parts to have available 800 leathern buckets, 50 ladders... also as many Hand-Squirts of Brass as will furnish Two for each Parish, four and twenty Pickax-sledges and forty shod-shovels.

Item: That every one of the twelve companies provide and keep in readiness thirty buckets, one engine, six pickaxe sledges and forty shod-shovels.

Item: That all the other inferior companies provide and keep in readiness buckets and engines proportionable to their abilities, of which those least able, to provide portable engines to carry upstairs into any rooms or tops of houses.

Item: That every alderman who hath passed the office of shrievalty provide four and twenty buckets and one hand-squirt of brass, and all those who had not been sheriffs, twelve buckets and one hand-squirt of brass, to be kept at their respective dwellings, and all other principal citizens and inhabitants to provide and keep in their houses a certain number of buckets.

Item: That all Brokers at the Royal Exchange attend major fires, along with the Lord Mayor and Aldermen, as salvage men to take care of such Goods and Household stuff as may be removed.

Item: At the cry of Fire every dwelling to hang out a light and place a bucket of water on the doorstep and then keep the household within doors, except for the designated stout man if summoned. The Lord Mayor to call on certain livery companies to supply trained men, not as firefighters, and others carpenters, bricklayers and tilers to make good damage.

Item: That no Gunpowder be kept within in the Walls, except in such secure places approved by the Court of Aldermen.

Printed for Nath. Brook at the Sign of the Angel in Gresham College 1668.

CHAPTER 8

FIRE OFFICES and FIRE BRIGADES

Houses frequently consumed before such fires could be extinguished

Memories of the Great Fire remained vivid well into the next century but, as the horror faded, old habits of negligence and fatalism reasserted themselves. It is unlikely during London's cold, damp winters that a decree ordering all hearth fires to be quenched at night was zealously obeyed.

Repairs and improvements to the City utilities were more practical. Waterwheels beneath London Bridge were soon operating again but replacement of damaged water mains took far longer. Stop cocks at ward boundaries were redesigned and hardened, with marked wooden plugs inserted into the wooden pipes at regular intervals to avoid *breaking of pipes in a disorderly manner,* as had happened in the Fire.

An engineer was appointed to advise the Lord Mayor when, and where, to blow up houses to contain future outbreaks of fire, and stores of gunpowder laid by in designated places. A scale of indemnities was drawn up to compensate owners whose premises might be destroyed by such preventive acts.

The Plague, like the Black Death, led to a labour shortage. In the months before the Fire the Royal Mail was reduced to 45 trained staff, and fewer still afterwards. Private enterprise saw its chance to break the monopoly, and one William Docwra planned a delivery and collection service to all parts of London, not just the centre served by the coaching inns. He promoted his business through a pamphlet entitled *A Penny Well Bestowed,* the cost of a letter from Westminster to Wapping in 1680. He extolled the rapidity with which lawyers could consult with their clients, traders give warning of their arrival in Town and correspond with all men of Business at a remote distance. Quick to take advantage of Docwra's postal scheme were the fledgling fire insurance companies boosting their own merits to potential customers, and denigrating the opposition.

The City lawyers remained obstinately jealous of their rights. In 1669 Lord Mayor Turner arrived to dine at the Inner Temple accompanied by officers bearing the ceremonial sword and mace. Outraged barristers and students jeered and jostled this show of armed corporation might until the mayoral party beat an undignified and hungry retreat. A few years later, another Lord Mayor went to inspect a fire in the Temple but was also forced to retire. Meeting a fire engine pounding up Fleet Street, he ordered it back to its base.

By 1679 the lawyers had invested in firefighting equipment of their own. On a bitter January night fire broke out in the Middle Temple; water froze in the supply pipes and the nearby Thames was icebound. Hopes faded until a merry quip was taken seriously and the *engine played away many barrels of beer to stop the fire, but the chief way of stopping was by blowing up the houses, in doing so many were hurt...one's skull was almost broken, but now in hopes of recovery.*

Ten years after the Great Fire much of Southwark was destroyed. Over 600 houses were burned including Chaucer's Tabard, other historic taverns and public buildings and several brothels. The stone gatehouse still bearing a few withered heads prevented the flames spreading to the Bridge. Charles II was *rowed down river to give such orders as found fit* and found the Duke of Monmouth and Lord Craven directing operations in an area better supplied than most with equipment.

Shortly after this Fire, the *London Gazette* announced that the King was pleased to grant *letters-patent unto Mr Wharton and Mr Strode, for a certain new invention for quenching fire with leathern pipes which carries a great quantity and a continual stream of water, with an extraordinary force, to the top of any house, into any room, passage or alley, being much more useful than any other which hath been invented, as was attested of the masters of St Thomas's Hospital and officers of the parish, as in the late great fire of Southwark, to their great benefit.*

These patented engines were powerless in 1682 against a blaze along the Thames shore at Wapping. A thousand houses were said to have been lost, most of them probably no more than shacks. Less destruction, but an alleged death toll of 50, arose from another fire among Wapping's wharves in 1715.

The fiery ruins in Cornhill in 1748 would have been more extensive but for the *ten Conveniencies, Engines invented by my late uncle Richard Newsham and now continued by Messrs Newsham and Ragg, Engine Makers to His Majesty appliances.* One of these is shown playing on the flames in the perspective view published by the manufacturers. Newsham, the late uncle, had abandoned button-making for invention, and his manual appliances with a pair of double-acting pumps and primitive cylinder and piston were twice as effective as most older models. He took out several patents, branched out into the export business but never thought of horsepower to pull his appliances through the streets.

Westminster suffered only smoke and smuts in 1666, but the first of two truly destructive fires occurred in April 1691. Before the flames were checked by blowing up houses, much of the Whitehall Palace was badly damaged and scores of adjacent mansions destroyed.

Extensive new apartments and galleries for the palace were designed by Wren but William and Mary had little time to enjoy them. A second fire in 1698, caused, as are so many still, by clothes hung to dry before an open fire, gutted the warren of buildings dating back centuries. Fire engines and water engines were soon on the scene, but made so little impact that by morning the palace was in ruins and a dozen people dead. The ruins of Wolsey's original York Place were never rebuilt and all that remains of Whitehall Palace are Inigo Jones's Banqueting House and Henry VIII's wine cellar. When the post-WW2 Ministry of Defence was built on the latter site, the stone vaulted cellar was moved up, along and down, into its basement, a challenging feat of civil engineering by Travers Morgan and Partners.

Admiration for Charles II's conduct during the Great Fire was slow to sour, but he did little to maintain the City's goodwill. His political inclination towards Catholic France was anathema to men who were by inclination, if not in name, puritan. Short of money for his pleasures, despite a secret pension from his cousin Louis XIV and failing to raise yet more loans from the City, he called in the Companies' royal charters. The specious excuse for this unprecedented act was *Quo Warranto*, 'by what right', were they held and enjoyed.

True, not all were impeccable; though many documents dated back two or three centuries, some were of doubtful origin and others copies of those lost in the Great Fire or earlier accidents. Confiscation of the pride and provenance of the most powerful group in the City caused outrage, inflamed by having to admit their 'errors' and pay heavy fines to have the charters restored. It may have led to short term financial gain for the King, but the harm done by *Quo Warranto* to the City/Crown relationship was never repaired under the Stuart monarchy. His father's levy of Ship Money in 1638 had proved even more politically disastrous in provoking civil war in the 1640s.

James II was ousted by the 'Protestant wind' that blew in William III and the Glorious Revolution of 1688. Aware of London's tinderbox reputation, the new king had several of the latest fire engines with improved sucking worms loaded aboard his flagship. These were designed by the Captain General of the Amsterdam brigade, Jan van der Heijden, author of the *Use of serpent-like fire sprays or hoses, how these should be kept at the ready with all their appurtenances in specially built sheds for use in the event of fire.*

Van der Heijden's models so impressed Peter the Great during his visits to the Koestraat factory, during his stay in Holland in 1697, that before returning home he ordered several for St Petersburg. News of their eventual arrival had the Tsar commanding a quayside building be set on fire so he could personally test the efficacy of his new toys.

Always mechanically inventive the Germans rivalled the Dutch, and one of Hans Hautch's fire engines was on the streets of Nuremberg in the 1650s. Like most innovations of the century it relied on a brass or copper air cylinder to improve the force and range of the water jet but was still hand-drawn.

In Britain His Majesty's Gunners were authorised to blow up with gunpowder buildings in the path of an uncontrollable fire—always a government monopoly.

(One unresolved mystery of Guy Fawkes's Plot is how he acquired the large number of barrels of powder discovered under the Houses of Parliament). A military drumbeat warned spectators to remove themselves before fuses were lit but most stayed to watch the explosions and often suffered the consequences.

The end of the century is literally shrouded in the mists of time, since one of the longest and dirtiest of London's fogs blanketed the capital for weeks. Unusual climatic conditions induced by cold air rising from the river turned a winter mist into a noxious fog by mingling with the filthy smoke and fumes spewed out by tens of thousands of domestic chimneys. This brew created a classic 'pea-souper'. The chief culprit, despite the banishment of the worst polluting trades from the centre, was still seacoal used for all home heating and cooking and fuelling the furnaces and braziers of craftsmen.

The corrosive effect of smoke pollution is less swift and dramatic than visible flames, but it brings its own casualties. Already the gleaming Portland stone of Wren's new churches was disfigured by grime, and many of the fanciful diagnoses in the *Bills of Mortality* blamed on the foul miasma are surely bronchitis, pneumonia and pleurisy. William III, choking with asthma, sought refuge in rural Kensington Palace, though recurring London fogs could hardly be held responsible for the chronic ailment of a man raised in the bone-chilling damp of The Hague.

Though Gresham's gold, 'good money' was fireproof, vulnerable paper money burns more than holes in pocket, a problem spared merchants of the Middle Ages. Mints of money continue to be made in the City, but there have been no coins since 1975, when all Royal Mint operations removed to Llantrisant in Wales.

The medieval merchant locked his coin away in an iron-bound chest with several keys. When not in use so too was gold and silver plate, his wife's jewellery and his aldermanic chain—safe against thieves and all but the most violent of fires. He spent lavishly on Russian furs and Venetian glass, along with imported wine, sugar and spices. His house might be glazed and made comfortable with feather beds, damask hangings and curtains and carved oak furniture. Surplus cash was kept by a local goldsmith, or invested in property, the City man's hedge fund.

By the 16th and 17th Centuries, seaborne trade was financed by much of this surplus cash. The risks of shipwreck, fire at sea, pirates and other maritime dangers were high, but so were profits. These untaxed gains were then re-invested in further expeditions, leading to a huge expansion of ocean-going shipping.

The dawning industrial and transport revolutions led to insatiable demands for imported raw materials, and an increase in exported manufactured goods. The growing network of canals facilitated carriage of goods in bulk and better roads ushered in a new age of fast, regular wheeled transport. In 1784, the first mail coach travelled from Bristol to London overnight and with it the advantages of entrusting valuable letters and goods to official coaches with armed guards were soon apparent to businesses. Time was money.

Potential for expansion was vast, but investment in machinery, mills, factories and transportation required financing on a scale hitherto unknown, and far beyond the cash reserves of individuals. Private, and then joint stock, banking came into its own, with Child's Bank in the Strand enjoying the doubtful privilege of Nell Gwynne's overdraft. Even so, as late as 1680 Sir Dudley North, an educated, well-travelled man, had no intention of entrusting his savings to *men who played at hazard with what had been earned by the industry and hoarded by the thrift of other men. If the dice turned up well, the knave who kept the cash became an alderman, if they turned up ill, the dupe who furnished the cash became a bankrupt.* Dr Johnson later expressed similar scorn for City stockjobbers, *an unnecessary collection of low fellows speculating in Funds of no benefit to anyone but themselves.*

Insurance now covered shipping risks, of which fire was always a prime hazard. One of the earliest maritime notices, dated 1627, was for *the sole making and registering of all manner of assurances, intimations and renunciations made upon any ship or ships, goods or merchandise in the Royal Exchange or any other place within the City of London.*

The Royal Exchange remained a hub of City life even after the first City coffee house opened in the 1650s, run by the servant of a Levant Company merchant. It soon became a centre for exchanging business, political and shipping news—the information technology website of its day. All merchants paid a penny entrance fee. Other coffee houses soon followed, each with a distinct clientele.

Stockjobbers started at Jonathons in Change Alley and expanded into the Stock Exchange Coffee House and Tavern. Edward Lloyd opened up in Tower Street before 1688, moving later to *Lloyds Coffee House within the Royal Exchange.* It profited from the reputation for being first with accurate news of the movement of shipping which was published in *Lloyds News.* This ran into trouble in 1696 but its successor, *Lloyds List* dating from 1734, remains London's oldest daily paper. A second Lloyd's Coffee House opened in Pope's Alley, specialising in insurance and ship auctions, the last being Brunel's steamship 'Great Eastern'.

Garraways sold coffee and wine in bulk, attracting many shipping men. In 1711 the Sun Insurance started insuring both ships and cargoes.

The Jerusalem developed into the London Shipping Exchange but burned down in 1748. The Virginia and Maryland and the Virginia and Baltic were the haunts of import and export traders; by 1810 merchants at the Antwerp Tavern in Threadneedle St were negotiating with the newly-independent United States. In 1823 the Baltic limited itself to 300 members, mainly tallow chandlers and shipping agents, many of them Greeks, or Anglo-Greeks. The 1891 merger of the

Shipping and Baltic Exchange led to the Baltic Exchange, whose elegant domed premises in Mary Axe were demolished by an IRA bomb in 1991.

The French, not the Dutch, were now the enemy, so the Bank of England was founded in 1694, enabling government to raise a *fund of perpetual interest* to pay for the war, and manage the national Debt.

Many of these enterprises contributed from the outset to what is now known as Britain's Invisible Earnings, profits from service industries rather than manufacturing. Today banks, finance houses, insurance companies, consultancies, Lloyds of London, Lloyds Register of Shipping, shipbroking, international law and accountancy all help to balance the nation's books.

A setback to the rampant capitalism of the early-18th Century was the South Sea Company 'bubble'. With few visible assets beyond an alluring title and backing from the Sword Blade Bank this trading venture swelled to unsustainable size before collapsing in 1720. Fortunes were made in its early days, but thousands of reckless investors were ruined in the final panic. Latent antagonism between Parliament and City was inflamed by the scandal, the first of many to dog the Square Mile, and the latter did belatedly attempt to impose some control on future speculations. The resentful poor, unable to borrow cash to play the market, took grim pleasure in the ruin of those who had, particularly politicians bribed with stock that overnight proved worthless.

Fires being as frequent as ever, developers like Nicholas Barbon realised there was money to be made from this ever-present danger and so expanded his original ideas. The Fire Office was founded in 1680, followed in 1683 by the Friendly Society and in 1685 by the General Insurance. The most famous opened in 1696 as the Amicable Contributors for Insurance from Loss by Fire, soon known from its badge as the Hand in Hand.

Handbills distributed by the Fire Office *kept against the Royal Exchange, and at the Rainbow Coffee-House* show rates in 1698 as 6s a year to insure a brick house for one hundred pounds, and double for timber. Discounts were offered for lump sum payments up to the full term of eleven years. The Office had assets of £60,000 from ground rents and listed a number of City worthies as trustees. Some of these gentlemen were *to be spoken with daily at the Exchange Office from eleven to One and at the Temple Office from Four to Six.*

The risk of fires was always present and so were the unpredictable risks carried by the new insurance companies. In the early days many were ruined by a sudden spate of fires or hastily amalgamated with others in order to survive.

All the companies employed Thames watermen, on call day and night. Watermen were a tough, independent foul-mouthed crew, famed even in a crude age for their abusive language and invective but, as a contemporary acknowledged, *active and diligent*. Serious fires bedeviled riverside wharves or on ships moored alongside but these experts on the City's main highway at all states of the tide were quick on the scene with their buckets and squirts. The Company of Watermen ruled the river, from its rebuilt Hall in St Mary at Hill, working closely with the new insurances offices.

Sailors were even tougher. Nimble fellows, resigned to a hard and dangerous life aboard ship, inured to living and working in cramped quarters, existing on sour beer, putrid meat and weevil-infested biscuit, they were fearless of heights and accustomed to harsh discipline.

Fire fighting offered novelty, excitement and a welcome addition to the meagre earnings of a waterman plying oars, so the companies were swamped by volunteers. Having been selected, a watermen then had to produce a reference from a worthy citizen such a member of the Common Council or prominent merchant. Once selected he was provided with an axe, distinctive arm badge and uniform. Tunics varied over the years from full-skirted, gold-cuffed masterpieces adorned with a huge silver arm badge to more serviceable tight, belted coats. Phoenix firemen sported coats of *crimson livery cloth lined with light Saxon green turned up with green shag, crimson waistcoat and breeches*; Norwich Union men wore red breeches and waistcoats with green frock coats and red epaulettes and Guardian men dark brown coats with red and yellow striped waistcoats; Caledonian firemen were identifiable by an orange thistle on their helmets. All, however, were outshone by the Westminster watermen in gold-cuffed and braided blue jackets, black knee breeches, white stockings and gold garters.

The more elaborate garments were probably only worn for the annual parade and banquet. Early insurance company fire fighters wore a variety of headgear, ranging from the peaked caps of the watermen, to military style iron caps and something resembling a coal scuttle. By the 1720s, a high-crowned type of bowler hat made of stout, boiled leather was common but a century later some company's men turned out in fashionable beaver hats with buckled headbands, some in low-crowned hats with a nautical air and others in waisted top hats, more suited to contemporary chimney sweeps. Leather helmets gained popularity during the 18th Century and already displayed some of the safety elements of modern ones: a peak to protect the face, a neck guard and a ribbed comb, in the style of a Spanish conquistador's morion, to deflect falling debris

Evidence of a serviceable fireman's uniform comes from Defoe's account of his countrywide tour in 1724. The men, very dextrous, bold and successful were on call day and night, furnished with tools proper for the job and *jack-caps of leather able to keep them from hurt if brick or timber or anything not of too great a bulk should fall upon them...[men] called firemen, but with an odd contradiction in the title, for most of them watermen.*

A later versifier gave a roll-call of the insurance companies and referred to uniforms of hobnailed shoes, worsted stockings, crimson plush breeches and red or blue jackets.

The badge of each respective crew, in tin or copper traced.
The engines thund'red through the street,
Fire hook, pipe, bucket, all complete.
And torches glared, and clatter feet along the pavement paced.
The Hand in Hand the race begun, Then came the Phoenix and the Sun,
The Exchange, where old insurers run, the Eagle where the new.

Those arm badges were base metal, but many were made of silver, and later of silver plate. All were very conspicuous, round or oval and up to six inches across and embossed with the company name and crest. At a cost of over £2 each firemen had to provide a surety that they would return their badge at the end of their service, or earlier dismissal. Barbon, sharp as always, quickly appropriated the phoenix as the symbol for his firemen's badges. This facilitated checking which men attended a particular fire, or were missing after it, and also as identification to the authorities and general public. Big fires attracted spectators, and frequently looters, so the militia was often called out to keep order, the fireman's badge acting as a passport to gain access to the site. By law the companies had to supply current manpower lists and identification numbers to the Admiralty, who kept a record of all firemen.

Rules were strict, if not always enforceable, and applied to porters as well as firemen. Disciplining a man for arriving the worse for drink by confiscating his axe and badge was simple, but more tricky was judging his failure of courtesy, diligence and fidelity in the heat of the moment. And was every man really capable of writing his name and address?

Charles Povey, once a coal merchant, started the Exchange House Fire Office around 1708 and is credited with organising the first salvage porters. These *able bodied men to give immediate assistance where-ever a fire shall break forth* and were recruited from City craftsmen skilled in the furniture trade. This expertise was required safely to remove the goods and merchandise, fixtures and fittings, from policy holders' premises which were on fire. Such premises were permanently identifiable by a sun-shaped fire mark nailed to the frontage with the subscriber's number inscribed on it.

Under an Act of Queen Anne of 1707, *for the Better preventing of Mischiefs that may Happen by Fire,* insurance office firemen were protected from the Press Gang, a valuable concession denied other lusty young men: ... *whereas the several Insurance Offices or Insuring Houses against Loss by Fire retain in their several services, and give Coats and Badges unto Watermen for attendance and extinguishing of Fires who are always ready at Call and are provided with Poles, Hooks, Hatchets ... which Watermen by Custom and Skill venture much further and give greater help than any other Persons not used to come into Danger...that the Watermen for the time being belonging to each Insurance Office, not exceeding Thirty for each Office ... shall be free from being Impressed or being*

Compelled to go to Sea, or serve in the Marine, or as Soldiers at Land, their Names and Places of Abode being Registered and Entered at the Admiralty Office.

The same Act pointed out unnecessarily that *many fires have lately broke out in several places in and about the Cities of London and Westminster and other places and many houses frequently been consumed before such fires could be extinguished.* It emphasised the inadequacy of water supplies and urged for greater awareness of fire prevention in buildings, but without suggesting how the oft-repeated regulations should be enforced. Stating the obvious, the Act suggested that these fires *rage and violence might have been prevented if a sufficient quantity of water had been provided in pipes lying in the streets, and if party walls of brick had been built between house and house from foundation to roof.*

The press-gang was on the look-out for sailors for the Royal Navy and the Shanghai gangs for commercial East Indiamen, with neither group fussy about whom the seized. As training took time and money, each insurance office provided its men with certificates, warning all Press Masters that the bearer was one of their thirty firemen registered with the Admiralty. To prevent impersonation the bearer's description was also given, stating age and height, in one case mentioning that the individual involved was *wearing his own dark brown hair.* However, any unlucky firemen caught off duty and without his badge or certificate was unlikely to convince the press-gang of his exemption before the ship sailed. Legend has it that one of Captain Bligh's Bounty mutineers was an illegally pressed fireman; years later a native Pitcairn Islander was indeed seen sporting his tattered uniform.

The logic behind another Act of 1707, which imposed fines of £100 for accidentally causing an employer's house to burn down, is unfathomable. Such a sum was far beyond the means of any domestic servant so the alternative of 18 months hard labour was inevitable. Had the fire been started deliberately, the penalty was the rope. (Arson in a naval dockyard, treason in time of war, piracy and violating the eldest daughter of the sovereign remain on the statute book as capital offences at the close of the 20th Century.)

Public appeals for destitute fire victims continued, so fraudsters latched onto touching kind-hearted folk for donations. A notice in the *General Evening Post* relates the miserable and calamitous condition of many *weavers, combers shoemakers, masons, lacemakers* after the devastation of the Devon town of Honiton. In order that money should

After some years all badges were individually numbered. not go astray, readers were begged to *pay what they shall please to Sir Richard Hoare and Company, Bankers in Fleet Street, which will be faithfully and impartially distributed to the most indigent.* The Portreeve, Rector and Bailiff of the town signed it and attested the *contents of the above advertisement to be true and the suffer-*

ers mentioned real objects of charity.

In 1760, after a big fire at Shadwell docks, a group of London watermen wrote to their employer, the London Assurance, asking for serviceable boots in place of the shoes provided with their uniforms. Their legs had been torn with nails, bars of iron and other such hazards as cluttered the site and *several petitioners were up to their knees in water, hot from the waterworks, and instantly after plunged in cold water, by which deplorable case great numbers of lives were endangered by the coughs and colds which they caught. Which calamity, might be in future be happily prevented were their legs defended by boots.'*

By the 1820s, most firemen had exchanged knee breeches, stockings and buckled shoes for canvas trousers and boots. Some still wore shovel hats like coal-heavers while others had low-crowned beavers, top hats or more naval headgear. Helmets were of leather, with improved neck protection and front peak.

The organised fighting of fire by the insurance companies provided welcome new business to interests ranging far beyond their own brigades. Initially there was work for tailors, boot makers and hatters in the provision of uniforms; for carpenters, wagon-makers, wheelwrights and coopers constructing the primitive appliances; for skilled iron founders and braziers making pipes, nozzles and squirts. As the number of brigades increased and equipment improved, trade increased in the manufacture and supplying of hoses, axes, ladders, lanterns, helmets and horse-drawn fire engines.

There was no lack of fires. In 1715 the *boy of one Walker who kept a small Gunpowder shop in Thames Street making Rockets and Squibs unwarily set fire to the Gunpowder upon which the House blew up.* The fire spread and, before its destructive career was stopped in Tower Street, over 120 houses were either burnt or blown up and, so the report claimed, *great Quantities of Oil, Wine and other rich Goods and Merchandises were consumed. The loss was computed at £500,000 and above 50 Persons perished in the Flames or were buried in the Ruins.*

As the efficiency of the trained firemen improved so did the numbers of clients signing up with the insurance offices. Companies were not above offering inducement, bribes or intimidation to attract or poach customers from each other. The Hand in Hand even thwarted the Exchequer by issuing its members with septennial policies attracting only one charge of stamp duty, not seven. This loophole was not permitted to survive long.

Policy holders were issued with a fire mark to fix to their premises in a prominent position, as Povey had initiated with his sun mark. Early ones were of lead, but 19th Century ones usually of tinned metal and, like badges, are now rare collectorsí items.

If a fire broke out on a house with the Hand in Hand firemark, then three out of the four brigades arriving on the scene might vanish again since there was no

FIREMAN & MANUAL ENGINE,
ABOUT 1750.

FIREMAN OF
ROYAL EXCHANGE ASSOCN., 1832.

"TOZER" FIRE-PUMP,
ABOUT 1870.

"VALIANT"
PORTABLE STEAM PUMP, 1863.

"QUADRICYCLE"
"FIRST-AID" HOSE-CARRIER, 1895.

OPERATING HOSE
FROM WATER-TOWER.

Illustrated cards were first introduced in as stiffeners for packets of cigarettes. The public soon became avid collectors and the shrewd cigarette manufactures realised they could be used to promote their products. They competed fiercely to publish a series, which would attract interest and lure smokers away from rival brands. Those illustrated are part of a collection of 50 issued by the Wills Tobacco Company. It was a popular series and demonstrates the wide interests in fires and fire fighting equipment.

NEWSHAM'S
FIRE-ENGINE,
1721.

1735.

FIRE APPLIANCES.

THE
"HODGE"
STEAM
FIRE-ENGINE,
1841.

HAND-DRAWN

HOSE-CARRIAGE
AND REEL, 1873.

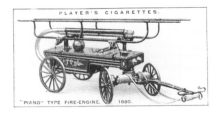

"PIANO" TYPE FIRE-ENGINE, 1880.

TYPICAL
AMERICAN
FIRE-ENGINE,
1880-90.

MANUAL FIRE-ENGINE, LATE 18TH CENTURY.

ELECTRIC
FIRE-ENGINE, 1910.

Circa 1660 pre Great Fire Panorama of London – after Wenceslas Hollar

1748 RUINS of the late dreadful FIRE which happened in Cornhill (with Newsham and Ragg manual fire appliance)

1780 Gordon Riots.

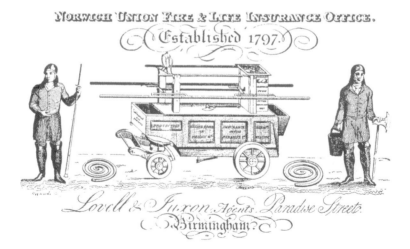

Circa. 1800 Norwich Union Firemen with equipment

Nineteenth Century Thames
Waterman.

Hand in Hand (wooden model) Note his
and other firemen's badges.

Circa 1818 Fireman Robbins with arm badge of
Norwich Union Fire Brigade.

Arms of the Guild of Fire
Fighters – Salamander Crest.

Arms of London Fire Brigade.

Fire marks. These were fixed to premises. It showed the company brigades who insured the building. These have become collector's items. Sun sign believed to be the oldest fire mark

Imperial grenade extin-
guisher.

Model of early 18th Century
Manual engine and fireman

Model of 19th Century
manual escape ladder

1863 Merryweather horse drawn fire engine

1861 Tooley Street fire, which killed the LFEE's Chief officer James Braidwood.
It was the largest London blaze since the great fire.

Braidwood's funeral procession passing St Pauls. Inset James Braidwood.
(Copied from old photographs)

profit in it for the Union, the Friendly or the London. This unhelpful practice waned as all the companies eventually realised that leaving a house to burn in the crowded city was not in anyone's interest, although it could lead to profit. Prompt action by one company to save a house might mean the grateful owner transferring his insurance cover as a reward. Several brigades would race to a fire, eager to claim their bonus of 5s for arriving first and then beer for manning the pumps. Malicious damage and bodily harm to competitors and their appliances were not unknown.

Despite better enforced regulations on new buildings of brick or stone, there was no lessening of the number of house and warehouse fires. None was on the material scale of 1666, though the death toll rose year after year, and not just of civilians. In a brutal age the fire offices treated their firemen well, paying decent wages for a dangerous job. They also made payments to the injured and felt an obligation towards the widows of those killed on duty.

The Union Fire Office of 1714, known as the Double Hand in Hand, from its badge of two pairs of clasped hands, did not engage in fire fighting until 1806. It employed a dozen porters, headed by a foreman, to salvage goods from burning premises. In the following century the annual meeting was marked by a parade of porters handing out insurance proposals, a poor advertisement since the men usually staggered around drunk.

Insurance is based on balancing of risks; although every major fire brought claims from policy holders, it also led others to insure their own premises for the first time and thus brought the companies increased business. Inevitably the poor and the feckless could not or would not insure their premises so, out of calculation and compassion, insurance brigades attended nearly all fires in the City. The government, quick to scent a tax opportunity, had imposed a charge every time HM's Gunners were called out to blow up premises to create firebreaks, a levy paid with fair grace to the Ordnance Board. What did cause ill-feeling between the offices and the Corporation was the refusal of the latter to impose a fire rate on householders to spread the cost of this public service. As the insurance brigades' efficiency increased, that of the parishes with their leaking buckets and rusty squirts had declined and, apart from prosecuting the odd beadle for neglect of equipment, the Corporation did nothing. Nor did it feel under any obligation either to shoulder or share the financial burden of firefighting. This was to be an acrimonious and very long-running dispute between the parties.

Long before it was resolved in the mid-19th Century, insurance brigades began to co-operate among themselves. In 1791 the Phoenix, Royal Exchange and Sun organised joint patrols after dark, and night centres were set up at Wood Street, Lincoln's Inn Fields, Conduit Street in the West End and dockside Tooley St. Rivalry was not extinguished since all brigades still rushed to be first on the scene.

Fires were often left to spread unchecked while rival crews fought for control of the water supply. Fines for brawling were imposed: a challenge to fight attracted a halfcrown fine, as did flinging water at colleagues or tossing firebrands; men trading punches were docked 5s, with an extra 3d for every oath. These were swingeing fines, since attendance fees for a foreman were only 5s and 2s 6d for an ordinary firemen for a six hour stint.

A dockland fire devastated the Ratcliffe Highway area, caused by an overturned pitch kettle in a shipwright's yard. The blaze stretched a quarter of a mile and threatened the Tower arsenal in a *scene so dreadful that the firemen discontinued their exertions from the threatening calamity...after the combustible matter [in a saltpetre store] blew up with an explosion that can only be likened to the burst of a volcano.* The loss of homes and businesses threw 1400 East Enders onto the scant relief of the Poor Rate. And so it went on.

Across the Channel, Louis XIV's fire service had been official and efficient for years. In 1699 he granted a sole patent to a M. Duperrier who, with a thirty year monopoly, turned out engines based on models seen in Germany and Holland. The King presented a dozen of Duperrier's French-made engines to Paris as *Pompes Publiques du Rois.*

Lottery funds in 1705 paid for twenty more Paris ones and in 1716 Duperrier was appointed royal superintendent of fire engines. He headed a paid force uniformed in blue coats and felt helmets with a mesh vizor. His widow held the same office until their son came of age and the family connection was not severed until the outbreak of the French Revolution in 1789.

CHAPTER 9

AGE OF ENLIGHTENMENT & THE GORDON RIOTS

Flames ascending and rolling in vast and voluminous clouds...
a Conflagration horrible beyond description

Georgian London was as dirty, noisy, insanitary and almost as flammable as ever. Its expanding population exacerbated by poverty, drink and over-crowding, led to greater lawlessness and violence. By 1700 England and Wales had about 7m people, by the 1770s 12m, many of them lured to the cities, especially London.

Pollution was worse than before the Great Fire. In 1771 Tobias Smollett was complaining of the acid smoke from seacoal affecting his lungs, and of filthy drinking water drawn from the polluted Thames. To the excrement, wash-tub scourings and putrefying carcases were now *added drugs, minerals, and poisons used in mechanics and manufacture.* Thirty years later the poet Southey found London's air no better, spending much of a visit coughing and blowing his nose due to the foul compound of *fen-fog, chimney-smoke, smuts and pulverised horse-dung.*

Social unrest simmered below the surface and, after outbreaks of rick burnings and of landlords' houses in country districts, draconian laws were passed against fire-raisers. Although firing standing grain, corn stores, hayricks or farm buildings became hanging offences, sporadic riots involving arson continued throughout the century. In England many were organised by the elusive Captain Swing and in Wales by men masquerading as the Daughters of Rebecca. The terror inspired in landlords was far in excess of any damage done and the gallows claimed many victims, though not always the guilty.

London felons of both sexes languished in the medieval jails of Newgate and Fleet but their fate did little to deter other malefactors. Robbery with violence, extortion with menaces, fraud, forgery and firing of property were rife. An armed highwayman robbed George II outside Kensington Palace, although with due deference. Firemen of the London Assurance wore swords on duty and were regularly seconded to the City Corporation to help maintain law and order throughout Lord Mayor's Day in November.

Prosperous citizens trembled at the violent potential of the sullen masses if they ever advanced from a mere rabble into an organised mob; fears which were to prove not unfounded before the century's end.

Housing conditions were dreadful but with trade booming property was at a premium. Shacks were crammed into stinking courts and alleys and extra storeys were added to already unsafe buildings. Existing building or fire regulations were routinely flouted, due as much to corruption as lack of enforcement officers.

Nor, many believed, had God's wrath yet been appeased. A storm, not to be equalled until the 1987 hurricane, struck in 1703. Hundreds of ships from Tilbury to Wapping were torn from their moorings, and so many vessels swept against London Bridge that the tide barely made headway upstream. Merchants bore heavy, uninsured losses in vessels and cargoes and many watermen, whose sole asset was their boat, being ruined. Though destructive fires were caused by over-turned lamps and candles, fortunately there was no major conflagration.

The Act of 1707 was directed at the mischief: *whereas many fires have lately broke out in several places in and about the Cities of London and Westminster and other places and many houses frequently been consumed before such fires could be extinguished...the rage and violence whereof might have been prevented if a sufficient quantity of water had been provided in the pipes lying in the streets, and of party walls of brick had been built from foundation to the roof.'*

One sensible demand on the parishes was for the location of every stopcock inserted into a water pipe to be clearly marked on the nearest house, the responsibility falling on the churchwardens who were also to maintain a fire engine and a leather pipe for filling it from the main. Fines were to be levied on defaulters, and rewards offered to the first three parish engines to reach any outbreak.

As words were not speedily followed by actions, a further act was passed to render the previous one *more effectual*. A new provision exempted the remaining houses on London Bridge from installing party walls; all other buildings had to comply.

The making of fire engines, squirts, hoses and pipes was given a huge boost after the Great Fire, but increased production went unmatched by any attempt at standardisation. Nor was there any consultation, let alone harmonisation, of equipment bought and installed by neighbouring parishes and insurance brigades. Hoses did not fit into every stopcock, pipes could not be joined together and damaged fire engines required a variety of incompatible spare parts. Not surprisingly diehards muttered against these new-fangled appliances, maintaining that buckets had been good enough for their ancestors.

A petition to Parliament of 1718 pointed out the deficiencies of fire engines calling them so *unlike in their make and dimensions that not above three or four can be playing at one time*. Similar incompatibility endangered the defence of the realm as applied to firearms and artillery, but nothing significant was ever done.

Building Act continued to follow Act, with one in 1776 to *explain, amend and render more effectual previous ones;* fine words, followed as before by minimal enforcement. Provision of more fire engines, at the charge of towns and city parishes, did lead to some improvement but one too often nullified by lack of maintenance. Fire fighting was of necessity at dangerously close range, so appliances were often burned or badly damaged by falling stone and blazing timber. A print of a dockyard engine marked by an anchor shows the chief fireman directing the hose from on top of the appliance and several men pumping hard at either end. One supply hose is inserted into the main through dislodged cobblestones but other men are filling buckets from the escaping water gushing upwards from this inefficient coupling.

Nonetheless, to be an insurance office fireman was healthier employment than many others. Poisoning, lung diseases or skin infections were commonplace among founders, braziers, typesetters, glassblowers, soap boilers, millers and painters. Blindness afflicted seamstresses and tailors, particularly those making scarlet uniforms for the army, as well as sawyers working double saws in sawpits, cutting planks for shipwrights and house builders. Lowest and foulest were the saltpetre men and purefinders, working respectively for gunpowder makers and tanners. The former skimmed effluent deposits off the floors and walls of cellars used as cesspits and the latter scraped up dog turds from the streets.

Though the City's political power had ebbed, carried upstream by the tide to Westminster, merchants and financiers did not pursue it, contenting themselves with sending combative MPs to Parliament. The government was headed by the Great Corrupter, Prime Minister Robert Walpole, who spent £100,000 building Houghton in Norfolk, £1000 a year on wine and died £40,000 in debt. He was unique only in the scale of his speculations.

The Port of London had never been busier. Over 2000 ships entered the Thames with foreign cargoes in 1728 in addition to 7000 colliers bringing seacoal from Newcastle and elsewhere. New docks were built to accommodate the giant East Indiamen sailing in with the wealth of the East in their holds.

The Bank of England, now on surer foundations, moved to its present site in 1734. In contrast much of the Royal Exchange was let out to tenants, one being the Royal Exchange Assurance Corporation, founded in 1720, and another was Lloyds who moved back in 1774. The REAC had own fire-fighting team, but despite this it was burned to the ground in 1838. Not much survived except the statue of the indestructible Gresham and several of the REAC's original firemen's badges. Gold coins to the value of £400 were also found but only ash remained of £2,500 of paper money in a safe. A third Royal Exchange was opened by Queen Victoria in 1844.

The philosophical and scientific advances of the Age of Enlightenment did not extend to civic amenities such as pavements, drains and clean water. Street lighting was appropriately the exception. A tax was imposed around 1750 on those City householders assessed for the poor rate to provide well lit streets, and incidentally employment of lamplighters. Five thousand lamps were lit nightly, fuelled with whale oil, but too often for safety the lamps were neglected, prey to louts or drunken gentlemen smashing them or tossing them through windows.

There were other unforeseen, if temporary, fire risks. London Bridge had been 'falling down' for centuries, and the remaining houses were removed in 1758. Several central arches were removed to make way for one wide span to facilitate river traffic. Stone from the demolished City gates in the Roman wall strengthened the foundations but before completion the temporary wooden bridge built alongside burned down, leaving Southwark isolated.

No matter what the cost, Georgian Society found imported products far more desirable than domestic goods: Venetian silks and damasks to Cotswold wool, Indian muslins and calico to Irish linen, shoes of Spanish leather to oxhide boots and furs from Muscovy preferable to coneyskin. No duellist would be seen dead without a Toledo blade. Above all French brandy maintained social distance from the Poor tippling on London gin, cheap since gin made from home-grown corn attracted no excise duty. Before the Great Fire there were an estimated 300 people to every City church, by the 1750s a gin shop to every 120.

Novelty, vanity, snobbishness and the dictates of fashion all played their part in the lure of goods on which government, always seeking its cut, levied a high tax. Nothing ever generated such hatred, evasion and violence as the Excise on wine, spirits and tobacco; a tax levied on goods released from bond, not on original importation. City companies opposed the tax, since contraband goods hit their profits by bypassing their own commercial channels, and all levels of society were shameless collaborators in the 'Trade'. It was *brandy for the parson, baccy for the clerk, and watch the wall my darling as the Gentlemen go by.*

Legal, untaxed imports included fire engines from Holland, still in the forefront of innovation since the tall, merchant houses of Amsterdam were death traps despite fronting canals. A wooden engine from about1720 in the National Brandweermuseum utilises air pressure to draw up water into its reservoir from the nearest source before pumping it out again through leather hoses. Similar inventions by English manufacturers led to battles over patents and licensing rights with Richard Newsham, John Grey, Nicholas Mandell and Mr Fowke the leading protagonists. Newsham seems to have won, and his engines were soon much in demand in the American colonies.

Fire engine manufacture was a family business. Elizabeth Nuttall advertised herself around 1770 as the widow of Adam Nuttall of Long Acre, offering for sale ingenious *engines of all sorts for extinguishing of Fires and watering Gardens which play with a constant stream and prodigious force.* Her husband had been Engine Maker to the Public Offices, Dock-Yards, Forts and Garrisons belonging to His Majesty's Royal Navy. Having access to good materials, his engines were made of *English Oak, quartered and well seasoned, the joints of the cisterns lined with copper and nailed with brass nails, and the wheels completely shod with iron.* They came in five different sizes, were easily portable, fitted through narrow apertures and cisterns and could be filled direct from ponds, rivers, wells, mains or by four buckets at a time. Intended for use on ship or shore, they worked with fresh or salt water, unlike competitors' *Engines that have racks and chains which become useless in a short time, and liable so to be when most wanted.*

In 1776 the Lord Mayor laid the foundation stone of a pillar on Wimbledon Common in memory of the inventor of a method of *securing buildings against fire.* David Hartley, who shared an enthusiasm for scientific advances with his friend Benjamin Franklin, relied on abutting metal 'fireplates' to separate the ceilings and wooden floors of successive storeys to impede, if not necessarily prevent, the spread of fire upwards. Earlier in 1776 he had invited George III and Queen Charlotte, as well as the *Prince and Princess of Wales, Noblemen, Ladies and Gentlemen,* to a fiery breakfast in his Wimbledon home, the guests well aware that the lower floors would be set ablaze during the meal. The royal family emerged unscathed as salamanders, the Annual Register reporting that the King oversaw the award of a Parliamentary grant, not exceeding £2500, to Hartley to defray the charge of his experimentsThe insurance offices were unimpressed and failed to recommend fireplates to their policy holders.

Harrowing personal tragedies continued unabated and were recorded in the parish church: *The whole offspring of James and Mary Woodmason Translated by sudden and irresistible Flame in the late Mansion of their sorrowing Parents. From the Sleep of Innocence to Eternal Bliss. A sympathising Friend of the bereaved Parents, their Companion in a Scene of Distress beyond the Powers of Language, perhaps of Imagination, Devotes this spontaneous Tribute of the Feelings of his Mind to the Memory of Innocence.*

The Woodmason parents had been enjoying Queen Charlotte's birthday ball when the news was brought to them, and this 1782 memorial lists the deaths of nine year old James through Mary, Charles, Harriot, George to the twins John and Elizabeth.

THE GORDON RIOTS 1780

Lord George Gordon completes an improbable trio with Boadicea and Wat Tyler as the third leader to incite the firing of London. Similarity between their followers lies in the underlying sense of grievance and impotence shared by the oppressed first century Iceni, fourteenth century landless peasants and the late eighteenth century urban underclass.

The Old Pretender, son of deposed James II, had been routed in 1715 and the Young Pretender in 1745. The third Protestant George came to the throne unopposed in 1760 but anti-Catholic prejudice still festered. Few actually believed in conspiracies to restore the Stuarts but many suspected Catholics in their midst of being papal agents intent on subverting the kingdom. More prosaically, as

Trevelyan suggested, the London workforce was ripe for trouble and increasingly resentful of itinerant Irish taking any available work at reduced wages—a complaint echoing down the years against any influx of impoverished immigrants.

The catalyst on 29 May 1780 was the passing of an Act repealing several repressive laws against Catholics, though still denying them access to universities or seats in Parliament. As additional safeguards they had to abjure any papal incitement to overthrow the Church of England, to accept the lawful succession and swear an Oath of Allegiance to George III.

This was not good enough for the unbalanced Lord George Gordon who, stirring a potent brew of religious bigotry and insular politics, denounced the Act as the thin end of a very sinister wedge. His hero being William III, triumphant King Billy at the Battle of the Boyne in 1690, he quickly raised supporters to defend the Good Old Cause, the enemy being the *dangerous confederation of Popish Powers* poised to *spread idolatry and corruption through the land.*

At public meetings thousands of trueborn Englishmen wearing blue cockades flocked to sign or make their mark on a monster petition. Then *since no Hall can contain 40,000 men so resolved this [Protestant] Association do meet on Friday next in St George's Fields at 10 o'clock.*

The momentous days that followed were recorded in a far from succinct pamphlet by William Vincent, a lawyer of Gray's Inn. Priced at one shilling,, it was officially entered at Stationers Hall and entitled *A Plain and Succinct Narrative of the Late Riots and Distress in the Cities of London and Westminster and Borough of Southwark.* The promised contents included *particulars of the Burning of Newgate, King's Bench, the Fleet and New Bridewell Prisons. Also the Houses of Lord Mansfield, Sir John Fielding, Messrs. Langdale, Rainsforth, Cox, Hyde and Romish Chapels, Schools etc. with an account of the Commitment of Lord George Gordon to the Tower and Anecdotes of his Life.*

On Friday 2nd June a procession 20,000 strong advanced on Westminster with the monster petition. Lords and MPs trying to enter Parliament were jostled, kicked and spattered with mud, encouraged by Lord George's inflammatory speechmaking from the sidelines. Bishops had their gowns and lawn sleeves torn and supporters of Catholic relief suffered picked pockets and wrecked carriages.

One peacemaking general vainly remonstrated *O Lord George, Lord George, for God's sake, Lord George do not lead the poor people into any danger* to a fanatic who had no interest in conciliation. Instead, sensing the government was on the ropes, Gordon stoked up the intimidation and violence. Parliament accepted the petition, tried negotiating with his Association and then adjourned the debate despite the disorder in the street. Monday was the King's birthday, marked by a proclamation offering rewards to anyone laying information against the rioters' leaders. Few responded, since more money was to be made by looting and extortion, the original thousands of Gordon's mainly respectable supporters now swelled unchecked by rabble from the slums and suburbs.

On Tuesday well-directed mobs attacked the decayed, verminous hell-holes of the Kings Bench, Fleet, Bridewell and Newgate jails. Doors and walls were broken down, inmates released and the buildings set on fire. A witness saw bemused prisoners dragged out by chains around their limbs, or by the hair. A *boy upheld by others* pushed incendiary material through windows so that *with a touch of fire handsful of tow dipped in turpentine was immediately in flames.*

Among the 300 released from Newgate were several murderers due to be hanged within the week. A fire was started in the adjoining house of Akerman the chief gaoler, and soon *the strongest and most durable prison in England, that had been newly erected and was not yet finished, on the building of which the nation had expended immense funds [£140,000], was demolished...the bare walls excepted which were too thick and strong to yield to the force of fire in the space of a few hours.* A popular print, issued within days, shows Newgate aflame and the crowd piling Akerman's furniture onto a bonfire.

A country visitor was aghast, but wryly noted that *Newgate was at this time open to all, anyone might get in, and what was never the case before, anyone might get out.* Dickens, born in 1812, whose father was jailed for debt in the Marshalsea, used the burning of Newgate in the plot of *Barnaby Rudge.*

Troops were called out and Lord Mayor Brackley Kennet read the Riot Act, but nothing made any impression on a populace inflamed by power, grievance and lust for plunder and destruction. Not since the Peasants' Revolt of 1381 had London been at the mercy of such lawlessness and fiery destruction, and the authorities so powerless.

Mobs, more violent than ever with the influx of vengeful prisoners, roamed the streets, wrecking and looting any house known, or rumoured, to belong to a Catholic or popish sympathiser. The chapels of the Sardinian and Bavarian ambassadors and the homes of Sir John Fielding JP and Chief Justice Lord Mansfield were set on fire. Mansfield's priceless collection of works of art and books was wrecked, with one scholar lamenting *the immense loss of some of the scarcest manuscripts in the possession of any private person in the world.*

Profiting from the panic, opportunists ran impromptu protection rackets so that the *inhabitants durst not refuse them money, though they paid and repaid,* to preserve their premises. One rogue on horseback, probably an escaped Newgate highwayman, refused to take anything but gold.

Langdale's brewery and distillery, owned by a Catholic, burned with colourful and intoxicating fury, but not before the rioters had drunk themselves insensible. Like the medieval peasants in the Savoy cellars, many died when the flaming building collapsed into its own vaults while others succumbed to alcohol poisoning or gulping unrectified raw spirits.

A callous citizen found it *impossible to ascertain how many deluded wretch-*

es lost their lives on the last dreadful night, but it is a consolation that very few innocent people, or people of credit, were among the killed. Another found a touch of the ridiculous amid the horror on hearing that the Jews of Houndsditch had attached notices to their shutters announcing *This house is true Protestant*.

By Wednesday night scores of large fires lit the sky the *flames ascending and rolling in vast and voluminous clouds, a Conflagration horrible beyond description*. A couple of hardy parish constables braving the mob were set on and their wooden staffs thrown into the flames, and they were among the few who attempted to do anything at all. There is scarcely a hint of the City authorities even thinking of calling out the fire engines and squirts to fight the flames: the danger to both men and appliances was too great so the fires burned on out of control.

Eventually Martial Law was declared and armed guards placed on the Bank of England* and the Royal Exchange. Ex-Lord Mayor John Wilkes MP, once darling of the London mob sided with the military, boasting that he *killed two rioters opposite the great gate of the Bank and several others in Cheapside*.

A final outburst of bloody rioting left a total of over 300 hundred dead and nearly 200 arrested, including Lord George Gordon. Twenty five rioters were later hanged after brief trials while the aristocratic ringleader was temporarily confined in the Tower. He was later released, re-arrested several years later for persistent libels and slanders and died insane in rebuilt Newgate in 1793.

The Gordon Riots were an example of 'usurped power and civil commotion', both of which usually invalidate any insurance claim. In 1780 the Sun Fire Office had paid out £56,000 on losses against £105,000 received in premiums but a year later, in the aftermath of the Riots, it disgorged £104,000 against premiums of £111,000, although not all claims referred to arson and wrecking. The owner of Langdale's Brewery fought for redress of £12,000 through the courts, and lost, although eventually receiving some compensation from the government. *Langdale v. Mason and others*, managers of the Sun, is a landmark case in early disputes.

The government had been scared witless by the riots, and the support they attracted by the Protestant Association throughout society. Antagonism to Catholic emancipation was set back for decades, with many convinced Lord George Gordon had suffered more from *a wrong head than a wicked heart*.

With no police force, the government had sent soldiers to suppress the riot, braving the instinctive English hatred troops in order to restore civil order. An ungrateful lawyer feared that the imposition of Martial Law without Parliament's consent could lead to tyranny. *The rights, Liberties, Constitution of England are objects of still greater consequence, dearer even than life and property were now at the disposal of the Court...[men] trembled for their Freedom...the possibility of Abuse was humiliating, derogatory and alarming.*

The uprising has an unforeseen effect on English penal system. The destruction of Newgate, the Fleet and other prisons, and the soaring number of criminals under ever-harsher property laws, exacerbated by the loss of the American colonies, made finding an alternative dumping ground essential. The answer lay in Transportation for non-capital offences to the empty continent of Australia, with dismasted old warships, the hulks, used as temporary jails. In May 1787 over 700 prisoners of both sexes—thieves, robbers, highwaymen, fences, swindlers and forgers—sailed in Captain Arthur Phillip's First Fleet, arriving eight months later in New South Wales. The following year in London there was a dramatic performance in St George's Fields of 'The New Holland', *being an exact representation of the landings of the British convicts at Botany Bay.*

Losses through fire and theft, caused during the six days of the Gordon Riots, ran into millions. Nine years later it was estimated that more property was destroyed and more people killed that May week than in the days following the Storming of the Bastille in Paris in July 1789. Nonetheless, in the light of what happened later across the Channel, both City and government felt in 1780 that they had escaped lightly in suffering brutal riots, not bloody revolution.

* An armed guard, known as the Bank Piquet, was mounted every night thereafter until 1973.

CHAPTER 10

PALACES, CASTLES & FIRE ISLAND

A huge red pile of embers representing half a million pounds
loss and a funeral pyre for three poor persons.

Any hint of unrest within the lower orders, from attempts at forming an agricultural trade union to seeking wider representation in Parliament, was seen by government as the precursor of social, if not violent, revolution, and harshly resisted. No-one was more reactionary than the Duke of Wellington, who was largely instrumental in delaying until 1832 the Great Reform Bill granting limited male suffrage.

Economic slump and unemployment followed the end of the Napoleonic Wars and, in the Luddite tradition, any mechanical invention likely to displace manpower was resisted, and frequently destroyed. London and provincial firefighters saw the new steam fire engines as job threatening, lowering the standing of the insurance office brigades, and putting paid to the free beer so lavishly bestowed on operators of manual pumps. These were the conventional type of engine, like those supplied by Lovell and Juxon of Paradise Street, Birmingham to Norwich Union around 1800: hand-drawn, wooden appliances needing relays of stout, thirsty men to keep them working at effective pressure.

The first steam engine came from Braithwaite and Ericcson, Inventors and Constructors of London, in 1829. It could throw 40 tons of water from its 1.5" hose nozzle every hour although the two brass boilers, one spherical and the other cylindrical looked better suited to distilling fine malt whisky. Steam was only used to propel water; mobility still relied on horsepower and would for decades more. Neither Shand Mason nor Merryweather entered the field until the 1850s, but long before that Braithwaite and Ericcson had built up an export trade to Europe which included the custom-built Comet for the Prussian king.

In 1833 the insurance brigades had been amalgamated into the London Fire Engine Establishment (LFEE), but unfortunately its combined wheeled steam appliances and fireboats were incapable of dealing with the catastrophe the following October.

For centuries, the realm's financial records had been kept on tally sticks, lengths of notched and split wood. Despite the subsequent inventions of paper, printing, double entry book-keeping and the Bank of England, this archaic system was maintained in the Exchequer until 1826—a year after Stephenson's 'Locomotion' first chuffed between Stockton and Darlington. Even after ledgers of income and expenditure were adopted, the cellars of the House of Lords remained stuffed with tally sticks—possible future reference material and certain present fire hazard.

Finally, on 16th October 1834, orders were given to workmen to shovel this archival kindling into the central heating furnaces of the Palace of Westminster. That afternoon the deputy housekeeper had shown two visitors around who, after complaining that the Lords was unbearably hot and stuffy, went in search of cooler surroundings. Mrs Wright returned to her own rooms, also surprisingly warm, but was reassured when told that the hot air in flues and chimneys was due to the heat generated by the burning tally sticks. Two hours later a doorkeeper noticed flickering light in a curious place and sought out the Clerk of Works.

The Palace, exempt from most prevailing safety or building regulations, was the fireman's text book nightmare—ancient, rambling, ramshackle, full of wide staircases, high ceilings, narrow passages, wooden panelling and draughty corridors. The fire travelled with frightening speed through the maze of passages, up and down staircases, towers and turrets, behind wainscots and below floors, devouring everything in its path. The LFEE turned out with a dozen appliances, joined later by many more, but their jets were powerless against the inferno. As so often in the past a high wind fanned the flames and water supplies were hampered by a low tide.

Knowing the Palace was beyond saving, peers, MPs, staff and passers-by joined in rescuing priceless documents, paintings and historical treasures. The deputy Sergeant at Arms entered a burning room by ladder to rescue the very symbol of Parliament's authority—the Mace. But for the rough handling of another helper, one peer directing the removal of precious volumes from the library would have been trapped and burned. He later rewarded this man with a pension for life.

As inevitable as the wind were the gaping crowds. They clogged the streets and bridges, crammed around every available window and the roof of the Abbey and even waded into the stinking Thames mud for a thrilling view. Boats were hired for exorbitant prices and everyone got in the way of the firemen. As public order was threatened by increasing numbers of spectators and by opportunist looters and pickpockets, the police were augmented by three regiments of Guards and a troop of cavalry summoned from barracks.

Next day the *Times* surprisingly praised the demeanour of the multitudes flocking to this spectacle of terrible beauty as *grave, decorous and becoming a thinking and manly population*, so unlike the boisterous, carnival atmosphere that usually prevailed at a good blaze. When flames erupted through the roof of the House of Lords another newspaper reported that the crowd was *so struck with the grandeur of the sight they clapped their hands, as though they had been present at the closing scene of some dramatic spectacle.* Knowing connoisseurs remarked for all to hear that not since the coronation of George IV had they witnessed ancient Westminster Hall so dramatically illuminated.

Quick off the mark, several members and students of the Royal Academy hired a boat and had themselves rowed up and down the Thames to revel in diverse aspects of this Apocalyptic holocaust. One sketching busily was James Mallord Turner, and seldom has the power and majesty of fire been so sensationally captured on canvas as in 'The Fire in Old Palace Yard' and 'The Burning of the Houses of Lords and Commons'. Too late to be much practical use, but in time to feature in one of Turner's paintings, was the Sun Insurance's fireboat arriving on the flood tide from its Rotherhithe base.

An ambitious, young architect, Charles Barry, saw the fiery glow when approaching London in the Brighton coach and rushed to the scene. He watched the destruction all night, never dreaming that he would be commissioned to design the new Houses of Parliament. But the honour of replacing a London landmark proved as two-edged a sword to Barry as it had to Wren, and the ensuing controversy and acrimony *ate up his life and corroded his peace of mind*. He even had to contend with the new Fine Arts Commission and the presidential supervision of Prince Albert.

Politicians were held in such low esteem that few Londoners regretted the loss of the MPsí privileged talking shop, the House of Commons. Westminster Hall and the Abbey, untarnished by faction or corruption, stood high in public affection and it seemed to many, if not the exhausted firemen, a miracle that both stood scorched but undamaged amid the desolation. Like Old St Paul's in 1666, the Hall had been under repair and rendered more vulnerable by timber scaffolding.

The gothic Palace was been reduced to seven acres of ruins, yet six days later Parliament met in a *temporary building not unlike a barn*. Before very long the Commons moved into the roughly repaired Lords. Though the Painted Chamber, the Royal Gallery, the Library and many priceless paintings and documents were lost, it was not total calamity: St Stephen's Chapel, where the Commons had sat since 1547 and where the Long Parliament met in 1641 to overturn England's constitutional history, was revealed in all its medieval glory unencumbered by concealing later buildings. The crypt survives today, much used for the weddings and christenings of politicians' offspring.

Parliamentary privilege rather than security dictated that firemen were never permitted to inspect the Palace. Nor was the building insured, since government bears its own risks and the Duke of Wellington had always shot down in flames any attempts to improve efficiency and public safety. Not even the ruins impressed him with the need for fire officers to reconnoitre public buildings or for the police to inspect, and if necessary fine, parishes for ill-maintained fire engines.

The following year, the fire Chief Officer Braidwood of the LFEE submitted a well-argued petition to Parliament, backed up by a blunt letter to the *Times* pointing out why the fire had proved so destructive: lack of party walls, funnelling passages, use of timber and repeated alterations to the Palace and *my own and the firemen's total ignorance of the localities of the place.*

The Duke, blandly admitting there might be occasional benefits from Braidwood's recommendations, insisted that his government had no intention of authorising or funding a fire service *which might, and probably would, relax those private and parochial exertions which have hitherto been made with so much effect and so much satisfaction to the public.*

Nobody argued with the Iron Duke: nothing was done.

The Tower, like the Palace of Westminster, was in the 'care' of the government, unprotected by insurance and dependent on its own ineffectual fire brigade. When fire broke out in the Armoury on a freezing October night in 1841, the inexperienced crews were as useless as their dilapidated appliances, possibly including those *300 buckets, 10 ladders and 12 hooks* ordered by the Lieutenant after the Great Fire. The LFEE, belatedly called to assist, managed to contain the fire, but not before the Armoury was in ruins. The loss was put at £.25m, a meaningless figure to set against the destruction of the nation's premier collection dating back to James II, of over 2,800 stands of irreplaceable, historic arms.

The people of Windsor, and the eleven year-old Prince of Wales enjoyed a right, royal display in March 1853: an ancient tower in flames, the Castle brigade commanded by the Prince Consort, a pregnant Victoria watching from a window and 700 guardsmen in battle order. Fire Chief Braidwood, his men, horses and appliances arrived eventually by train from Waterloo only to find that Dearest Albert had everything under control. Windsor Castle burned again in 1992.

Idle gazers rivalled the speed of firefighters to the scene, careless of their own danger and revelling in the misfortune of others. Many travelled long distances, courtesy of railway companies laying on excursions, to see the aftermath of a real cracker. In October 1854 a woollen mill on the Gateshead quayside burst into flames, spread to an adjacent warehouse stored with fertiliser, arsenic, soap, saltpetre and sulphur which exploded. Over fifty people were killed, some of them sightseers on the Newcastle shore, and the appliances of the Newcastle and North British insurance brigades were destroyed. Next day trains were stopping on the high-level bridge so no passengers should miss the smouldering devastation on both sides of the Tyne. Later the royal train paused en route to Balmoral for the Queen to make a donation to the afflicted.

In 1886 a serious fire at Hampton Court took 15 brigades to bring it under control and damage was estimated at £20,000. Far more serious destruction was caused in 1986, the only fatality being a resident of a Grace and Favour apartment thought to have started the fire by falling asleep when smoking in bed.

Docks were known to be lethal, but dockers still searched volatile cargoes with naked flames, and paid the price, until they adopted the safety lamp, invented by Humphrey Davy, which had proved its worth in the coal mines. The principle of the miner's lamp was a wire gauze surrounding the flame, thus reducing the temperature that could ignite firedamp or methane gas. Davy lamps increasingly replaced conventional ones for illuminating empty storage tanks, ship's holds and damp cellars where gases accumulated.

Even canals were not exempt from fire. In 1874 one of a string of barges carrying several tons of gunpowder on the Grand Union canal blew up, killing three people and damaging nearby property.

London's 19th Century inhabitants were a walking fire risk in their own right. Roman citizens of both sexes had worn variations on the simple toga, gown, tunic and cloak, with few if any underclothes. Scope for fashionable displays of taste or wealth was in the richness and diversity of colour, materials and jewellery. By contrast the early Victorians, particularly the women, were over-dressed and over-decorated to a ludicrous, lethal degree from buttoned boots to feathered hats by way of lampshade crinolines and layers of petticoats. The number of domestic tragedies caused by crinolines catching fire was appalling. Mothers burned to death in front of their families unable to wrap the immense flaming skirts in a curtain or roll the victim in a rug due to the unyielding wire framework.

An authority on accidental fires raged against any *luckless female, who, in spite of constant and fearful warning of the extremity of danger and folly of wearing the preposterous crinoline, persists with characteristic obstinacy in distending her apparel, gets in contact with fire and...pays the penalty of her life.* This same critic, counselling damp blankets to smother chimney fires still recommended firing a pistol to dislodge the burning soot. Did citizens keep a gun lying across the andiron, along with poker, shovel and brush for this ancient ploy?

Whole sectors of the City and its immediate surrounds were devoted to cutting, sewing, stitching, embellishing and packaging to satisfy the demand for apparel. The tailoring business and the rag trade provided employment for tens of thousands, many of them young women who paid with their lives when fire swept through the crowded tenement workshops. Many sweatshops were in the East End, though the narrow streets of Cripplegate north of Cheapside became so notorious for outbreaks that it was dubbed 'Fire Island'.

Storerooms and attics were crammed with fabrics, feathers, furs, artificial flowers, ribbons, beads, wadding, stiffening, horsehair, celluloid, glue and solvents. The neighbourhood was poor, the buildings old, much of the lighting still gas lamps and most fire precautions blatantly ignored. Retailers of these frills and furbelows in the area included drapers, haberdashers, milliners, hatters, tailors, and bootmakers.

The Great Cripplegate Fire occurred in the very centre of Fire Island on 19 November 1897. Fire engines from the Whitecross St station were on the scene of Waller and Brown's mantle manufactory within four minutes of the alarm. By then top floors of two warehouses were well alight and a strong wind spreading the flames fast. Containment was the prime concern and, though many buildings in the path of the fire were saved, others provided targets for the thwarted flames.

At its height *51 steamers, one manual engine, one hosecart, three long ladders, two fire escapes, three hose and coal vans* and 293 firemen were battling amid the smoking, smouldering labyrinth of *enclosed courts, well-holes, communications in party walls* narrow alleys, and dead ends.

For once there was no water shortage. The *City Press* reported that 15m gallons, over 67,000 tons, had been drawn from the New River Company *who, it may be added, will receive no payment in respect thereof. Many injuries were received by officers and men, but no one was incapacitated or expressed any wish to be relieved.* Also commended was the Salvage Corps, under Major Fox, for saving a great deal of valuable property under dangerous conditions. At one time there were 550 firemen and police on duty, many of the latter controlling the crowds hampering the former. Flying sparks were more effective in forcing the idle gazers to *take to their heels since several persons were slightly burned by these fiery messengers and many had their headgear damaged.*

A hundred large buildings were destroyed, 4000 workers rendered jobless, St Giles Cripplegate slightly damaged, and Barber Surgeons' Hall threatened. In an echo of the Great Fire, but unlike the two paintings lost in the Steelyard, their endangered Holbein portrait of Henry VIII was removed to safety in time.

Companies were quick to advertise in the Great Cripplegate Fire supplement issued by the *City Press*, among them Griffiths and Sons, fire-and burglar-proof safe manufacturers and dealers in second-hand safes, and also iron doors for strong rooms. Archibald D Dawnay Ltd, whose fireproof floors withstood a tremendous fire in a six-storied druggist's warehouse and proved to be absolutely indestructible. The Granite Silicon Plaster Company were suppliers of granite plaster to her Majesty's Government with the slogan *You can render and float in one coat and set same day.* Its manifold virtues included being fireproof and a perfect non-conductor, presenting a finished smooth surface and hard as stone, being the best thing for quick repair and having no rival as a structural material. James Lewis and Co, Fire Surveyors and Assessors, wished sufferers from the great fire to place themselves in immediate communication, their experience of nearly 30 years in this especial business enabling them to settle with any company.

Finally Merryweathers, the most famous of fire engine manufacturers, urged all owners and occupiers of City warehouses to adopt the London Brigade hand fire pump as illustrated, invented and made by the company. It was safe, durable, powerful, reliable, and required no chemicals. It quoted Fire Chief Captain Shaw's report that *out of 4,733 London fires in one year no fewer than 1,871 were extinguished by the London Brigade hand pump.*

For centuries the only buildings in which large numbers of people gathered had been churches. Being stone they were not fire prone, and if an outbreak occurred during divine service there was time enough for the congregation to escape to safety. Indeed, no-one died in St Paul's in 1561 or 1666. Cathedral fires resulting from earthquakes were not a British, and seldom a Protestant, misfortune.

Although public theatres, initiated in Shakespeare's day, had been death traps from the outset (see chapter 15), rivalled in the 19th Century by department stores.

Owners of large retail shops were aware of the peculiar vulnerability of their premises, yet fires continued to endanger both live and property. Since such fires were public relations as well as commercial disasters, it is difficult even now to obtain full details and check death tolls with certain famous stores.

Whiteleys in Bayswater was damaged so frequently by fire between 1880-90 that the management was convinced an arsonist was at work. The early outbreaks caused accumulated damage of more than £200,000, but on a Saturday evening in 1887 the store was destroyed in what was to date one of London's largest fires, drawing in most of its appliances and huge crowds. Insurers by now jibbed at full cover on this jinxed enterprise, so only a fraction of the total loss was recoverable.

A witness described the *huge red pile of embers representing a half a million pounds loss and a funeral pyre for three poor persons.* More accurate was the later report listing four firemen killed and a thousand employees' thrown out of work. A major fire in a shop or factory meant not only lost jobs, even if only temporarily, but irrecoverable losses to smaller businesses which supplied goods on credit to an under-insured company.

In a few terrifying hours in Christmas week in 1909 the prosperous furnishing and drapery business of Mr Arding and Mr Hobbs went up in flames, the worst outbreak in the London suburbs. Their Clapham Junction store was the culmination of thirty years steady retail expansion, and admirably served by trains, trams and buses bringing customers from both central London and the country. The original shop had been enlarged by inclusion of adjoining buildings, and despite complying with current London County Council fire regulations, and having its own brigade, this type of hazardous expansion yet again led to disaster.

Illuminated Christmas window displays attracted shoppers into the store; when one incandescent fairy light failed, causing a short circuit, it ignited swathes of cotton wool, tinsel decorations and celluloid toys. Within seconds the snowy scene was blazing, assistants did not know where to find or how to use extinguishers and, when the store's fire brigade swiftly appeared, they compounded the danger.

Rushing in, and leaving the outside door open, they directed their jets onto the blazing window causing the melting glass to burst and admit a sudden rush of air onto the growing flames. Within two minutes panic-stricken customers and staff were struggling to escape, many swept helplessly towards blazing staircases, smoke-filled rooms and falling glass. In the desperate rush fire doors were wedged, open allowing the fire to spread with terrifying speed from floor to floor, all packed with flammable merchandise, curtains, carpets and wooden counters. Plate glass was now much used in shops, creating a terrible risk in the event of a fire. Broken glass falling from a height could, and did, slice through a man's arm or neck with fatal ease.

Unprotected steelwork melted and buckled, bringing down the upper floors and finally, with a resounding crash, the roof and landmark cupola. Fire crews who had raced to the scene from all over London could do little but play their hoses on adjoining premises to damp them down against the intense heat. The nation, led by Queen Alexandra, expressed their shock and sympathy at the loss of nine lives, mostly female assistants, and the Drapery and Furnishing Trades association offered practical and financial help to one of its flagship stores.

Three hundred men laboured for three months clearing rubble, the new Arding & Hobbs on the same site opening for business the following Christmas. The public were reassured that the new store of steel and concrete clad in brick and stone was equipped with all the latest fire precautions—iron fire doors throughout, four fire-proof emergency staircases and 1600 ceiling sprinklers. This 1910 Arding & Hobbs was built to last, its cupola-topped turret being clearly visible from trains passing through Clapham Junction. During the Blitz bombs wrecked several neighbouring buildings but the only damage to the store was caused by a blast blowing out all the rear windows.

Though five shop assistants were killed in a fire in John Barkers of Kensington in 1912, the recurrent press coverage of such disasters failed to deter customers in their search for necessities, bargains or novelties. Fire was just one among the hazards of London life.

The original Civil Service Stores in the Haymarket was seriously damaged in both 1881 and 1903. The new store in the Strand was being upgraded and refurbished when fire started in 1982. Ignited by the intense heat, the contractor's stock of compressed gas cylinders turned into jet-propelled rockets, several launching themselves through plate glass windows out into the street and dispersing onlookers with greater speed than usual.

Even greater hazards than those posed by stores, theatres and later cinemas faced guests or inmates of hotels, schools, hospitals and asylums. Fire breaking out at night when the young, the old and infirm were asleep caused particular horror and high levels of death and injury.

Twenty six abandoned children died in an orphanage in 1890. When fire swept through the Colney Hatch Asylum in 1903, over fifty mostly elderly, mentally confused patients were unable to find a way out or leave their beds despite the efforts of staff. The same year two boys died in one of Eton's boarding houses, their fate made more ghastly to distraught onlookers on account of the firemen's inability to cut through security bars before the flames reached them.

CHAPTER 11

THE RISK BUSINESS

The best risk is a marble temple under water

The inventive Nicholas Barbon's fire office at the Royal Exchange spawned many competitors but he over-reached himself and died in debt in 1698, his mantle being claimed by Charles Povey. In 1709 Povey founded the Company of London Insurers but by then London's monopoly of insurance was crumbling. The Bristol Crown of 1718 was one of the first independent offices in a provincial town, followed by the Friendly Insurance Society of Edinburgh in 1720. By the time Povey died in 1743, *upwards of ninety*, town and country were keen rivals.

Much later, around 1780, Thomas Bignold left Kent for Norfolk, dismayed that no company would cover his person and goods in transit. His assertion that nothing was uninsurable, *the question is merely, would those who fain would be insured pay the price,* had fallen on deaf ears at the Sun Fire Office but set the course of his own career, and of five generations of Bignolds. An early venture was the Norwich General Assurance of 1792 followed by the launch of a mutual insurance association of twenty eight members, with all profits returnable to the assured at the expiry of successive seven year periods. In February 1797 this Norwich Insurance Fire Office placed its first advertisement, but within days had became the Norwich Union Fire Insurance with its own uniformed firemen. A life assurance society followed in 1808 which merged into the Norwich Union group in 1925, and floated as Norwich Union plc in 1997.

The London insurance companies were well aware of the deficiencies in their fire coverage but were still left to do the job by both government and the City Corporation. In 1832 it cost £8000 to operate 19 fire stations with around 80 firemen. A year later most of the big companies amalgamated their brigades into the London Fire Engine Establishment. Original members, with dates of foundation, included the Sun (1710), Union (1714), Westminster (1717), Royal Exchange (1720), Globe (1720), London (1720), Phoenix (1782), Norwich Union (1797), Imperial (1803), Atlas (1808), Alliance (1824) and Protector (1825).

The Patent Office archives are crammed with stillborn inventions of countless English eccentrics, among them many fire fighting contraptions thought up by amateur scientists. These individuals also pestered the insurance companies with their devices, some of which would have strangled or suffocated victims long before the flames reached them.

Any extinguisher relying on gunpowder was unlikely to find favour with insurers. One early device was *a waterbomb to scatter, by explosion of gunpowder, a fluid to quench any burning material and reduce it to a black coal.*

On the right track, but only after his erratic rockets had scared his own artillery far more than the Napoleonic enemy, was Sir William Congreve. Later, as Comptroller of Woolwich Arsenal, he showed more concern over the dangerous materials in his care, installing in buildings stacked with weapons and ammunition a sprinkler system of metal pipes fastened to the ceiling. When activated in an emergency, these pipes could be continually supplied with water from a mains source.

Complacent Londoners had no time for the revolutionary slogan property is theft: property was sacred. The sole purpose of insurance fire brigades was to save their premises and for salvage porters to rescue the contents. Not that anyone trapped or injured was deliberately left to die, but the rescue of residents or workers was only incidental.

Following a *Times* letter in 1817, and several more lethal fires, community-minded citizens set up a Society for the Preventing of Loss of Life from Fire. It was based on similar principles to those of the Royal Humane Society and operated from offices in Cheapside. Despite its noble aims it soon closed, having received no encouragement from government and few subscriptions from the public. The idea was refined and reborn in 1836 as the Royal Society for the Protection of Life from Fire (RSPLF).

Six central London areas were chosen as bases for wheeled, wooden escape ladders managed by conductors. When an alarm came for a neighbour-hood fire, the conductor and a team of volunteers manhandled to the site this unwieldy monster, weighing nearly a ton. Slow and awkward though the ladders were, nearly a thousand lives were saved in the first twenty years, mostly before crowds of enthralled and impressed spectators. Donations poured in so generously that by mid-century the Society increased its ladders to 85.

Though some London street names dated back to the Romans, house numbering remained unknown until necessitated by the spread of postal services in mid-19th Century. Individual properties had always been identified by adjacent churches, livery halls, inn signs or craftsmen's emblems. In 1476 William Caxton had set up his printing works 'At the Sign of the Red Pale' in Westminster and three centuries later Child's Bank established itself in Fleet St at 'The Sign of the Marygold'. The issue and attachment of distinctive firemarks to properties, many carrying policy numbers, were essential to the efficient organisation of the fledgling insurance brigades whose offices kept lists of the locations of insured premises. The authorities slowly followed their lead, but not with any consistency. Some streets had odd and even numbers on opposite sides while adjacent streets were consecutively numbered from one end to the other. Even so, 'arbitrary power' could not, and cannot, force Londoners to display publicly a number on their own premises, to the inconvenience of more than postmen.

Though firefighting was a job for men, in addition to widows taking on the family business, women were frequently found in allied trades. In 1745 Ann Bagley received £15 for casting 1000 Sun firemarks of lead and in 1748; Mary Maynard was paid £13 for gilding 500 firemarks and there must have been other unnamed females at work too. In the 1770s, Hester Bateman was commissioned by the Hand in Hand and the Sun fire offices to make silver arm badges for their employees. As a renowned silversmith, and a widow, Hester had her hallmark registered at Goldsmith's Hall.

The selection of watermen, and later sailors from the Royal Navy and merchant marine, was continued by the LFEE. They were all highly suitable: sailors *are taught to obey orders and the night and day watches and the uncertainty of the occupation are more similar to their former habits than those of other men of the same rank in life.* They also responded to the commands of the bo'sun's whistle, far more effective than the human voice in the noise and confusion of a fire. The men kept 24 hour watches for weeks on end and, being seamen, were not expected to object to this close confinement in station quarters since at least they were on dry land at home with their families. *Although the discipline is severe,* wages were *liberal* 21s per week, rising to 24s 6d—above that of omnibus drivers or dockers.

The insistence on choosing only sailors led one youth to run away to sea in order to qualify as ex-Navy and join the LFEE. After several provincial promotions, this Samuel Wilkins ended his career as Firemaster of Edinburgh.

Observation towers equipped with compasses were installed at all fire stations and constantly manned by firemen still sailors at heart. When smoke or flame were sighted, messages were relayed to other stations by runners with a note of the compass bearing, by a fireman riding one of the horses, or later by telegraph. Even ex-mariners could be confused by the Thames's sinuous course and despatch appliances to docks or warehouses on the wrong side of the river.

Rules varied slightly from brigade to brigade but the early emphasis on obedience, punctuality and cleanliness remained paramount, as did heavy fines for fighting, swearing and appearing *drunk and abusive* in uniform. At a time when there was no official police force, men of the Norwich Union were reminded that *the fire engine establishment [and equipment] is the property of and is supported at the sole expense of the Norwich Union Society and therefore is not subject to the control or orders of the police, military or any other person or persons whatever.* It also spelled out that *when premises are on fire they automatically become the property of the Office in which they are insured . . .*

Carelessness caused most domestic fires: overturned oil lamps; candles left near billowing curtains; clothes hanging too close to fires; overstoked furnaces;

seeking out gas leaks with a naked flame. Rats, London's ineradicable vermin, gnawed through electricity cables causing many loft and roof fires.

Records of central London fires in retail premises for 1832 showed bakers and oilmen top with ten outbreaks apiece. Carpenters followed with seven, chandlers and cabinetmakers with six and grocers and eating houses with five. Booksellers suffered four fires, with bootmakers, chemists and haberdashers just behind, with three apiece.

In factories and warehouses negligence was augmented by other hazards: overheating and spontaneous combustion from damp grain or hops; fumes building up in empty oil or gas tanks; cabinet makers' glue pots boiling over on gas rings; examining brand marks on tea chests or packing cases with matches.

Particular businesses were subject to particular hazards but the worst risks were not always best covered—notably docks, mills, factories and warehouses.

Around 1800, with the Gordon Riots still an awful warning, some of the steepest premiums were paid by breweries, of which there were dozens in the capital. Four big ones covered by the Sun Fire Office—Browns, Clowes, Hanburys and Meuxs—were insured for £390,000. In comparison the Duke of Bedford's stately home of Woburn Abbey with all its artistic treasures was covered for £80,000.

The Pantechnicon Furniture Depository in Belgravia was the largest modern, 'fire-proof' warehouse in the capital with numerous hydrants and steel partitions. It was therefore filled to capacity with the possessions of *ladies, gentlemen and members of the Nobility and Quality*, The value of these carriages, furniture, paintings, fine wines and household effects was £2m. But one February evening in 1874 an undetected outbreak of fire, a high wind and inadequate water supply resulted in huge losses, of which only £200,000 was covered by insurance, proof that it was not only the poor who failed to take out adequate cover.

The Wallace Collection would be richer still in works of art but for the Marquis of Hertford's losses in depository fires. Apart from the antiques destroyed in the Pantechnicon, the unfortunate peer lost another £75,000 worth when Dixon's Depository in the Edgware Road burned out in 1902.

Hudson's Depository collapsed in flames onto the railway lines outside Victoria Station in 1919, and a memorable Blitz blaze took place in that Boat Race landmark on the Surrey shore, Harrods Depository.

Piano factories were high on the scale of risk. In 1825 Stoddart's and several adjoining premises in Marylebone were totally destroyed but, out of a total loss of almost £.25m only £17,000 was covered by insurance. Broadwood's premises, on a two acre site in Horseferry Road, were razed to the ground in 1856 at a loss of £100,000. A year earlier, a big fire off Fleet Street destroyed many shops, homes and warehouses, despite the efforts of *several brigades supported by those of London Insurance Companies*.

Hop warehouse fires were made deadly by water. Cascades of water drenching bagged or loose hops caused them to swell, eventually bursting through floors and ceilings and causing walls to collapse outwards.

Timber yards burned like kindling, a fire in Silvertown docks in 1902 dramatically showing the differing combustibility of hardwoods. After the flames subsided, some stacks of seasoned timber were no more than outlines in ash, while those of Australian Jarrah redwood not only withstood the flames but acted as a barrier to their progress. An even worse fire in 1921 by the River Lea displayed the same phenomenon, with some stacks of 20-year old seasoned wood reduced to blown dust and others burning through while retaining their shape. The intense heat buckled steel cranes and melted railway lines before the fire was controlled by thirty appliances and three river boats at a loss of £650,000.

Fires in sugar mills and warehouses were especially feared by firemen owing to incandescent flows of sticky, burning caramel; however, they offered idle gazers a glorious, pungent display of leaping blue and purple flames.

Many flour mills were in the Southwark riverside danger zone. Fires occurred by the spontaneous combustion of dust particles or sparks from millstones and grinding gear. Damping down was the only way to lay the ubiquitous flour dust, until the installation of electric extractor fans reduced the fire risk and improved the air quality for the work force.

In 1846 fire enveloped wharves and warehouses near St Katharine's Dock packed mainly with tobacco, tea and coffee. It smouldered for three weeks after being contained, the final cost owing to one overturned oil lamp being yet again £.25m. In addition two sailing ships and several lives were lost.

Arson was the last resort of shop, factory and warehouse owners in financial difficulties. Fraudulent bankruptcies—with the connivance of scurrilous attorneys—resulting from suspicious fires were common, as were fires started by disgruntled employees or competitors.

Once the flames are contained there is a long way to go before a fire brigade declares a site safe. Danger lurks in basements and cellars, beneath fallen timbers and masonry and in adjacent buildings where intense heat builds up undetected and bursts out when exposed to the air. Many such fires broke out days and weeks after the Great Fire as the ruins were being cleared, rumour eagerly attributing these to *incendiarists and foreign agents*.

Concealed fires smoulder overnight or throughout a weekend undetected, only to explode into flames when the premises are unlocked on Monday morning. The aim of damping down is to prevent such outbreaks, fire officers returning to a site several times after an incident to check all is well.

The Mark Lane fire of 1850 in the centre of the City's provisions distric broke out in mid-September. It was under control within 24 hours but not until Christmas did the fire brigade finally withdraw supervision. Only a small proportion of the £200,000 damage was covered by insurance; so intense had the heat been that for ten days an underlying main ran with boiling water. The problems of forming one unified local authority, let alone a fire service, had grown with London's explosive growth and its unique demography—a self-governing, self-financing City and its sprawling, ill-defined hinterland of hundreds of separate, independent parishes.

Typical of many Englishmen of his day, Captain G W Manby devoted much time and money to social and scientific causes. He took a professional interest in lighthouses and invented ship-to-shore rescue cables fired by rockets. Saving of life at sea led to increasing concern for those in peril from fires on land, so he published a pamphlet on *The Extinction and Prevention of Destructive Fires*.

He and his friend J M Turner, the painter, had witnessed the flaming destruction of Parliament in 1834 but, despite the efforts of the firefighters, Manby was unimpressed. He complained of the lack of a single figure of authority to co-ordinate activity and the absence of any *pre-concerted arrangements, in a word, want of an organised National Fire Police*. In 1835 he published *A Plan for the Establishment of a Metropolitan Fire Police*.

Another concerned citizen was Samuel Brown, complaining in print that Londoners were surrounded by hazardous trades and combustible materials, *exposed from the age and nature of construction to the most fearful conflagration, if a fire once begins*. He excoriated the politicians but paid tribute to the London Fire Engine Establishment and the public spirit of the insurance companies who financed this body of devoted, zealous, intelligent men. Had they not taken a *nobler view of their responsibilities* two million inhabitants would have received scant succour from the *tender mercies of the Government*. Protection from the *ravages of fire...would be left to the notorious inefficiency of parish engines, or the desultory efforts of individuals impeding each other*.

Brown's attack, together with Manby's broadsides, were further salvoes in the long-running battle to establish either: a) a police force, b) a fire service or c) a fire service under command of the police as in Liverpool. Fruitless argument raged for decades over when or even if, a unified fire service was to be formed and whether it would be municipal or national. Would London's be controlled by the new Metropolitan Board of Works of 1855, or the reactionary City Corporation? Who would pay? Was it necessary at all?

The last question was answered in Tooley St in June 1861.

Unlike the dense stacking of goods in the holds of cargo ships, unloaded baled cotton, tea chests, spirit barrels, sacked grain, hops and sugar were stored in multi-storey buildings interspersed with wooden floors. When fire broke out passageways, doors, windows, hoist ports, stairwells and chutes acted as conduits to the air, fanning the flames and hindering the firefightersí attempts to reach the heart of the fire.

As an alternative to timber, cast-iron was excellent for supporting wide-span roofs without intervening columns. It was fireproof except to extreme heat, but being frangible was paradoxically vulnerable in a fire. Cold water hosed onto heated iron beams or girders caused them to shatter, resulting in immediate collapse of ceilings or roofs. So great was the danger *apprehended from the treachery of cast-iron in buildings on fire that men of the LFEE are prohibited from going into parts or places which depend upon supports of cast-iron whilst they are allowed to trust themselves to burning timber almost at their own discretion.*

In 1858 James Braidwood, London's first overall fire chief, had spent weeks inspecting the riverside from Queenhithe by St Paul's to the West and East India Docks. His subsequent report was damning. Known hazards, that should long since have been eradicated, had proliferated not diminished: from rotten wharves and unsafe bridges; to barrels of spirits stacked alongside explosives and tarred timber propped against tall warehouses holding thousands of tons of mixed goods, with no party walls. Interested parties expressed concern, but carried on as before. Insurance rates rose but dock owners paid up rather than install costly safety precautions.

The reckoning in 1861 cost them dear. It cost Braidwood his life.

The Southwark shore presented a fortress wall of warehouses flush to the water, interspersed by narrow alleys leading into the main thoroughfare of Tooley St which ran between London Bridge and the future site of Tower Bridge (1894). An evening breeze ruffled the Thames, insufficient though to cool cobbled streets and tall buildings which still retained the heat of the hot summer Saturday of 22 June. This combination of factors turned a commonplace incident into the fiercest blaze since the Great Fire, and one not to be equalled until the Blitz.

The six storey Scovells warehouse that first caught fire was filled with edible commodities of tea, sugar, rice and spices, together with a treacherous mixture of saltpetre, tallow, jute and cotton. Ironically, the owners had acted on Braidwood's repeated recommendations by separating different cargoes into specified areas and installing fireproof iron doors. Fatally, sweating workers had opened some of these during the day, leaving them ajar to fan the burning bales and spread the fire rapidly until every storey was ablaze.

The Southwark brigade was on the scene within minutes but, by the time Braidwood's Watling St force and many others galloped over London Bridge, any hope of containing the fire within Scovell's was gone. Cotton's was ablaze, followed by warehouses on Chamberlain's Wharf. Paint, oil, flour, cheese and spirits were added to the unholy brew spilling out of the burning buildings and pouring over the wharf walls into the water. Ten thousand splintered casks of molten tallow scummed the river, a fiery flood ignited by exploding barrels of rum and brandy and heaving with swarms of drowning rats.

Nearly every brigade of the LFEE made for Southwark, hampered both by dense crowds on London Bridge and the arrival of various independent insurance company appliances. Most effective were the two fire boats, floating platforms with steam-powered pumps, but less so was the odd parish engine which trundled to the scene. The fire spread downstream, generating such heat that these fireboats and their crews were badly scorched and their craft in danger of incineration.

A messenger was sent to obtain new orders from the chief officer, so Braidwood and a colleague hurried down an alley to the river. Moments later another fireman heard above the roar of the flames the ominous crack of collapsing walls and yelled *run for your lives*. It came too late to save the two men who were crushed under tons of burning masonry.

The fire burned out of control for two days. It devastated numerous wharves and buildings downstream from Hay's Wharf and the area was not declared safe for weeks. The crowds had not enjoyed such a blaze since the Palace of Westminster in 1834 and their appetite for excitement was matched only by their thirst for beer. As the fire continued to rage night and day, pubs along the Thames remained open round the clock in defiance of the law.

The two firemen were not the only fatalities. Several opportunists, rowing out to snatch liquor barrels from the water, were caught in the current and swept into the tide of blazing tallowThe heat and danger were so great, and the fallen debris so compacted, that it took three days to recover the bodies of Braidwood and Hodges. In a gesture reminiscent of the sailors manning Nelson's barge tearing strips off his funeral pall, the still-warm metal buttons from Braidwood's tunic were distributed among his weary, grieving crew.

His death left the LFEE stunned and rudderless. James Braidwood had headed it for 28 years, with no deputy groomed to step into his boots on retirement, or death.

The Tooley Street Fire was *of an extent never equalled in the metropolis since the foundation of the Insurance Offices*. Of the estimated property losses of £3m only a little over half was insured but, coming on top of a spate of dock, warehouse and factory blazes in the 1850s, paying out had the insurance companies reeling. Several smaller ones were brought to the brink of collapse; for the combined years 1860 and 1861 even the mighty Sun saw losses of £493,000 exceed premium income of £462,000.

The lessons of Tooley Street, even had they been implemented in full, were undermined by the increasingly hazardous cargoes traded in the docks. These were stored in old and new warehouses, most exempt from the provisions of various building acts. To the ancient enemies of oil, spirits, sugar, tallow, pitch and saltpetre were added rubber, petroleum, naphtha and the volatile modern 'improvements' of gas lighting and later electric power. Successive building acts were repeatedly ignored.

The increasing risks and escalating pay outs on fire policies provoked the insurance companies to a final effort to unburden themselves of the LFEE. Far from leading the nation, London continued to lag behind other centres in provision of fire services paid for by ratepayers as in Manchester, Liverpool, the main Scottish cities and most European capitals.

To staunch the flow of losses, and impose on owners greater awareness of the need for improved safety standards in warehouse buildings and storage, rates were raised within a few days of the Tooley Street fire. By agreement between members of the London Mercantile Tariff, those covering the Waterside District went up by 300-500%

The outcry was immediate and, since Lord Mayor Cubitt of the building family was an interested party, he hosted a public meeting at the Mansion House. Owners, merchants, bankers, builders, wholesalers and wharfingers all aired their grievances which coalesced into resentment against the insurance offices who were accused of cynically abusing their monopoly and acting against the public interest by operating a cartel. The justifiable complaints of the insurers against the culpable, profit-hungry, risk-taking builders and property owners went unheard in the uproar.

A committee was formed, but so irreconcilable were the two sides that several members raised £2.5m to start a City rival to the LFEE insurance offices. This Commercial Union Fire Insurance Company advertised fire, life and marine insurance and the opposition soon felt the heat from this and other newcomers, including the Mercantile Fire Insurance.

Two founder directors of Commercial Union had personal and commercial interests in warehouse safety, one being a wine and spirit importer, the other a tea, coffee and spice merchant. Later the board included a wholesale grocer, a coalmine owner, a woodbroker and one of the mustard Colmans of Norwich. The exotically-named Falconer Larkworthy was a director from 1863-1928.

A ceasefire was declared in this undignified and expensive campaign between the old and new guard in 1863, when all parties approved an umbrella Fire Offices Committee and subscribed to a new London Mercantile Tariff. This stated that *each class of goods should be charged a premium proportionate to the risk*, there being three classes for dockside premises and five for goods. Acceptance of greater business risks and life cover by the companies, and increased shareholder investment, came from the 1862 Companies Act limiting liability.

The transition from sail to steam brought little relief to hard pressed marine insurers. Ships continued to capsize, run aground, founder in storms, ram each other and catch fire. In 1875 Samuel Plimsoll MP, the sailor's friend, stormed against *murderous shipowners, speculative scoundrels, ship-knackers* interested only in profit. Reprimanded by the Speaker for his language, Plimsoll repeated his insults and threatened to *unmask the villains who send their sailors to death.*

Thanks to this Bristol-born politician, and with the blessing of the insurance companies, the Merchant Shipping Act was passed in 1876. A key safety clause was that every loaded UK vessel should still ride high enough in the water to show the Plimsoll Line marked on its bows.

In 1799 'HMS Lutine', once a French naval frigate, foundered in a storm with all hands en route to Hamburg, with a cargo of specie and bullion valued at £1m. Lloyds paid out on the insurance loss, although after several salvage attempts much of the gold and the ship's bell were recovered in 1859. The bell hangs in Lloyds of London and, though shipwrecks and piracy are less frequent, the old horror of fire at sea remains. Missing ships are posted *overdue* at Lloyds. When rung once, the Lutine bell heralds bad news, twice signals all is well.

Fires were frequent in the spinning and weaving towns, so several northern mill owners pioneered self-help for the wool and cotton industry. Based in Manchester they founded the Mutual Fire Assurance Corporation and, when their experimental sprinklers and extinguishers proved their worth, offered attractive rates to factories purchasing and installing them. The Mutual became the Palatine and, along with the Globe, was absorbed into Commercial Union.

The companies advertised almost from the outset, an early 20th Century London Transport booklet inviting samples from those who had done so on its omnibuses for more than 50 years. One veteran advertiser was the Sun Insurance Office, claiming to be the oldest in the world, with a reproduction of an 18th Century painting of a brigade answering the 'First Alarm—A Struggle for the Start'.

Porters were still employed by the insurance companies to drag goods and chattels out of burning buildings, though they were overwhelmed by the expansion of warehouses, factories and offices. After the brigade had done its work, they were then expected to check premises for fire damage, as well as examining them for supplementary damage caused to property and goods by water, steam, foam and chemicals. Unarmed themselves, they were at the same time supposed to deter or apprehend looters. To meet the new demands, the London companies formed the specialist London Salvage Corps in 1866 which lasted for over a century until disbandment in 1984.

The state of the capital's fire protection, apart from the LFEE and the Salvage Corps, was a shambles, and a useless, perilous one at that. Parishes were still required to maintain and turn out to a fire with equipment that was frequently broken, missing parts or in one case walled up in a shop. The City was a honeycomb of almost a hundred separate parishes each governed by its own vestry. Old women and children were on the pay rolls and most volunteers turned up at fires only to claim the beer allowance. As the total cost of fire protection by the parishes did not exceed £600, everyone remained content to rely on the insurance companies brigades. Why change a free service to a municipal one chargeable to householders?

The increasingly resentful insurers and their new LFEE chief, Captain Eyre Massey Shaw fresh from heading the Belfast brigade, thought otherwise. Hints were dropped that all 127 fire fighters from its twenty stations would be withdrawn from service if new proposals were not considered seriously. It was no more the responsibility of insurance companies to maintain fire brigades, argued the Globe, than for life assurance firms to provide a staff of doctors to the public. The cost of the LFEE's protection of the community was now an annual £25,000.

With hints taking on the tone of threats, the alarmed government offered the sop of a Royal Commission, to include Lord Mayor Cubitt and Sir Richard Mayne, commissioner of the Metropolitan Police. Its role was to examine existing legislation for the *Protection of Life and Property against Fires in the Metropolis*. This the commission did with remarkable speed, delivering its brief report within six weeks. London's vulnerability to fire shocked everyone.

Its main recommendation was a fire service on the lines of the LFEE, under the command of the police, restricted to the area of the Metropolitan Board of Works. Captain Shaw was asked to draw up a workable, economical budget, his £70,000 annual estimate being instantly dismissed as too extravagant. It took three years of haggling, argument, concessions and compromise before the *Act for Establishment of a Fire Brigade in the Metropolis* was passed.

In 1866, two centuries after the Great Fire and eight after the Norman Conquest, the Metropolitan Board of Works took over from the LFEE. As the Metropolitan Fire Brigade, it was funded by a halfpenny household rate raising £31,000, a levy on the insurance companies of £35 per million on the gross value of property insured within an agreed area, and a sum from central government. It was independent of the police, although acting in close liaison in emergencies.

All the buildings, appliances and most of the staff of the LFEE were taken over by the MFB. Captain Shaw, who had replaced Braidwood, was appointed chief officer and the old Watling St station remained as fire HQ. The London insurance companies were finally rid of the burden they had borne since the days of Barbon, the Fire Office and the Hand in Hand. In a timely gesture, after various financial adjustments between the parties, the balance of the funds in the companies' favour was donated to develop the Fire Brigade Research and Training Trust.

Not until the *1938 Fire Brigade Act* were all local authorities in England, Scotland and Wales made responsible for fire services, an unwieldy 1668 separate, statutory bodies.

CHAPTER 12

VICTORIAN LONDON

To abide by certain wholesome regulations as regards
the security of buildings from fire. (1843 Act)

By 1801 the population of Central London was around 125,000, less than half the Great Fire total. Teeming suburbs, sprawling ever outwards from the Great Wen, quickly pushed 'greater' London over the million mark. In the 1830s the human exodus accelerated with the arrival of the railways which, along with steam ships, could also transport goods in and out of the capital in quantities undreamed of previously.

A horse could carry one sack of wheat. The pulling power of a horse and cart was two tons of goods, whereas a horse pulling a truck along a mine rail track could manage 8 tons, a river barge 30 tons and a canal barge 50 tons. The 'iron horse' powered by steam, drew 20 wagons loaded with 5-10 tons apiece.

After the first passenger train ran from Deptford to Bermondsey in 1836, mainline terminuses followed in quick succession: Euston (1837), Paddington (1838), Fenchurch St (1841), London Bridge (1844), Waterloo (1848), King's Cross (1852), Victoria (1860), Broad St (1865), St Pancras (1868) and Liverpool St (1874). Though passenger trains killed off long distance horsedrawn coaches within a decade, carts and wagons were essential for collecting and delivering goods to rail heads until well into the next century.

Railway fires were frequent but, except in collisions, seldom fatal. Sparks from the smokestack set light to grass or trees in the country and roofs and wooden buildings in town. Smuts and smoke polluted everything within range. Track fires, many fraudulent, were just one more hazard for the insurance companies who received daily returns from the LFEE, reporting every incident in detail and giving the supposed causes.

More than half the non-railway fires causing structural damage were attributable to furnaces and stoves, defective or overheated chimneys, blocked flues and other apparatus for heating and lighting. All traders and manufacturers in the City were bound by the current *Metropolitan Building Act* and existing fire regulations. Most commercial fires were still caused by negligence, linked to non-compliance with regulations.

Though one clause prohibited furnaces being placed neither *upon nor within a distance of 18" of any timber or woodwork*, loopholes were everywhere. A line of small burners laid on a wooden floor to provide a kitchen hotplate caused a serious fire in Gresham Street; in this instance, it being a gentlemenís club, no rule had been breached as these were not covered by the Act.

In 1848 Professor William Hosking, architect and civil engineer, compiled *A Guide to the Proper Regulation of Buildings in Towns as a means of Promoting and Securing the Health, Comfort and Safety of the Inhabitants.* It spelled out much of what should have been obvious and routine construction practice but was not, and never had been, since the first building decrees of Mayor Fitzailwyn in 1189.

He defined regulation as *both restraint and compulsion...such as to command general acquiescence in the necessity and propriety of the imposition.* He believed few reasonable citizens would quarrel with this though *to certain individual interests some rules will be felt or be fancied to be repugnant.*

Seals of approval were given to new incombustible materials for party walls and to the ability of solid doors, plastered ceilings and brick chimneys for checking flames from spreading to adjoining dwellings. Stairs were essential, but with the *safety of the inmates so important there was no excuse for making wooden staircases so exceedingly inflammable in England.* Condemned too were wooden skirting boards, hollow wall partitioning and floor and ceiling cavities. More technically, Hosking found brick-nogging much inferior to the French application of a plaster of Paris mortar. French exterior shutters were also superior to the interior deep boxing of English wooden ones. In urban buildings thatched roofs, tarred felt and projecting upper storeys were deplored: building materials and styles officially banned since the Great Fire.

Multi-ownership as well as occupancy of several adjacent houses for manufacturing purposes, was fraught with dangers. The original buildings may have complied with fire regulations, but new owners knocked through party walls, erected flimsy partitions, installed dangerous equipment or stock and blocked staircases. Throughout the 19th Century, lives were lost and millions of pounds of goods destroyed in these rabbit-warren conglomerations, many in and around the City of London. Many continue to die in cheap hotels and tenements converted in like manner today, in fireman's parlance Multi-House Occupancy, MHOs.

Professor Hosking ends his chapter on Security against Fire with a swipe at the *let-alone people railing at meddling, and would have it preferred that poor people should still be taxed by their landlords for the means of insuring against loss in the event of fire doing damage to the houses, instead of paying to no greater extent for insuring themselves [by safety improvements] against loss, in the use of buildings insured by their structure against fire.*

Though do-it-yourself was not a widespread Victorian hobby, magazines did offer householders a simple formula for producing fireproof paint. All that was required, in varying proportions, was alum, potash, salt, quicklime and skimmed milk, with plaster of Paris added for a white finish.

Graduate paint-makers could then progress to home-made matches, known as Friction Lucifers. The ingredients were marginally less dangerous than the antimony, potassium chlorate and sulphuric acid of earlier products, though they did have drawbacks. Rats gnawed at the sulphur or phosphorus heads, and the matches could ignite if accidentally trodden upon. Unsurprisingly, there was great demand for the wonderful, fireproof material of the day—asbestos.

The increasing size and capacity of warehouses was marked by a similar increase in serious, costly fires. Numerous investigations and reports followed although little was actually done to put their recommendations into effect.

200,000 cubic feet has been arrived at as the largest capacity of which any single warehouse, or several compartments in a series of warehouses, should be permitted...upon the assumption that it is built of brick or of stone. A low building covering a large surface area was less dangerous than either a tall multi-storey one or a high, vaulted one on a restricted ground base. Many with river frontages were bounded on at least two other sides by narrow alleys, difficult of access for fire engines as in the Tooley Street fire, and with no space to erect ladders at safe angles. Grain and hops required custom-built warehouses but these were often sold and used for storing different, mixed goods.

Above a capacity of 100,000 cubic feet, the London Fire-Assurance Offices imposed an additional 30% on both buildings and contents. *And let it not be forgotten* Hosking warns that these costs are added on to the *price of every yard of cotton or woollen cloth, of every pair of stockings and skein of thread, of which material have passed through buildings dangerous in respect of, or rather not secure against fire.*

High though rates were on dangerous goods stored in dockland warehouses, they were a bargain compared to higher risk Liverpool. The highest premiums in London touched 12%, compared to ordinary rates of 2-3%, whereas the minimum in Liverpool was 8% per cent rising in extreme cases to 35% or 45%. The majority of householders were uninsured and between 1832-1842 insurers paid out over £1m on Liverpool fire losses, a fraction of the real cost of those killed, injured, bereft of businesses or employment. Until the trade embargo during the Civil War the main culprit of Liverpool warehouse fires was American baled cotton from the southern states, always flammable and liable to spontaneous combustion.

Rates did not fall until, by Act of Parliament, Liverpool merchants were compelled *themselves to abide by certain wholesome regulations as it regarded the security of buildings from fire,* and the city installed a better water supply.

The ubiquitous Manchester goods warehouses, a generic term like a Dutch barn, were usually found close to city centres and served as both wholesale and retail outlets. The ground floor was a conventional shop, the upper floors stacked with goods, and the attics housed staff, warehousemen and domestic servants.

Originally intended for the sale of Manchester cloth in bales, these warehouses were popular with the general public for offering fashion, drapery and household materials.

Insurance rates issued in 1845 applied to usage by *wholesale dealers in cotton, linen, silk, woollen, worsted piece-goods, and by wholesale glovers, haberdashers, hosiers, lacemen and thread manufacturers*. Cover was available only on brick-built buildings with tiled or slated roofs, and rates increased for multiple tenancies and if any manufacturing process was carried on.

A typical Manchester warehouse fire broke out near Guildhall in 1845, destroying the building plus £100,000 worth of goods in less than an hour. But for the prompt appearance of LFEE brigades, it was estimated that within a hundred and fifty yards over a £1m of property also would have been lost. The subsequent enquiry disclosed a catalogue of ignored and violated regulations. Two large buildings had been joined by covering over the intervening courtyard, no fireproof walls had been installed, no fireproofing of the roof attempted and no additional exits been provided. Tragedy had only been averted by the swift notification of the fire; a few hours later scores of people would have been asleep upstairs and unable to escape.

In another legal case brought against an owner, the magistrate upheld the man's plea that his premises did not come under the regulations since they were warehouses, not dwelling houses. The clear impression given was that warehouse staff living on the premises were as expendable as rolls of cloth and boxes of buttons.

Commercial and domestic fires, then as now, were frequently caused by matches, early examples being known as Lucifers or Vesuvians. Flints and tinderboxes had been superseded by phosphorus matches in the mid-18th Century, at first advertised for the use of travellers, those at sea or *in a rural situations such as fishing*. All match factories were from the outset repositories of flammable and toxic materials, including sulphuric acid and hydrogen, with one igniter activated by biting apart a glass phial containing phosphorus-soaked paper. Less deadly may have been the philosophical wax matches of Mr Barrett, who supplied to the court the pocket luminary, the ethereal match and instantaneous light box. Better still were the first friction matches in 1827. Fire brigades used re-igniting, sulphur-headed matches to drop on ready-laid kindling in the fire box to raise steam.

The Whitechapel factory of the two Quakers, William Bryant and Francis May, was piled high with flammable paper, board, timber, ink, glue, wax, manganese, zinc oxide and potassium dichromate. Fire, however, was not the worst hazard facing the women staff, but rather cancers of the mouth and tongue, known as 'phossy jaw', and caused by licking brushes loaded with sulphur and phosphorus.

Spectators at fires, descendants of generations of idle gazers, grew to be such a menace that official action was taken to control them. Around 1857 Stephen English of the Norwich Fire Brigade issued his men with ropes to restrain the crowds at any major outbreak. These had to be replaced with wire after incensed onlookers cut the hemp ones with their pocket knives. London and other brigades soon followed the example of Norwich, whose chief crossed the Atlantic and rose to be Lt. Colonel English, in time for the American Civil War.

A more serious London threat to firefighting was lack of water; the expansion of fire brigades and water suppliers ran almost in tandem during the 18th and 19th centuries. Both for a while were united under the Metropolitan Board of Works.

Conduits in main thoroughfares providing free water had been phased out by mid-18th Century so the poor relied on stand pipes or suspect wells. Most wooden or lead pipes were replaced by iron, which lasted longer but rusted and leaked at the joints. The enlarged network of mains laid beneath the City streets was a great improvement but too often only provided erratic supplies and fluctuating pressure.

Water still came from springs, wells and distant rivers, most being pumped straight from the Thames, always a central sewer and increasingly polluted. The New River Company and the London Bridge Waterworks had faced growing competition since the Great Fire, their rivals' subsequent construction work causing intense annoyance to the populace through *perpetually laying down of pipes and amending them*. By 1821 the demarcation disputes between the companies and the constant disruption of highways led to a Parliamentary enquiry into the *State of the supply of water to the Metropolis*.

Before matters got better they got worse with the visitation of King Cholera in 1831, an epidemic to rival the Noisome Pestilence. At the time of the *1844 Metropolitan Buildings Act* it was reckoned that 3m people lived in 270,000 houses, mostly with cellar cesspits but, when the Commission of Sewers had these abolished, the Thames became the recipient of their effluent through 350 foul drains. The search for clean water became more urgent in 1855 when, after a prolonged summer drought, the Thames flowed sluggishly beneath a mephitic, shimmering scum of algae and excrement. So intolerable was the Great Stink that Parliament adjourned and no living creature was seen in the river for months afterwards.

Two unsung heroes of Victorian England were the social reformer Sir Edwin Chadwick, of the General Board of Health, and the civil engineer Sir Joseph Bazalgette, of the Board of Works. These tireless pioneers brought clean water and efficient drains to London despite entrenched opposition from vested interests. They deserved sainthoods, not knighthoods.

Fish gradually returned to the Thames, but the first salmon not until 1974.

The key Act concerning fire brigades was the 1847 consolidation of certain provisions of the *Waterworks Act*. These enshrined the right *at all times to take and use water for extinguishing fires without making compensation for the same*. It also ordered the installation and maintenance of fire plugs in the mains at hundred yard intervals, and the placing of notices showing the whereabouts of every such plug on the wall of the nearest convenient building.

By the time of the 1876 Select Committee on Fire Brigades, the number of water companies was down to nine. These provided just over 50% of households with 116,000,000 gallons a day.

The heroic but anonymous Fireman was a popular Victorian figure, prints by artists of the day adorning many a parlour wall. Keen to redress the balance of brave military and naval deeds so often depicted on canvas, Millais painted *The Rescue* in 1855, after seeing two firemen plunge from a roof into a burning building. Fifty years later *Saved*, the rescue of an unconscious girl in her night-gown, sold in thousands as prints and postcards, boosted by the fact that the swooning maiden was a fireman's daughter.

The Press Gang no longer preyed on London's watermen, but the belief that *one volunteer is worth ten pressed men* was strongly held by some attached to their own parish engine and opposing the new LFEE. A rare certificate of 1840, issued by the alderman for Walbrook, commands the churchwardens of three parishes to pay the rewards sanctioned by Parliament after a fire in his ward. To the first engine on the scene, St Mary Abchurch, £1.10; the second, St Martin Ongar, £1; the third, St Mary Basshaw, 10s. The turncock received 10s.

A paper read to the Society of Arts in 1865 on the *Best Mode of Protecting London from the Ravages of Fire* listed over 70 active volunteer brigades in the United Kingdom, plus 10 in London. Of the latter, Burnett's distillery in Vauxhall owned fire plant worth £1000 and Price's candleworks works in Battersea over £2000 worth. The author disagreed with the common belief that *the most important thing for every Englishman to know was how to use a rifle*. What use was marksmanship when a state of utter ignorance prevailed *in regard to fire engines and how to proceed when fire broke out?* Radical change was called for, but still on a volunteer basis.

Meanwhile fires continued throughout Victoria's long reign.

In 1890, on one of the coldest winter days ever recorded, fire broke out in Queen Victoria Street. It spread with such speed and fury that lunching City workers ran for their lives and it took 30 appliances hours to contain it. On every gutter and gaping window frame water glazed into huge icicles, suspended like daggers over the heads of the firefighters below, whose beards and eyebrows were already coated in ice. Like the aftermath of a massacre in Siberia sodden heaps of mink, sable, ermine and astrakhan lay in the ruins, part of the £.25m loss suffered by

Revillon Fréres, furriers of Paris.

The City, concerned as always over property losses and suspected arson, pushed a *Fire Inquest Act* through Parliament. Impartial, if irresponsible, the nation's legislators continued to show as little concern for their own personal or domestic safety as they did for that of the general public. A proposed Bill giving councils the right to appoint fire inspectors to check escapes and alarms in hotels, factories, theatres, hospitals, schools and workhouses was thrown out that same year as *too Utopian.*

The wonders of gas and electricity heralded neither the end of coal fires nor of pea-soupers: indeed, the unsolved murders attributed to Jack the Ripper were rendered more hideous by the foul murk usually shrouding his nocturnal activities.

Not until Parliament passed the post-Second War *Clean Air Act,* enforcing the burning of smokeless fuel, was the battle won. What Dickens called his London Particulars were romantic and picturesque only in retrospect. Though well within living memory, the great smogs that used to claim thousands of lives every winter are now, happily, things of the past. A blessing to all, not least fire crews turning out for a blaze in nil visibility and relying on a man leaning out of the cab to discern the flares highlighting the kerb.

Queen Victoria's 1897 Diamond Jubilee was celebrated throughout the Empire, England being still dotted with celebratory buildings of varying degrees of architectural splendour and civic utility designed to honour her. Unfortunately, as Blackstone notes in his 1957 *History,* many jubilee fire stations still in use were *inadequate and cramped and unenhanced by a regrettable tendency in 1897 to combine the new fire station with another municipal amenity, a public lavatory.*

CHAPTER 13

FOES OF THE FIRE KING

The Thames all over was in flame, as with lighted oil 'twas running.
The Fire King laughed when he found he could tame
The Fire Brigade with his funning.'

Neither of the capital's two great Victorian fire chiefs were Englishmen, let alone Londoners. James Braidwood, born in 1800, was a Scot who had commanded the Edinburgh Fire Engine Establishment before moving south in 1833, as superintendent of the London Establishment. Captain Eyre Massey Shaw, an Irishman of the North Cork Rifles, succeeded Braidwood in London in 1861, after several years heading Belfast's combined fire and police force.

These two very different men transformed the London fire fighting scene, becoming in the process hugely popular figures, media celebrities of their day.

Parliament had established Britain's first police force in Northern Ireland in 1830, prompting wags to christen the Home Secretary responsible *Orange Peel*. Having overcome entrenched resistance to arbitrary powers and agents of tyranny, Sir Robert Peel's innovation spread to England where the new enforcers of law and order were equally promptly nicknamed Peelers, Bobbies or Coppers.

No such popular identity bestowed on London firemen of the period survives, so who knows who, or what, was a *Jimmy Braider* or the *Long 'Un*? Even the title of *Fire King* was ambiguous. In his prime it was allotted to Captain Shaw but in popular myth it was the spirit of the destructive fire fiend, depicted in cartoons as a cross between Jack Frost and a malevolent, pantomime Demon King.

Early 19th,Century Edinburgh, its handsome facade masking teeming courts and squalid tenements, was almost as great a fire hazard as its neighbour Glasgow or pre-Great Fire London. Like other cities, it had relied on an assortment of insurance company firefighters before becoming the first to combine all these into one efficient, trained municipal brigade under a Master of Fire Engines.

When only twenty four James Braidwood, a local builder's son, was promoted to command from one of the volunteer forces; thereafter, further advancement was rapid. Within a few years Edinburgh had the best trained and equipped brigade in Britain. Uniforms were heavy and cumbersome, so scorching was far less common than a thorough soaking while fighting a blaze and the smell of damp, steaming cloth hung over every fire station. Helmets were painted red, blue, yellow or grey denoting their appropriate watch and the men wore midshipmen's naval jackets and loose white duck trousers over leather boots.

Braidwood took over the new London Fire Engine Establishment in 1833 at the impressive salary of £400 a year. Unlike most firemen of the period, he was interested in the practicalities and administration of his profession, instituting regular examination of all fire fighting equipment and practice. His expertise and the publication of important technical papers later earned him associate membership of the prestigious Institution of Civil Engineers, founded by Thomas Telford.

Though water was still the main extinguisher, Braidwood was the first to realise the importance of penetrating to the heart of a fire to overcome it, rather than deluging the flames from a distance. It was dangerous work for men using hand-held jets, with no reliable communication systems; nevertheless, the success rate in containing major outbreaks soon justified the risks involved.

Braidwood was proud of the LFEE and its men, and keen that any misdemeanours or dereliction of duty should be swiftly dealt with. The public was told to note the red number on the left breast of any offending fireman's dark grey uniform, and notify the superintendent of the chief station at No.68 Watling Street.

This being the century of mechanical developments, a great advance came with the invention of steam fire engines, known as steamers. The appliances were still horse-drawn, and it was the water tank heated from below that activated steam-driven pistons to power pressure hoses. Though they were infinitely more powerful than the old hoses primed by men operating manual pumps, initially they had a fatal tendency to run out of fuel, and thus steam, during a long fire.

There were, however, limits to Braidwood's modernity, so it took time for innovations to meet with his approval and adoption. No breathing apparatus or steamers had been ordered for Edinburgh in his day and this conservatism, or prejudice, travelled with him to London. The gift of a fireproof suit with attached breathing helmet and air hose from the Parisian *Sapeurs Pompiers* did win him round to such gear, but steamers took longer to gain favour. He insisted that such powerful water jets would injure firemen, add to the damage to buildings and ruin their contents. More importantly men might rely too much on the power of the hoses and revert to the old long-shot propulsion, rather than penetrate deep into a burning building to locate the heart of the fire. Eventually he did authorise a steam fireboat in 1855, moored at the King's Stairs, Rotherhithe, but not until the year of his death in 1861 did the LFEE have a wheeled steamer.

With good reason Braidwood was sceptical of most commercial inventions to prevent fires, fireproof houses or save lives. Phillips Patent Fire Annihilator gained public acclaim, scientific approval and a medal from the Great Exhibition, but not the Fire Chief's endorsement. This complicated hand-held device consisted of a cylinder within another cylinder, containing a glass phial and metal rod. Water, sugar and charcoal were among the more harmless chemicals distributed between this trio of vessels, along with nitrate and chlorate of potash and sulphuric acid. When thrown at a fire the cylinders broke, the burning chemicals emitted steam and the resultant gases allegedly extinguished the flames.

Although one company offered householders reduced premiums if they purchased these devices, within months Braidwood's scepticism was vindicated. The Annihilator factory went up in flames and the British Fire Prevention Insurance Company foundered.

Braidwood's tenure saw the momentous fires at the Palace of Westminster (1834), Royal Exchange (1838), Tower of London Armoury (1841), Windsor Castle (1853) and the explosion aboard the paddle-steamer 'Cricket' (1847).

London was shocked by Braidwood's death in the Tooley Street fire. He was honoured by a funeral the like of which had not been seen since Wellington's—his old adversary—in 1852; similarly it brought the capital to a halt. City church bells tolled, Queen Victoria was represented by the Duke of Sutherland and the Earl of Caithness, both amateur firefighters and friends of the Prince of Wales, Braidwoodís three sons, a thousand policemen, officers of the London Rifle Brigade, a fire protection society band, members of the public and every firemen who could be spared joined the 1.5 mile procession to Stoke Newington cemetery. Flowers from admirers all over the world decorated the hearse and accompanying carriages, a memorial poem selling briskly to those lining the route.

The first letters spelled out James Braidwood, and it concluded:

Where shall we seek so firm, so brave a mind,
Or where, his men reply a heart so kind?
Oh not in vain didst thou resign thy breath,
Devoted hero, conqueror in death

Braidwood had also featured in a prophetic poem about the Fire King in 1839:

'I'll do for that Braidwood said he, and the whole of the brigadier brood.
I'll make them respect my dignity as every fireman should.
I'll set the Thames on fire and see if he bilks me of my food.
Then away he tooled to Tooley Street and selected a warehouse of oil ...
The Thames all over was in flame, as with lighted oil 'twas running.
To save his craft was each man's aim but his craft exceeded their cunning.
And the Fire King laughed when he found he could tame
The Fire Brigade with his funning.'
When they threw the tide on the burning mass quite fruitless was their
desire,
And the bravest heart cried out 'alas' and shrank from the Fire King's ire.
Things were come indeed to a pretty pass when water wouldn't put out
fire.'

Braidwood's silver epaulettes and black silk neckerchief, scorched and blood-stained, are exhibited in the Southwark Fire Brigade Museum.

Braidwood's successor at the LFEE was Captain Eyre Massey Shaw, whose tenure saw it transformed into the Metropolitan Fire Brigade, in 1866..

Modernisation had seen the striking uniforms and impractical footwear of the early insurance brigades give way to more practical attire, a few post-Waterloo companies kitting out their men in other than drab coloured tunics, trousers and boots. Braidwood had altered the LFEE uniforms to black leather tunics, silk neck-scarves to guard against sparks, re-enforced leather helmets and stout boots. Shaw preferred the dragoon, or Napoleonic, boot providing greater protection to the wearer's legs though at the price of impeded mobility. Buttons, epaulettes, belts, gorgets and whistles varied, with some brigades indulging in military undress uniforms decorated with frogging and gold braid.

Shaw was familiar with Paris, the *Sapeurs Pompiers* being the inspiration for the LFEE's new, metal helmets. These had padded interiors, chain link chin straps, high ridge combs and distinguishing badges. Protective face and neck peaks curved down either side of the ears, the resulting gap intended to facilitate the hearing of shouted orders. Constructed of several sections, they allowed damaged parts to be removed and replaced by the station workshops. A popular officer might be presented with inscribed helmet on retirement, and the helmet of a fireman killed on duty was placed on his coffin.

Shaw, like Braidwood, was plagued by inventors, few of whom would have survived if relying on their own contraptions. One enthusiast admitted his device was a failure, but kept working on it. Another ingenious individual mastered poisonous gases to the extent of inventing a versatile machine that could dowse fires and exterminate rats. Many hedged their inventions with secrecy, demanding money before revealing the benefits they were willing to confer on the community.

Steamers were efficient once on the scene and working, but useless if the boiler fire refused to light, or went out, a problem to which Shaw found a solution. After numerous experiments he settled on a gas burner, kept permanently alight on a low flame to maintain the heat of the water in the boiler above, and kindling laid on top of Welsh coal in the firebox. Immediately a call came in, while the horses were being harnessed, the kindling was lit and, once underway, draughts forced through the perforated firebox as the horses hurtled through the streets, fanning the coals, and boosting the temperature of the boiler.

Shaw was all for innovation, if it proved its worth. Under his command every station was linked with others by electric telegraph, but he was initially unsympathetic to reform of the arduous working conditions, long hours and rigorous discipline in the force. Though firemen's pay was better than in the past, older firemen still looked back to the days when the insurance companies had granted pensions, treated the injured with generosity and cared for the widows and orphans of those killed.

Open to argument, if not coercion, Shaw did change his mind about the conditions and backed various humble memorials sent by the engineers and firemen to *your honourable Board...trusting our case may be thought worthy of your earnest attention and that in its most essential points it may meet with your kind approval and support.*

These ineffectual pleas only worsened relations between the self-important Board of Works and its autocratic fire chief. By now Shaw was alarmed that so many expensively trained firemen were resigning because of the conditions, the brigade being well under strength and recruiting almost at a standstill. He spoke out loud and clear, with typical absence of tact, which did little to endear him or his cause to his employers.

The Board was certainly beset by problems other than the brigade, but forfeited all public respect in 1871 by its treatment of the widow of Joseph Ford, a fireman who had been trapped on a ladder and burned alive during a rescue attempt.

A horrified, helpless crowd had seen Ford's terrible, prolonged death:

> *He falls, he falls, is there none to save?*
> *Ah, cruel to think that one so brave*
> *Who snatched six souls from a fiery grave*
> *Should perish by the same.*
> *...Like Jacob's ladder, years ago*
> *Perchance that fire escape would glow*
> *With angels passing to and fro*
> *To point the way to Heaven.*

The Board initially awarded Mrs Joseph Ford a small weekly pension, which they subsequently withdrew after a newspaper appeal raised over £1,000 for the bereaved family.

With his growing family Captain Shaw 'lived above the shop', the brigade HQ in Watling Street, although the search was already underway for a more spacious location to accommodate the expanding MFB. Acrimony and argument bedeviled the final choice of Winchester House in Southwark Bridge Road. Not without reason although it consisted of a pair of pleasant houses, a garden and plenty of room for staff lodgings, stables, engines houses and a training yard.

Lambeth was a disreputable area, it was not in the City and there was no river frontage. In addition the building was opposite a disorderly public house, part of the site was occupied by an abandoned workhouse and adjacent to a pauper's burial ground bordered by an open sewer. Nonetheless, the project went forward and the Shaws moved into a commodious, refurbished portion of Winchester House in 1878. There the HQ of the London brigade remained until the move to Albert Embankment opposite the Tate Gallery in 1937.

Shaw's mixing in aristocratic circles and his friendship with the Prince of Wales attracted venomous journalistic criticism. Sneers grew louder after a visit to the Isle of Wight to advise on fire precautions at Osborne House, and his return with an inscribed timepiece from the Queen. Perhaps not unjustified were the heavy hints in the press that he regularly accompanied the Prince on amorous forays among the capital's clubs, theatres and houses of assignation. One price to be this friendship was laying on entertainment for distinguished guests, including a Russian grand duke and the Shah of Persia, with everyone wanting to be *in on a good fire* or failing that taking the salute at a parade.

In 1886 Shaw was lucky to escape *without a shadow on his fair name* from a divorce case brought by Lord Colin Campbell. The delicious scandal riveted London's attention and was the stuff of tabloid editors' dreams: charges and counter-charges of adultery, friends of royalty including the Duke of Marlborough and Captain Shaw cited as co-respondents, the wife's accusations of husbandly liaisons below stairs with the maids and titillating revelations of what the butler saw through assorted keyholes.

Socialite Shaw might have been, but he was also a fireman's fireman who never sent his men into dangers he was unwilling to face himself. He was much in demand overseas in his role as an exponent of modern fire fighting and he visited America several times. However, his Limey accent and abrasive manner made enemies as well as friends, so it may have been no accident when he was drenched during a display in New York. European journeys took him to Spain, Germany and France, where he examined the gutted shell of the Opera Comique. In Egypt, his hosts offered him the impossible task of rendering Cairo immune from fires.

Despite his popularity and undoubted success as fire chief, some newspapers never moderated their venom. *Reynolds News* chose his retirement and knighthood in 1891 for a final salvo. *Flunkey Shaw has not only got his savings and his pension, but also a KCB [Knight Commander of the Bath], and is now presumably happy, since he is just the kind of small-minded man likely to set a high value on a empty title as well as a solid pension.* All this attention paid to him, in the paper's view, was Tory snobbery and a slap in the face of the democratic London County Council (LCC). It was as well the editor did not know that Shaw had confidentially informed the Prince of his impending letter of resignation days before it was made public.

Another newspaper reckoned sarcastically that London could just about manage without Captain Shaw and, if the MFB could not cope, then there were equally good men in the provincial brigades *to take the place of the late lamented Adonis*. *Punch*, in more mellow mood, published a cartoon of Shaw divesting himself of helmet and axe at *The Fire King's Abdication* and alongside an adulatory poem:

> *...his Crown's a brass helmet, his Sceptre a hose,*
> *True Fire King—all others are spurious.*
> *For he rules the flames, he has done so for long*
> *And now that he talks of retiring*
> *Men mourn for the fire-queller, cautious and strong*
> *Whose reign they've so long been admiring.*

Then came a dig at the bickering committee of the LCC:

> *Our Big Boards might jib and our Bigwigs might jaw*
> *But spite of their tricks and their cackle.*
> *Our Chief we could trust, we were sure that our Shaw*
> *His duty would manfully tackle.*

The tribute in *The Fireman*, published by Merryweather the manufacturer, was muted. While acknowledging Shaw's excellence as an organiser, it commented on the rigour of his discipline, the exaggerated claims in the press of the affection of his brigade and his shortcomings as a technical engineer. It ended with the back-handed compliment that the *public* had always unreservedly placed its confidence in him. The writer was possibly one of the old guard smoke-eaters, hinting that in one respect Shaw was inferior to Braidwood whose *firemanship was the wonder of competent critics*.

Shaw's relationship with the elected representatives on the Fire Brigade Committee of the LCC was as prickly as that with its predecessor, the Metropolitan Board of Works. These years of incompatible partnership failed to end in reconciliation and his retirement was not a harmonious episode.

Incontrovertible testimony to Shaw's service are two lists, the first column representing the state of affairs on his appointment as LFEE chief, and the second on his retirement from the MFB. In those thirty years he attended a 55,004 fires, and 32,335 false alarms.

fire stations (1861)	13	fire stations (1891)	59
firemen	11	firemen	706
miles of hose	4	miles of hose	+33

Once distinguished as Sir Eyre Massey Shaw, the ex-chief was invited to bring his specialised knowledge onto the board of the Palatine Insurance Company and the Metropolitan Electrical Company. His last years were saddened by the death of his wife, followed by acute thrombosis necessitating the amputation of first one and then the other. He died in 1908.

Edward VII, when Prince of Wales, met Shaw through his firefighting cronies, the Duke of Sutherland and the Earl of Caithness. It is tempting to say the pair got on like a house on fire, as indeed they did. Messages relayed to Marlborough House would send the Prince hotfoot to the Chandos Street station off Trafalgar Square to don his fireman's uniform, identical to all the others except for his silver helmet. Keeping the Prince out of real danger probably distracted officers from more important duties but the value of such a fireman's friend in high places tilted the balance in favour of his participation. In the very early days of his friendship with Shaw, the Prince spent a happy day at the first Crystal Palace fire engine trials.

Involved in the action at the Alhambra theatre fire, in Leicester Square in 1882, the Prince almost suffered the fate of Braidwood. Shaw, knowing royalty could not be commanded, solved this dilemma by sending a man to request the Prince to assist him on the opposite side of the square. Before the message was delivered, Shaw saw a bulging wall crash into the street, burying several men only yards from where the Prince was standing.

Though Bertie, Prince of Wales, never let anyone forget who he was, he nevertheless had a genial, common touch which endeared him to many. Assistant Officer Ashford died after terrible suffering, and a few days after the Alhambra fire the Prince visited other surviving, injured firemen in the Charing Cross Hospital, handing out boxes of cigars to cheer their recovery. On another occasion he noticed one man tucking his cigar away in a pocket, and asked him why. When told it was to enjoy later, he promptly gave him another to smoke there and then.

Londoners had a soft spot for their Prince and his human failings. Bertie was a bit of a card, a ladies' man and a stylish sinner, unlike his stern, unbending father, and he always rated a cheer when spotted in fireman's uniform. He features in the long memorial poem published in *The Fireman* after the Alhambra fire:

...Now will the Firemen cease the fight or dauntless courage prove?
Yes, still they face the dreadful roar nor backwards do they move.
Tho' a whirlwind rushes round them, they at their post remain,
Mid the hissing, mid the roaring, mid the hurricane of flame.
...They stand like a noble army with banners all unfurled,
They execute their orders from the 'Skipper' they revere
Full well they know, to him each man, is as a comrade dear.
...Then honour to our Fire Brigade, whose men possess such zeal,
Proud heroes of their native land their grief all hearts must feel.
And honour to our gracious Prince who nobly leads the van
Of public grief and sympathy, for Ashford, brave fireman!

Queen Victoria was unamused by her heir's foolhardy exploits and put a stop to his fire fighting, though nothing could quench his passion for it.

As King, Edward VII did not forgot his friends in the brigades and the dangers they faced in a job that to him had been no more than a diverting hobby. In 1909 he presented the first King's Fire Service and Police Medals to those throughout the Empire who had shown outstanding courage, skill or devotion to duty.

The establishment of the LFEE had not meant the end of all insurance or volunteer fire brigades; there was still competition to be first at the scene of an outbreak.

'Captain' Frederick Hodges inherited a distillery, and a fortune, so his passion for firefighting was based on the permanent threat of an inferno engulfing the family business in Lambeth. Breweries were still high risk to insurance companies and Hodge's highly flammable premises were set among warehouses, lucifer factories and tallow works.

Victorian snobbery disdained retailers as tainted by Trade, but fortunes gained in manufacturing, mill owning, engineering, mining or brewing transformed the heirs thereof into gentlemen, even lords. Hence the Peerage and Beerage. George Stephenson remained a rough Yorkshire engineer till the day he died, but son Robert was quite at home in London Society as was Isambard Kingdom Brunel, son of a French emigré

In 1851, the year of the Great Exhibition, Hodges formed his personal brigade from forty uniformed employees equipped with two manual appliances. A novelty, copied by the LFEE, was the observation tower. Look-outs scanned the rooftops for smoke or flames, not only in anticipation of a 'shout' but in an attempt to negate the number of false alarms from mischievous folk eager to see a fire engine in full, galloping splendour. The brigade cost Hodges £400 a year and turned out for any local fire in a spirit of philanthropic good neighbourliness. His employees benefited from any monetary reward when first at a fire, a frequent occurrence which did not endear them to rival LFEE crews.

Hyde Park in 1861 was the venue for the first fire engine trials ever held. Star turn was Merryweather's steamer *Deluge*, with a double-acting horizontal pump and single horizontal cylinder, that threw a water jet 140 feet high. At Crystal Palace in 1863 Merryweather showed off an even grander pair of steamers, the double-cylinder *Torrent* and the *Sutherland*, in competition against three American and six British manufacturers. Surprisingly, the double-cylinder *Sutherland* was purchased by the Admiralty, seldom to the fore in innovation, for use in naval dockyards. Since Hodges could afford the latest and the best of everything, his brigade was equipped with both a *Deluge* and a *Torrent*, to the envy of all.

His hobby had gained him entry into the very highest circles and he would call up his noble friends when a good fire was in the offing. To their astonishment

South Londoners, expecting an appliance manned by half a dozen salty-tongued ex-sailors, would see a *Deluge* galloping to the scene manned by the Prince, the Duke, the Earl and Hodges.

Amateur or not, Hodges's team tackled hundreds of fires in the years of its existence and, on his retirement, *in recognition of his heroic and unparalleled exertions to protect life and property from fire,* the grateful neighbourhood presented him with a fire engine. Embellished with glittering panels and polished brass it more resembled a hearse, but was no less magnificent for that.

Hodges's business and his hobby also amused his neighbours:

> *If fire you want to put in*
> *Try Hodges' cordial gin.*
> *If fire you want to put out*
> *Try Hodges' engine and spout.*

CHAPTER 14

THE CRYSTAL PALACE

...thousands that raced from all over London to see the mighty blaze

Prince Albert headed the Royal Commission set up in January 1850 to plan the Great Exhibition. By June a site had been staked out in Hyde Park but with no agreed 'temporary' building to go on it. An architectural competition, attracting 245 entries, had inspired nothing but disharmony in the judging committee, one particular monstrosity of brick and iron being by Brunel. In desperation the committee decided to do it themselves, entrusting engineering and architectural niceties to one of their most distinguished members.

Soon even Prince Albert's temper was fraying from the unceasing attacks of press and public. The *Times* could scarcely believe that the Prince's advisers *dared to connect his name with such an outrage [in Hyde Park]...can a building erected on such a scale ever be removed? Under one pretence or another it will remain a fixture.* Other critics muttered that this misbegotten industrial trade fair should be sited far away on the Isle of Dogs.

The whole project might have foundered but for a country visitor attending the Commons with an MP friend. Problems with the Great Exhibition building came up and, within a few days, Joseph Paxton dashed off a sketch of his own ideas. While the building committee havered over this design of glass and iron, Paxton pre-empted their decision with a design printed in the *Illustrated London News*, whose weekly circulation was 20,000. The public loved it, and belatedly Prince and committee loved it too. Long before the glittering, glass building was finished, *Punch* christened it the Crystal Palace and the name stuck.

Paxton, a farmer's son and head gardener of the Duke of Devonshire's Derbyshire estate, had designed and built magnificent greenhouses at Chatsworth. By 1850 he was acknowledged in the highest society as both an innovative gardener and expert in the design of anything from reservoirs to gas works. He enjoyed the genuine friendship of his patron, and the Duke of Wellington once told Devonshire that he *should have liked that man of yours for one of my generals.*

The scale of this Cathedral of Commerce was vast for any age, a building covering 19 acres of a 26 acre site. Many doubted that it could never be built, or, if built, would collapse under its own weight, overheat in the sun, catch fire by lightning or shatter in a thunderstorm. Scoffers had to eat their words after 2,000 workmen had installed 4,000 tons of iron, 25 miles of guttering, 200 miles of framing and transformed 400 tons of glass into 293,000 window panes. Two hundred soldiers marched, stamped and shouted inside it to test its viability in accommodating thousands of pushing, shoving, excited people at one time.

Built in five months at a cost of £800,000, no lives were lost in the construction. One engineering journal marvelled that *considering the perils [and] workmen's habitual imprudence arising partly from real indifference to danger and partly from bravado [that there had been few] accidents, with two or three exceptions of a slight nature.*

By January 1851 Prince Albert was exhausted by the strain: he was worried by the lunatic fringe and remarked that *strangers are certain to begin a revolution here and to murder Victoria and myself. The Plague is certain to start again and for all this I am responsible.* But with the arrival of the first exhibits in February, the critics joined the public in being madly in favour of this wonderful project— which naturally they had supported from the outset.

Few books on the Great Exhibition give even passing mention to any fire or crowd safety measures; such information has to be found in technical journals. One committee member, Henry Cole, had submitted a report on the *Security of the Building from Fire*, but commented acidly that the term 'fireproof' was only relative. Complete fire safety would be too costly and was at any event incompatible with a vast, vaulted, draughty edifice with no dividing walls. Nor would it make any difference what degree of fire-proofedness was the aim since it would not *sensibly affect the rate of insurance, an infallible gauge. . . security from fire should be obtained by vigilant watching, and efficient preparations to extinguish fire, if it should unfortunately happen.*

A 24 inch main was laid from the Chelsea Waterworks with a pressure sufficient to propel a jet 70 feet, a manual, wheeled, pumping engine being stationed close by. In addition to scattered buckets and hoses, there were 25 fire points throughout the building attended by Sappers, men of the Royal Engineers. There were also a number of firefighting appliances among the exhibits, including the innovative steamers, though none was intended for emergency use.

Steam power to drive many large mechanical exhibits was provided by five 150 horsepower boilers, served by coal-fired furnaces installed in an adjacent purpose-built building. The boilers were fed by a water tank supplied from the 6 inch main installed around the entire Palace. Firecocks were placed every 240 feet, and interspersed with sixteen 4 inch pipes branching off to carry water into the building for various purposes, including the nave fountains. Firecocks could be attached in an emergency, and a 120 ft. circle from any one would overlap another, thus covering the whole interior

An adequate water supply was doubly essential since the public was entitled to free glasses of pure water on demand. *Punch* quickly jibed that anyone producing London water fit to drink would exhibit the *best and most universally use-*

ful article in the entire building.

The organisers, after assessing past events both at home and overseas, imposed a trio of prohibitions in the interests of safety and public order: *No Smoking—No Alcohol—No Hot Food.* There were complaints about the lack of all three as the Exhibition progressed, particularly when the autumn days grew chilly and no heating was allowed, but the bans stayed in force.

The Great Exhibition of the Works of Industry of All Nations opened on 1 May 1851 and closed on 11 October. During those five months, 141 days with no Sunday openings, over six million paying visitors passed through the building. The paying public was admitted through three main entrances but left the building by 17 exits. To prevent unauthorised entry these were fitted with one-way turnstiles, difficult for ladies in voluminous skirts to pass through at leisure, and absolutely lethal in the panic of a fire.

The tender to supply refreshments was won by Messrs. Schweppes with a bid of £5,500. Hot drinks were not included in the hot food ban: by the last day the caterers had served mountains of buns, pastries and ices and enough tea, coffee, selzer, sodawater, chocolate, cocoa, ginger beer and spruce beer to fill a reservoir, or extinguish an inferno. Their total profit was £45,000. Even more welcome than refreshments were the public conveniences, the first ever provided at a public event. Some were free while others, more luxurious, made a profit of £1,769; all in pennies?

That charter of social progress, the *Illustrated London News,* had noted in September 1850 that *the working classes in Manchester, Liverpool, Sheffield, Birmingham, the Potteries, and Glasgow, as well as other places, have commenced laying by their weekly pence to form a fund for visiting London...Were it not for cheap excursion trains this great source of amusement and instruction would have been unobtainable.*

Innumerable items challenged for the title of most bizarre among more than 100,000 exhibits. One display of hats was *made from the leaf of the cabbage-tree by prisoners in the Darlinghurst gaol exemplifying the industry and discipline of the prisoners in the Australian gaols.* Almost as useless was the *fire-escape dressing table intended to be always ready and in instant motion, without the least preparation, and to be drawn up from above or below as many times as there are persons to be rescued. The first motion of raising the table-top opens the window, and lets down iron blinds to any number of lower windows.* Fire Brigades and water companies had more sensible exhibits, including the latest appliances, fireproof doors and materials, escape apparatus and street water hydrants.

Disraeli laid on flattery by the trowelful, declaring the Crystal Palace an *enchanted pile which the sagacious taste and prescient philanthropy of an accomplished and enlightened Prince have raised for the glory of England and the delight of two hemispheres.*

Victoria's diary for the closing day echoed that of the opening: *One of the greatest and most glorious days of our lives with which, to my pride and joy, the name of my dearly beloved Albert is ever associated.*

The final attendance was 6,039,195, and a breakdown of the ticket sales shows how affordable the exhibition was to all but the very poorest:

Season tickets, 3 gns. men, 2 gns. ladies, 141 days	773,766
£1 visitors, exclusive two days	1,042
5s & 2s 6d tickets, next 58 days	824,968
1s tickets, final 80 days	4,439,419

The highest attendance, of 109,915, was on Wednesday 7 October, during the last week of the Exhibition, 93,224 people being in the building at the same time. (This is the official figure, but could that number have been contained in the 19-acre building even with its upper galleries, after making allowance for 100,000 exhibits, many of them exceedingly large?) Whatever the true figure, if fire had broken out it would have resulted in the worst loss of life in a public building in history. Miraculously, and mercifully, during the entire 141 days the only incident was a small fire in a waste bin, dowsed by a bucket of water.

The final profits of £186,000 exceeded the most optimistic forecasts. Augmented by Treasury grants, they were devoted to the high ideals of culture and learning on a designated site in South Kensington: the Victoria and Albert, Science, Natural History and Geological Museums, the Imperial College of Science and Technology, Royal School of Mines, Royal College of Art, Royal College of Music and the Royal Albert Hall of Arts and Sciences.

The Albert Memorial, unveiled in 1863 after the Prince Consort's death, shows him holding the catalogue of the Great Exhibition.

The Crystal Palace in Hyde Park was temporary. It was soon dismantled and then rebuilt, enlarged, on Anerley Hill, Sydenham. Queen Victoria reopened it 1854 as a place of public entertainment which it attracted huge crowds at weekends after the direct rail link from London Bridge Station was opened. The Palace was now over 1200ft. long, 450ft high, 200ft to the roof of the transepts and flanked by two 250ft high towers which provided the head of water for the fountains. Within and without were housed or presented a menagerie, an amusement park, prehistoric animals, concerts, circuses, theatricals, exhibitions, firework displays, Cruft's Dog Show and, until Wembley opened in 1924, the Cup Final.

A lecture advertised in 1876 by the Rev. R M Hart on the subject of *Fire, and How it is Extinguished* was regrettably cancelled. Two days before the event most of the North Wing, housing several galleries, the tropical apartments and Orangery, went up in flames and several exotic beasts in the menagerie perished. Not all this part of the Palace was rebuilt, owing to shortage of funds.

As a finale to Captain Shaw's career, the London Fire Brigade staged a gala review in 1891, attended by over 1400 men from 131 brigades and 56 gleaming fire engines. As a 'visiting fireman' the Kaiser took the salute, dazzling in white uniform, blue Garter ribbon and eagle-mounted gold helmet. The day concluded with the finest firework displays ever staged at Crystal Palace.

The splendour and novelty of Paxton's Great Conservatory at Chatsworth had earned the gardener-cum-architect his commission for the Great Exhibition building of 1851. This Derbyshire glasshouse continued to nurture exotic plants until the Great War, when a series of winter fuel shortage closed down the furnaces and left the exhibits to die of cold. The dangerous, neglected structure was blown up by the 9th Duke of Devonshire in 1919.

The following year the Great War Exhibition was a huge success at Crystal Palace although few saw much future in Logie Baird's later television experiments within its seemed quite obviously impossible to send pictures through thin air.

By the 1930s the Crystal Palace was showing its age, leaking at the joints and succumbing to rust and weather. The cracked gutters and glass panes had earlier been caulked with pitch, thus introducing a fire risk absent from the original Hyde Park building.

On the frosty evening of 30 November 1936 the Palace caught fire. First on the scene, but half an hour after the first flames were reported, was Penge Fire Brigade. Eight fireman manning the single motor appliance did their inadequate best with a single jet of water but, even with 70 pumps in action, an hour later the Palace was beyond saving. As they battled on past midnight, firemen were seen wearing their helmets back to front in an effort to protect their faces from the glare and intense heat. The twin towers blazed like beacons, visible from as far as Hampstead Heath, and people poured out into the streets or took to their cars to witness at closer quarters the landmark's fiery death. Children were woken up to view the blaze, in the same spirit that their parents had been taken to witness a moment of history in the passing of Queen Victoria's funeral train in 1901.

Spectacular to the last, the Crystal Palace, famous for its magnificent firework displays went out in the greatest and most awe-inspiring show in its history reported the *Daily Mirror*. There had not been a blaze to equal it since Tooley St in 1861, beyond the memory of all but the most ancient of idle gazers.

At least one of Edward VII's sons had inherited his passion for fires. Major Cyril Morris, London's Chief Officer, had to take time off from directing operations to escort the Duke of Kent around the perilous site. He had come hotfoot from an official dinner in full evening dress and, when the canny Morris insisted that only one helmet and pair of boots could be spared, the disappointed equerry had to stay with the car. *The ruse worked and the Duke trudged along through all the water and mud that collects round a large fire. We all had a splendid time with him,* Morris wrote in his memoirs. After introducing several senior officers he called up some of the younger men who had been in the thick of the firefighting. *Like other members of the Royal Family I have met in connection with my work he took the keenest interest in all he saw, asked numerous questions that were always to the points, and I really believe he enjoyed his experience.*

By morning the building was a forlorn, menacing wreck. 100,000 panes of shattered glass hampered salvage work and 15,000 tons of twisted iron girders and framework solidified gradually from the molten metal into grotesque shapes and rivers of frozen steel. In these *halls of havoc girders, planks, turnstiles and cast-iron fittings are strewn in a tangle, distorted mass. The twin towers, which it was feared at one time would fall on the thousands that raced from all over London to see the mighty blaze, now stand gaunt and lonely above the twisted metal.*

Another reporter described the spectacle when flying at 1000ft, with the flames only 200ft below the plane. Through gaps in the swirling smoke he peered into the *blazing crater of a volcano. Red-hot metal piled up in huge, shapeless heaps...Roads around were thronged with congested traffic, and the crowds of people who gathered in the glare made it a scene like hell.* A spectator commented that *Brock [the manufacturer] in his wildest dreams had never conceived such a firework display.*

An unexpected ally of the idle gazers had been the BBC, broadcasting the progress of the fire to an enthralled nation and drawing anyone within miles to the conflagration They were later bitterly criticised by the London Fire Brigade whose efforts were hampered by the ever-increasing throngs of spectators. This may be the first instance of radio, and now television, abandoning any sense of responsibility to those coping with disasters, from motorway pile-ups to air crashes, in their eagerness to be first with the news.

The official enquiry blamed the initial outbreak on a gas leak, the fire spreading undetected through the huge unrestricted space to set the building well ablaze before the first appliance arrived. Within a week Lloyds paid out £110,000 in fire insurance, plus a further £10,000 for the loss of the great organ. Several witnesses recalled that as the flames consumed its pipes, this splendid instrument let out unearthly wails in its death throes.

Rumour, never completely silenced, insisted the fire had been neither accidental nor arson, but started by the authorities intent on destroying so conspicuous a landmark before enemy bombers headed for the capital. This is surely improbable since the full horror of aerial destruction unleashed during the Spanish Civil War did not culminate in the bombing of Guernica by the German Condor Squadron until 1937. There was no immediate threat against Britain in 1936. Nor was there any way to disguise other landmarks such as the course of the Thames, St Paul's or the Houses of Parliament. Why destroy the landmark and leave the towers glittering in the sunlight, or had the fire brigades not been informed of governmental pyromania? Ironically, the towers were demolished in 1940, for exactly the reason rumour had mooted for the entire structure in 1936.

Eye witness accounts of molten glass flooding the streets of Penge are discounted by modern physicists claiming that both the heat and the quantity of glass were inadequate for such a long-range phenomenon. Maybe, but lumps of shapeless metal and chunks of fused glass from the site were certainly eagerly snatched up as souvenirs. Publisher Russell Miller remembers these as coveted trophies in the school playground and remembers the bombing rumours about the towers.

Fred Redding, archivist of Selfridges, recalls the *boys who lived next door knocking on our door to tell us what was up, and as I had finished my homework was allowed to go to Hillside Road where we had a grandstand view—between us and the Palace—a valley and nothing to get in the way. I remember the whole golden outline of the building shining from inside. A far better show than the annual fireworks. This outdid it all. We visited the burnt-out site a few weeks later—a devastation of blackened timber, twisted iron and congealed, jellied glass. Little did we realise how good a preparation this experience had been to prepare us for the London Blitz, and it remained a small boy's warning not to play with matches.*

The destruction of Alexandra Palace, back in 1873, was attributed to embers spilling from a workman's unattended brazier, another forerunner of the dreaded misplaced blowtorch. The loss of that gutted palace topped £0.5m. Though it was quickly rebuilt, in 1980 another fire ended its role as the pioneer television centre, decades after Logie Baird's experiments at the Crystal Palace.

CHAPTER 15

PLAYING WITH FIRE—Theatres

By the benefit of a provident wit, put it out with bottle ale.

Theatres might have been designed for no other purpose than to give a leading role to the Fire King. Even when timber and thatch gave way to stone and tile these huge, high caverns were still full of highly flammable galleries, floors, seating and curtains, quite apart from the scenery, costumes and realistic displays of fire and flood so beloved of audiences. All were lit by sconces, hanging lamps, candelabra or candles, and within inches of the actresses' swirling skirts were the footlights of naked flame. Smoky tallow or clear wax candles made no difference to the danger.

Until the advent of department stores and grand hotels, the greatest loss of life in single incidents had usually involved theatres.

Miracle plays performed on carts or temporary staging delighted townsfolk of the Middle Ages, but post-Reformation Londoners demanded more dramatic and secular entertainment in custom-built premises. By 1600 there were four, public London theatres: the Globe on Bankside, Red Bull in Clerkenwell, Curtain in Shoreditch and Fortune in Whitecross Street. The Whitefriars and the Blackfriars had the curious status of private houses. At the whim of their patron actors from any of these could be called upon to perform at court or homes of the nobility.

The City Fathers threatened to close down Burbage's wooden Shoreditch Theatre in 1597. Overnight the owner and his players dismantled it, trundled it over London Bridge and re-erected it on bawdy Bankside out of their jurisdiction. Burbage's new company included a couple of playwrights, Fletcher and Shakespeare, and achieved respectability when James I designated them the *King's Servants to exercise their art within their usual house the Globe*, alongside the Southwark Bear Garden.

Sir Henry Wotton wrote to a friend in 1613 after a lively visit to the Globe to see *a new play called All is True, representing some principal pieces of the reign of Henry VIII...at Cardinal Wolsey's house, certain cannons being shot off at his entry, some of the paper or other stuff wherewith one of them was stopped, did light on the thatch where, being thought at first but an idle smoke and their eyes being more attentive to the show, it kindled inwardly and ran round like a train [of gunpowder] consuming, within less than an hour, the whole house to the very ground. This was the fatal period of that virtuous fabric, wherein nothing did perish but wood and straw and a few forsaken cloaks. Only one man had his breech-*

es set on fire, that perhaps had broiled him if he had not, by the benefit of a prov-ident wit, put it out with bottle ale.

Having no financial interest in the playhouse, the urbane ex-ambassador to Venice could afford to be witty, but the total loss of the Globe was a disaster for the company and one of the earliest accounts of a theatrical fire.

Private theatricals reached new heights in elegant, if interminable, Jacobean masques, a blending of poetry, music and stylised dance. They were usually events of exquisite refinement, but not the *Masque of Solomon and the Queen of Sheba* performed for James I's Danish father-in-law in 1606. The performance degenerated into a drunken orgy featuring the two lecherous monarchs, dishev-elled nymphs and staggering goddesses. The culmination was Faith, Hope and Charity *sick and spewing in the lower hall.*

In the next reign, William Prynne condemned playhouses, players and play-goers for *concupiscence and filthie lustes of wicked whoredome.* Since the French were capable of any depravity, his main target was Queen Henrietta Maria, whom he accused in print of being *whorishly impudent as to act, to speak publicly on the stage, perchance in Man's apparel?* His ears were cropped in the pillory for the insults, and when, he repeated the libels, the stumps were cropped again.

Between 1642 and 1658 there were no theatre fires in London. An admirable record owing nothing to improved safety and everything to the Civil War, during which all playhouses were closed. *The Lords and Commons in this Parliament assembled* thought fit that *while these sad causes and set times of humiliation continue, public stage-plays shall cease, and be forborne.*

There was a impassioned response from *comedians, tragedians and actors of all sorts and sizes within the city of London and the suburbs.* Why should play-houses be closed when barbarism, beastliness, pick-pocketing and brawling con-tinued at the Bear Garden? Why were they singled out when at *civil and well-governed theatres none used to come but the best of the nobility and gentry?*

In 1616 an old cockfighting pit in Drury Lane was converted into a theatre, only to be burned down by a gang of drunken apprentices. It reopened as the Phoenix and put on clandestine plays during the Civil War but was killed off at the Restoration by the Theatre Royal in the same street. The Fortune in Golden Lane owned by Edward Alleyn, a colleague of Burbage, cost £550 when it was built in 1600. It burned down in 1621. Its brick replacement was also used clan-destinely during the war, which probably led to its destruction by puritan sol-diers.

After the Restoration, Pepys's playgoing several times a week led to admitted neglect of Navy Office business and January 1661 was the *first time that ever [he] saw women come upon the stage.* The King's liaison with the actress Nell Gwynne was no secret, and Pepys lusted after her too, but without fulfilment. Ever observant, he noted in 1667 that one theatre had removed the filthy rushes from the floor, two fiddlers had been replaced with ten and tallow dips were hardly to be seen, in fact *all otherwise...wax candles, many of them.*

One theatre that bore anything but a charmed life was the Theatre Royal, Drury Lane, in its various guises. The first burned down in 1672. Rebuilt by Wren, it was replaced with a new one in 1791. Richard Brinsley Sheridan, was among the shareholders watching their investment disappear in flames in 1796. When told not to obstruct the firemen, he complained *that surely a man might take a glass and warm his hands at his own fireside.*

The Theatre Royal was again rebuilt, this time with a water tank on the roof and the novelty of a cast-iron safety curtain. This marvel was cranked down during the interval and struck by hammer to show its worth to the appreciative audience. Theatre and fire curtain went up in flames in 1809 during a performance starring John Kemble. The Phoenix fire officers were quickly on the scene, but not before the fire had spread to an adjacent storehouse used for additional scenery, costumes and oil for stage lighting. Several men were killed and many others injured. The theatre reopened in 1812.

Many theatres still playing to packed houses in the West End have burned at least twice, including Covent Garden and the Lyceum, previously the English Opera House. The record number of destructions is held by Astley's Amphitheatre in Westminster Bridge Road which burned down in 1794, 1803, 1830 and 1841.

Astley's was an enormously popular equestrian venue for all classes, the Olympia and Horse of the Year Show of its day. Starting as a tented arena in 1769, it was rebuilt as an amphitheatre in 1794 when its ex-cavalry officer owner put on displays of horsemanship, pony racing, circus acts and any other crowd-pullers he could think of. After the fourth fire Astley's disappeared, only to be reborn as the New Westminster Theatre Royal which lasted until 1893.

Beneath the great Rotunda, and in its several card and supper rooms, the Pantheon in Oxford Street could accommodate 1500 people when it opened in 1772. It impressed even the cynical Horace Walpole with its splendour, while to many others it was the most magnificent place of assembly in Europe. Tickets for the complete programme of twelve subscription entertainments were much sought after, even at six guineas. Its genteel reputation was as short as its life, and after becoming a theatre in 1791 it burned down the following January amid dark rumours of arson from rival attractions. The Pantheon's final moment of glory came next morning with sunlight glittering on cascades of icicles suspended among the ruins—an echo of its debut as an enchanted palace conjured by the *potent wand of some Fairy.* Since 1937 it has housed no fairies, only St Michael, as the Oxford St store of Marks and Spencer.

London's three riverside pleasure gardens, Vauxhall, Ranelagh and Cremorne, attracted huge crowds in summer, not all of them in respectable pursuit of music, dancing and refreshment. In its late-18th Century heyday, Vauxhall drew 60,000 people to a fancy dress ball illuminated by 30,000 lamps. On other occasions a thousand soldiers had re-enacted Waterloo complete with cannon and rockets, an early parachutist had fallen to his death and a successful balloon ascent was made by Charles Green. The young Mozart performed at Ranelagh and, at rival Cremorne, *intrepid astronaut Green* soared skyward again, this time sharing the basket with a leopard and a lady. The only fire precaution in these place was the banishment of gentlemen wishing to smoke to designated booths distant from the main galleries.

Owners of theatres and pleasure gardens were far less concerned with the safety of patrons than the value of their expensive premises, and thus insured them against loss by fire. The Sun Fire Office was well ahead of its rivals, the Royal Exchange and the Phoenix, in providing cover and by 1790 was collecting premiums to the value of £100,000. The Pantheon was covered for only £2,000 but Drury Lane for £10,000 and the Royal Opera House, Covent Garden, for £25,000. The pleasure gardens of Ranelagh were covered for only £,4000 but Vauxhall for the precise sum of £20,800. Other Sun clients included many of the Oxford and Cambridge colleges, the Hudson Bay Company and, for £16,000, Carlton House, home of the spendthrift Prince Regent, the premium surely paid by someone else.

Londoners expected every victory, coronation or royal birthday to be celebrated with fireworks so all three gardens obliged with dazzling displays on these occasions, and lesser ones weekly. Trapeze artists swung through salvos of rockets, tightrope walkers trod between blazing walls and Handel's Music for the Royal Fireworks was rehearsed at Vauxhall before 12,000 people. The actual event for which it was written, celebrating the Peace of Aix la Chapelle in 1749, took place in Hyde Park. The unintended climax to the four-hour show was the pyrotechnic palace set alight by a firework, two people trampled to death, the Duke of Richmond making off with the unfired rockets and the distraught Italian organiser arrested for drawing his sword in the presence of George II.

Built in the Moorish manner with minarets and a dome, the Alhambra opened in Leicester Square as the Royal Panopticon of Science and Art to display the latest marvels of the two. However, it failed to please and bankrupted the owner. In 1856 it re-opened as a circus but, despite a visit by Queen Victoria and the royal children, four years later it was transformed into a music hall as the Alhambra Palace. Londoners loved it for the variety of its acts: singers, ballet dancers, tightrope walkers and trapeze artists. Francois Leotard, the original *daring young man on a flying trapeze*, was a highlight of the 1861 season only to be outshone by the great Blondin, fresh from his exploits at Niagara. Promenade concerts were popular but what really pulled in the crowds were the Alhambra's saucy dancing girls. Trouble followed when one particular lass kicked her gartered legs higher than her head, to the cheers of the audience. The owner was fined and the theatre closed when the killjoy authorities took the view that layers of silk petticoats were no substitute for the lack of a pair of cotton drawers. Physical danger to the public counted for nothing, but moral depravity was checked at source.

After yet another re-opening, the Alhambra managed to stay within the law only to catch fire in December 1882, despite newly installed hydrants and iron safety doors. Although the building was empty at that hour of night, and Captain Shaw and his crews arrived *with commendable promptitude*, two firemen were killed during the blaze. The flames spread to an adjacent Turkish bath and temporary police station after gutting the auditorium, although the ornate facade of was barely scorched. Most of the larger orchestral instruments and £10,000 worth of costumes were destroyed, but luckily those for the forthcoming *Love of the Flame and Icicle* were not yet in house. The North British and Royal Insurance Companies paid out a total of £34,000. In its final incarnation, the Alhambra lasted until 1936, hosting Diaghilev's ballet, the Russian ballet, the Monte Carlo Ballets Russes and George Robey's Music Hall, along with more saucy ladies. The Odeon Cinema now stands on the site.

Unlike the Alhambra, when the Theatre Royal, Exeter, caught fire in September 1887 it had been playing to a full house. The fire took hold back stage but swiftly engulfed the whole building precipitating panic in the audience who rushed and stumbled for the smoke-shrouded exits. Though many escaped, the final death toll rose to 188, many of the dead found piled on top of one another in charred, choking heaps. One of the audience who risked his life to rescue several people was a sailor, Able Seaman Hunt, who was later promoted and received a Royal Humane Society medal.

The coroner's jury deliberated for eight days before returning a verdict of accidental death and condemning the licensing authority and the architect for the faults and dangers inherent in the building. A macabre classification of the dead listed 114 recognisable or charred human bodies, 30 reassembled bodies among the heaps of bones and a further 35 likely bodies in the ashes.

Limelight, much used to create brilliant effects on stage, was a dangerous device created by heating particles of pure lime through the constant application of a gas-fired torch. Accidents and deaths as a result of its use were frequent.

The damage and fatalities in British theatres were serious enough, but far worse happened elsewhere in the 19th Century with over 1200 people killed world-wide in 1884 alone. Not included in that figure was a tragedy in the Star Theatre, Glasgow when a drunken shout of *Fire! Fire!* led to a stampede and fourteen deaths. A theatre fire in St Petersburg claimed hundreds of lives, one in Karlsruhe resulted in over six hundred casualties and not long after nearly 300 died in Brooklyn. When Vienna's Ring Theatre caught fire over five hundred playgoers were burned, suffocated or trampled death in the rush towards the smoke-shrouded, unlit exits

Captain Shaw of the Metropolitan Fire Brigade was appalled at the unending tragedies at home and abroad, and the almost total lack of concern shown by the authorities. Such regulations as did exist for safety in places of entertainment were blatantly ignored so Shaw undertook an exhaustive study before publishing *Fires in Theatres* in 1878. This damning indictment was enough to make any Londoner foreswear the pleasures of the theatre for ever, if they valued their lives. Shaw denounced *monstrosities in the way of theatres which have disgraced our cities for years and should never have been allowed to exist.* Every single one of the 41 theatres inspected was a potential deathtrap and collectively they nightly endangered the lives of thousands of citizens with the threat of fire.

Monstrosities or not, little was done beyond extending the power of the Board of Works to insist on minor improvements to existing theatres. It was mere tinkering since it involved no more than modest expenditure and applied only to those above a certain seating capacity, thus excluding most music halls and all public houses. This inertia was compounded by the division of responsibility for theatres between the local authority and the Lord Chamberlain's office, the latter more concerned with jeopardising the public with staged obscenity, sedition or naked flesh than naked lights.

Although candlelight and gas were on their way out, 'The Electricity', first used at the Savoy in The Mikado, brought its own hazards of faulty installation, worn cables and proximity to water. Shaw's first hand knowledge of the perils did not dampen his enthusiasm for the theatre but like most victims he did not relish being a target for satire on stage himself. In *Iolanthe* W S Gilbert's pointed allusions to their chief's amorous gallantry went down exceptionally well with his force:

> On fire that glows with heat intense I turn the hose of common sense
> And out it goes at small expense.
> We must maintain our fairy law, that is the main on which to draw
> In that we gain a Captain Shaw.
> Oh, Captain Shaw, type of true love kept under.
> Could thy Brigade with cold cascade quench my great love, I wonder?

In 1897 a committee of public-spirited men set up the British Fire Prevention Association. Among its members were men with first hand experience of theatres. One was actor-manager Sir Henry Irving, who had recently lost all his company's sets and costumes in a storage fire in Bear Lane, Southwark, another was Gilbert's partner in the Savoy operas, Sir Arthur Sullivan. The driving force was architect Edwin Sachs, who had once worked as a temporary scene shifter on stage and later designed several theatres incorporating safety features.

The urgent need to protect the public led to the publication of the

Association's Red Books, soon to become the fireman's invaluable manual. These evaluated technical advances in firefighting and prevention, improvements in fire resistant materials and advocated a laboratory for testing such materials.

In 1897 Sachs published *Fire and Public Entertainments* opening with the horrifying statistic that between 1797-1897 11,000 notable fires in public buildings caused more than 10,000 deaths—most of them in theatres. He had found no appreciable improvements in building safety, nor change in public attitudes, since the gladiatorial days of the Roman Empire. However, the recorded fires of Antiquity at the Theatres of Pompey and Marcellus, the Circus Maximus and the Amphitheatre, which claimed hundreds of victims, did not appear to have dampened the populace's appetite for *bread and circuses*.

Bringing his survey up to date Sachs listed the horrors of fires in the Amalienborg Palace Theatre, Copenhagen (1689), 210 dead; Royal Palace Theatre, Dresden (1701); Residenz Palace Theatre, Munich (1750); La Scala, Milan (1776); Municipal Theatre, Nice (1881), over 70 dead; a Brooklyn theatre (1878), 283 dead; two Russian circus disasters (1883 and 1898) with a combined total of dead of 320.

Analysing recent figures he listed the causes of nearly 200 theatrical fires as:

lamps	*18*
open lights	*37*
defective gas	*44*
defective electricity	*7*
defective heating	*32*
guns, fireworks & explosions on stage	*56*

Edwin Sachs, Captain Shaw and others must have felt that the *Theatres Act 1843* and the *Metropolis Management and Buildings Act 1878* were about as fireproof as the paper they were written on.

CHAPTER 16

GOING TO BLAZES

Stop me not, but onward let me jog,
For I am Chance, the London fireman's Dog

The London Fire Brigade never owned its horses but relied on a regular supply from contractors, almost exclusively Tillings of Peckham. These jobbing livery stables 'horsed' anything from an omnibus to a hearse and serviced the capital's fire brigades for over fifty years.

To the warning cry of *Hi! Hi!* a fire engine could thunder through the streets at full gallop—but for the traffic congestion. In 1885 an estimated 30,000 horses worked in London with over 100,000 vehicles traversing the City streets every twenty four hours. When the Blackwall Tunnel was opened by the Prince of Wales in 1897 to relieve overcrowding on London Bridge, it was designed to carry over 1000 horsedrawn vehicles daily. (A century later it was choked with 40,000 motorised ones).

Thomas Tilling had begun a dairy business in 1847 with a horse and cart then, branching out, offered a single horse and carriage for hire. By 1849, with four horses in the stable, he set his Times omnibus on the road. It made four return trips a day from Peckham Rye to Oxford St with Tilling always making the early morning drive. In its heyday Tillings ran 250 buses, and many of its 7000 horses were hired out on long term contracts to fire brigades and the London General Omnibus Company (LGOC), forerunner of London Transport.

The railways had quickly claimed most long distance transport, but all intermediate journeys and deliveries within towns were by horsedrawn vehicles. As late as 1901, Tilling still horsed fire brigades and had 220 horse-buses on the London streets.

Steam powered-propulsion, with a few exceptions, was never adopted for fire engines, although it was used for some stage coaches. The *Royal Patriot* ran between London and Bath from 1827 and the 1836 *Automaton* travelled at a rapid 11.5 mph. The *1861 Locomotive Act* referred to steam 'road locomotives', curious vehicles permitted to go 10mph in the country and 5mph in town. The *1865 Red Flag Act* reduced these speeds to 4mph and 2mph, to avoid running over the man walking ahead with a red flag or frightening horses and cattle. In 1928 a limit of 12mph was imposed by the *Heavy Motor Car (Amendment) Act Order*.

A Tilling horse was valued at £20, and its working life with the London General Omnibus Company six years, according to the *Illustrated London News* of 1865 which described the work undertaken by the animal as *a fair term of servitude for the poor animal during which time he seldom fails to perform his daily task of 12 miles [pulling a bus]...and consumes 15lb oats, 3lbs beans, and 5lbs straw*. Fire horses ate the same amount and, if short of exercise for a few days, became very excitable at the next alarm, one pair allegedly bypassing their appliance and dashing straight out of the station.

Over time Tilling bred the ideal fire horse, a cross between a shire and a charger, standing 16 hands tall, and of notable strength and stamina. A horse needed to pull a fully equipped fire engine through cobbled, often hilly streets. Equine recruits were trained for their role by pulling trams or one of Tilling's regular omnibuses through heavy traffic. Unlike their continental and American counterparts, his horses learned the ropes in a mere three months instead of twelve, and were usually six years old before joining a brigade to pull five tons of appliances loaded with water, fuel and crew.

Greys were traditional, mainly for their visibility at night, and their collars carried several small bells and the neat initials 'TT'. Tilling's animals enjoyed an inbred calm temperament but, when firemen rescued other horses from burning stables, it was necessary to blindfold them to avoid panic and injury.

Though brigade horses worked hard, compared to their human counterparts in Victorian London they led a life of luxury—warm shelter, good food, loving attention and specialist medical care. Stables were an integral part of the fire station and coachmen and grooms would return any sick or injured horse to Tilling for treatment, or instant replacement. Despite working on hard-surfaced City streets horses were lightly shod, if at all, making them deft and sure-footed on wet streets or surfaces flooded by fire hoses.

Fire stations had several pairs of horses on the strength with one pair on watch at all times. They learned quickly and, as soon as the alarm went and the stable door opened, they made straight for the shafts of the vehicles without any command or direction. Harness was suspended from the ceiling of the appliance room and it took only a few pulls on the ropes to release the collars and bridles, then a couple of snaps of buckles and tightening of girths before all was ready to go in less than two minutes.

During a blaze, the coachman unshafted his team and lead them out of danger down a side street, although, in the days before the telegraph, a fireman might ride off on one to summon reinforcements. The waiting horses knew they were in for treats since many in the crowd materialising out of nowhere to watch a blaze invariably arrived with buns and apples.

A working life lasted about five years when, though still active, they were despatched to the knacker's yard as they were not much in demand for other activities. Once a fire horse, always a fire horse, and they were so conditioned to respond to the rumble of a fire engine and the clangour of bells that, oblivious of any new role pulling a milk cart or cab, they would gallop off in pursuit of action.

A 1905 photograph of Norah and Sarah harnessed to a turntable ladder at Kensington fire station, is one of the last examples of London fire horse power. The last LGOC horsedrawn omnibus was withdrawn in 1911.

Country brigades, particularly small volunteer forces, could not afford to retain their own horses. They relied on local farmers and tradesmen to bring their animals along when the alarm bell rang and there was keen, often rough, competition to be first and claim the bounty. Horses pulled country fire engines until after the Great War, and for a time ran in tandem with motorised appliances.

The scale of charges for Westerham, Kent included those for *horse per pair, bellman and turncock* for the years between 1904-1919, altered only in 1923 to *horses per pair, motor lorry and motor car.* The charge for horses was according to distance and duration with a minimum charge of 2gns per pair. The turncock was paid according to time, refreshments being *as ordered by Officer in charge.* Use of the engine was 2 gns, and an extra 10s 6d if accompanied by the hose cart, which if sent out alone to a small fire cost 1gn. The captain received 5s for four hours duty, firemen 3s and pumpers and labourers 2s 6d for similar stints.

An early place of honour among fire horses goes to the unnamed mount of Lord Craven, a mettlesome steed that *smelt the battle afar off.* Craven did notable service during the Great Fire and ten years later was active in combating the Southwark conflagration. In 1682 he was out again at Wapping where a domestic fire spread so rapidly that twenty people were burned in their beds and great damage done. Several manual fire engines directed by Craven proved their worth, the prompt appearance of this nobleman at London fires being credited to his horse being able to sniff smoke from a great distance.

During the Second World War, with petrol strictly rationed, horse drawn transport was suddenly in great demand. Old carts and drays rescued from scrap heaps and farmyards where they had long been abandoned in favour of motors were sold on to butchers, grocers, milkmen, laundries, market traders, the post office and railway companies. There were no air raid shelters for animals so, before making for safety themselves when the sirens wailed, drivers unshafted their horses and tied them head on to the *back* of the cart to prevent bolting. For decades after the bombing the Barbican lay derelict while rebuilding plan after plan was drawn up, discussed and rejected. One of the few buildings still standing in those bomb-scarred acres was the Whitbread Brewery. Built in 1782, the roof of the Porter Tun Room has a span surpassed only by that of William Rufus' Westminster Hall. One massive oak king-post in the brewery supports the roof and beneath it rows of vats once held over 5,000 barrels, 205,000 gallons of maturing beer.

Samuel Whitbread was apprenticed in 1736 to a member of the Company of Brewers. Later the three Whitbread brothers went into business on their own account and with the King's Head Brewery launched the family fortunes. At the time, goods arrived in the City by river and canal, and later by train, but once unloaded all deliveries still depended on carts, waggons and drays. At the outset Whitbread's stabled 60 horses, and in around 1900 over 300 delivered beer to the capital's hundreds of pubs and taverns. In the 1950s, under Colonel W H Whitbread, a Master of the Brewers' Company, the company went public but within 25 years London's independent breweries had shrunk from 703 to 177. Production at the last one ceased in 1976, although Whitbread's headquarters remain in Chiswell Street.

In the great raid of 30/31 December 1940 the Barbican area was almost levelled by bombs and fire, but Whitbreads suffered minor damage compared to its neighbours. This was due to forethought not luck, since 'Mr Harry' Whitbread had several years earlier organised a company fire brigade, trained by an ex-officer of the LCC service. Fire watchers manned the Malt Tower pinpointing fallen incendiaries for swift destruction by the fire fighters. The worst damage was the loss of a warehouse containing £40,000-worth of hops.

As the scale of this monstrous raid became apparent, the stable doors were opened and the dray horses released to take their chance in the blazing streets. There was little to rejoice at next morning amid the stench of cordite, wet ash, smouldering timber and roasted hops, save for the re-appearance of all the company's horses.

A witness never forgot the sight of the shires trotting back in ones and twos bringing with them *quite a number of friends picked up during the night. These friends made themselves at home in various stalls and we were able to return them to their owners within a few days.*

The modern stables of 1897 in Garrett Street, frequently renovated since, allowed the shires to climb a shallow, circular ramp to their own named bays in the multi-storey building. Fire precautions and fire drill were as strictly enforced as for any other London inmate, including the Household Cavalry barracks in Hyde Park.

Not all horses escaped so lightly in wartime. One livery stable near Oxford St took a direct hit from a doodlebug in 1944. A witness likened the aftermath to a battlefield of reeking charred flesh and spilled blood and guts, accentuated by the cries of crippled animals struggling to get to their feet. The fireman's axe, similar to that of an army farrier, effectively put them out of their agony.

Though cats, birds, even a goat and a monkey were kept as Victorian station pets, dogs were the firemen's special friends. Tall tales grew up around some of these legendary animals. Chance ran away to join the fire brigade, and when his Spitalfields owner reclaimed him he bided his time before escaping back to the station. This act was repeated so often that his owner gave up and Chance achieved his ambition to be a regular member of the Chandos St crew. Quick off the mark when the alarm rang, Chance was often the first sign to anxious house-holders that help was on the way. He learned to pull burning timber aside to assist in rescues, had a sharp nose for sniffing out buried fire plugs and was himself an interested observer at the Houses of Parliament fire in 1834.

A performing bear in Spitalfields Market once touched a chord of sympathy in the dog. Some weeks later when the Islington Philharmonic caught fire, one of the crew followed Chance into the empty, smoking wreckage convinced the agi-tated dog sensed a hidden victim. So he had. Abandoned by his owner, chained to the wall and dead from suffocation was the pathetic bear.

Chance died in action. He had been hurt in a fire a few days earlier and was resting at the station when a call came; rushing out to climb onto the engine proved too much for him and he had a fatal collapse. Several firemen contributed to a taxidermist's fee to have him stuffed and he was then displayed in a glass case at Chandos Street. To raise funds for a fireman's widow and three children, a raffle was organised with Chance in all his glory as the prize. Every fire station in the metropolis took part and, together with public purchases of the sixpenny tickets, £123.10. was collected. The winner carried off his bizarre prize but no record exists of his last address. If anyone discovers a stuffed dog in a glass case, please notify the Southwark Fire Brigade Museum.

Another London fire dog, Billy, ended up as a stuffed exhibit at Madame Tussauds' waxworks. Furthermore, Baron, a Great Dane adopted by the Whitefriars station off Fleet Street, figured on one of set of postcards lauding London's noble fire brigades. He too died on active service, run over by a fire engine. In 1885 a fireman and his dog featured in the Lord Mayor's Show, hav-ing rescued a Rochdale family from their burning home. Fireman Craggs received a Humane Society medal but Carlo the retriever won the loudest cheers of the day.

Wallace, Chance's Glasgow counterpart, was credited with psychic powers in his ability to race far ahead of an appliance to get to a fire. He nipped round cor-ners and made unexpected turns to the astonishment of onlookers, unaware that the canny dog paused at any intersection to glance back and check the direction the coachman was pointing his whip. Like Chance and Billy he finished up stuffed, and displayed in a glass case alongside a pair of rubber boots once pro-vided for his sensitive paws by a sympathetic lady.

During the Blitz an abandoned mongrel found a friendly home in a Fulham fire station, and like all fire dogs put himself on the strength. Red survived to see peace and earned the honour of a fire engine to take him to his final billet.

Though working fire horses are now no more than a nostalgic memory, fire dogs are coming back into their own now as official members of the force. Sophisticated electronic equipment is far less effective in detecting and isolating chemicals used as fire accelerators by arsonists than a dog's nose.

Star, a one year old labrador, went on active service in December 1996, following in the paw marks of his father and mother who are explosive experts, and a drug-hunting sister. Graham Meldrum, West Midlands Chief Fire Officer, hopes Star will be the first of many fire dogs in UK. He cites as an example the Americans, who have over 400 in action. The forensic evidence attributable to their dogs stands up, if not literally, in court.

In March 1997 Phoenix signed on with Northumberland Fire and Rescue Service, complete with heavy-duty boots to protect his paws from being burned or cut by broken glass. The yellow labrador is specifically trained to sniff out suspicious chemicals and liquids used to start fires deliberately. Once alerted by an alien smell he comes to attention and barks for attention. David Myers, his ex-army dog handler, is full of praise for his lively pupil, finding him quick to learn and eager to please. Phoenix is never let loose in a burning building but sent in after the fire is under control and kept in contact with the handler through a long leash attached to his chest harness. Dubious finds are sent for analysis to specialist laboratories and if declared positive, the evidence is forwarded to the police.

Nelson, who lives with his firefighter handler, Richard Gibbons, has made the leap from abandoned puppy rescued by the RSPCA to team member of the Cornish brigade. He is a cross between German shepherd and collie and like Phoenix and Star is trained to sniff out hydrocarbons used as accelerants. One drop of petrol or paraffin detected can be enough to change an 'accidental' fire into a case of arson.

Insurance companies appreciate the value of firedogs, and several brigades are seeking sponsorship of around £15,000 to train their own canine recruits.

Anyone looking for an appropriate name for a fire dog need look no further than Dr Nicholas Barbon, aka Barebones!

Dogs have minds of their own, and not all are receptive to orders or sympathy. During the Blitz, and at great personal risk, a fireman rescued a dog from high in a partially demolished house. Immediately it was set down on the ground, the dog scrambled back up the ladder and retreated to its familiar lair.

CHAPTER 17

FIRE KNOWS NO FRONTIERS

Pay all our policy holders in full, irrespective of the terms of their policies'.

Fire was romantic, as was the gallant firemen, the hero of many a heartrending melodrama on both sides of the Atlantic. Young ladies recited poems, sang sentimental ballads and played rousing pieces on the pianoforte, such as the *Midnight Fire Alarm* and the *Fireman's Galop*.

As in London so in New York, Paris and Berlin, a good fire drew the crowds. Press pictures of blazes anywhere show spectators enjoying the drama, ignoring the peril of the victims and frustrating the firemen's efforts. The risk of being injured, even killed, merely added a whiff of danger to the participants' pleasure. Americans were not idle, but well-informed, gazers, following the fortunes of particular crews with the passion of football fans. The basic fireman's uniform was a thick, double-breasted red shirt, black trousers and metal helmet but badges and crests made rival crews instantly recognisable to their supporters. When brawls between firefighters broke out there was never a lack of partisan onlookers to join in for the hell of it.

Though early appliances had been imported from England, Holland and Germany, but the Americans soon manufactured their own and earned a share of the expanding export market. 19th Century mergers and amalgamations obliterated some old-established names and created new ones that became even more famous: Lote of New York, Hunneman of Boston, Emphraim Thayer of Boston, Amoskeag of New Hampshire, Lee and Larnard of New York, Macks of Brooklyn, Maxim, Merrick and Seagrave of Columbus. The Waterous Engine Works were in Minnesota and American LaFrance based in the 'Fire Engine capital of the World', Elmira, New York state.

Big money was at stake, and manufacturer pitted their machines against their rivals with all the commercial fervour of Formula One racing car teams. Engine trials involved lighting the fire box, raising steam from cold which took an average of 15 minutes and then pumping water for a set time of 20 minutes. Accidents and breakdowns were frequent, disputes breaking out between crews whose engine had managed one gigantic spurt before expiring and a rival that kept going but at feeble range. Judging how high rather than how far appliances could throw a jet of water was simpler, and not open to argument. A tall mast was erected with a series of metal cups at regular intervals attached to a running halyard which was lowered and the contents checked after each contestant had used up their allotted performance time.

All manufacturers were criticised by *Mechanic's Magazine* for their machinesí lack of technical or mathematical excellence. Organisers of events were not spared either, Paris being *if possible, worse managed than those of the English of 1851...distances to which water was projected were only ascertained by stepping!* Napoleonic metres or imperial yards?

International contests for manual engines were held at the Great Exhibition in 1851 and in Paris (1855). The 1859 Philadelphia Trials were fought out between eight American steamers: the *Good Intent, Weccacoe, Baltimore, Independence, Washington, Mechanic, Hibernia* and *Southwark*. The winner for height, distance and water pressure was *Hibernia*, and for steam pressure, *Southwark*. At Hyde Park 1862 in the cause of English fair play against dodgy foreigners all appliances were operated by men of the Grenadier Guards. Competing with Merryweather and Shand Mason were Perry of Canada, Lemoine of Canada, Metz of Heidleberg, and three French companies, Letestu, Flaud and Delpech.

The Crystal Palace Trials of 1863, were advertised as open to all the world, a challenge taken up by seven English and three American engines, the *Victoria* and *Alexandra* from Amoskeag and the *Manhattan* from Lee and Lanard. The event was organised by the London Fire Engine Establishment and so Charles Young, expert on everything pertaining to fire fighting, took a dim view of the committee whose most notable feature was the *entire absence of any person, Englishman or foreigner, at all acquainted with the working or manufacture of fire engines*. This was fair comment since the committee consisted entirely of insurance men, keen to discover the most effective appliance and prepared to offer premiums to the winning manufacturers. No engine, however, was without problems—fire bars fell out, pipes leaked, nuts worked loose, cylinders cracked, fly wheels came off and piston rods strained beyond endurance. The hybrid *Sabrina*, an American design but British made, overturned and was completely disabled *through the mismanagement of the LFEE*. There were no irreproachable Grenadier Guards on this occasion.

The overseas contenders suffered the worst accidents on the day and were slated by partisan, ill-informed press criticism. This offended the Americans, as well as all decent Englishmen and lovers of fair play. Eventually, and with several qualifications, Merryweather's *Sutherland* was pronounced the winner, with *Shand Mason* second. In Holland the following year, the latter reversed the placings with a gold medal

Charles Young reckoned that a volunteer fire brigade had become a *popular and national institution in America, to a far greater extent than in any other country in the world. It may almost be said, than in all of them put together.* Writing in 1866, having evaluated fire services from Australia and China to Holstein, Prussia and Saxony, this was no inspired guess.

Berlin had a Braithwaite steam fire engine dating from 1832, and most Belgian communities relied on the stout citizens of the Town Guard. Holland came in for high praise, with both Amsterdam and Rotterdam having efficient brigades and imported English steamers. In one German principality the gymnastic companies doubled as firemen with the object of saving life and property from the ravages of fire, while in Hanover all citizens could be called out in an emergency with the exception of priests, doctors and royal servants. The Stuttgart fire engine was an American model that had been runner-up in the 1863 Crystal Palace Trials. The most respectable Swiss citizens vied with each other in eagerness and zeal to gain places in the restricted fire brigades of their communities. Efficient as clockwork, two or three men would hold matching keys so one was always available to operate the turncock and activate the water supply, an idea that had never occurred to London's parish worthies.

Quoting a witness, Dr Rennie reported that firemen in northern China were summoned by drums and gongs to fight a fierce blaze in Tientsin, and their efforts were aided by Russian and French sailors whose ships were frozen in for the winter. When night fell the wavering lanterns and banners reminded Dr Rennie, if not the sailors, of *a gigantic teetotal procession back home.*

St Petersburg had only two steamers, one American and one English, and the firefighters in heavy jackboots and metal helmets resembled dismounted Lifeguards. But, being subject to a despotic government, most of them were military defaulters and *altogether the whole affair is calculated to provoke a smile for its pretentious inefficiency.*

Turkey was accorded similar scorn. The year previously Constantinople had suffered its latest, dreadful fire and Young endorsed the *Times* correspondent's view that the authoritiesí reaction was worthy of reproach. The appliances were a *miserable mockery, far inferior to the paltriest parish engines at home...served by a swarm of half naked semi savages whose entire turnout constitutes one of the local sights that strangers stare at in amazement.*

Coming in for glowing praise were the *Sapeurs Pompiers* of Paris, now numbering 1250 men, servicing 180 appliances from 130 stations. They were under the supreme command of the prefect of police and, since all recruits came from infantry regiments, they remained soldiers under military discipline.

Young also reported on a huge parade of 20,000 volunteer firefighters in Philadelphia, staged less than six months after the end of the American Civil War. With seven bands interspersing 57 steamers, 11 hand engines, 102 hose carriages, 12 hook and ladder carriages and 21 ambulances, it took over three hours for the procession to pass the saluting base. The very first fire engine imported from England in the 17th Century was a star of the show.

The city had historic links with Benjamin Franklin who had founded a force shortly after his return from England. There is a fine portrait of him in the towering helmet of the Union Fire Company of Philadelphia, decorated with a manual fire engine, almost certainly one of Newsham's imported from London. Franklin's interest in fire had led to scientific studies differentiating between positive and negative electricity and its relationship with lightning. From his discoveries stemmed many innovations, including the widespread installation of lightning conductors on tall buildings.

A company for the Mutual Insurance of Houses, pre-dating Franklin, was burned out when most of Charleston was destroyed by fire in 1740. His 1752 Hand in Hand Company of Philadelphia was surely a case of 'passing off' as the original company in London, meriting a writ in a more litigious age, unless they had filched his lightning conductors without licence in return.

When committed as military strategy arson is classified as scorched earth policy, and the retreating Americans set fire to New York rather than have the British capture it during the War of Independence. George Washington, Father of the Nation, was personally interested in fire fighting and prevention, but encouraged his troops in this fire-raising in 1776. Flaming brands were thrown into buildings throughout the city, fire engines sabotaged and, since the bells had been melted down and re-cast into cannon, no tocsin warning could be rung from church steeples. In 1814 the British took their revenge, burning Washington to the ground before their final, ignominious withdrawal.

Thanks to Napoleon and Tchaikovsky, the burning of Moscow in 1812 is as famous as that of London in 1666. The wooden city was fired by the retreating Russians, leaving the enemy only a tenth of its houses and palaces habitable. Napoleon glowed in the reflection of *billows of fire, a sky and clouds of aflame, mountains of red, rolling flame, like immense waves of the sea, alternately bursting forth and elevating themselves to the skies of he flame above. Oh, it was the most grand, the most sublime, the most terrific sight the world ever beheld.*

Muscovites viewed the disaster rather differently. *The fires went on for six whole days and nights so that it was impossible to tell night from day. . . everything was crackling and falling in and the wind was howling so...All the time pillaging continued...[soldiers] stripped the sacred ikons of their frames, bayoneted them and poured filth on them.* When 'General Winter' forced the French to abandon the charred ruins, vengeful Cossacks harried the remnants of the Grande Armée on the terrible march home.

Long before European settlers penetrated the American West, fires caused by lightning swept across the plains, but logging and locomotives were often to blame later. Prairie fires could cause terrible loss of life, but financial damage was never on the scale of urban outbreaks. On 8 October 1871, the worst killer fire in American history raged through the Lake Michigan area of Wisconsin, claiming nearly 1200 lives and burning a million acres. The wooded land around Pestigo spread out like a hand into the waters of Green Bay, and hundreds of people fled down these deadly fingers only to be trapped between the flames and the lake.

On the same October day Chicago, which had a dreadful fire record unrivalled by any other place in the United States, was destroyed. Surrounded by stock yards and meat-handling factories it was a central railroad junction, the main grain market of the Union and a magnet for immigrants. Its city centre was still mainly of timber with wooden sidewalks. Legend has it that a cow, Daisy, kicked a milking bucket that overturned a lantern that started the fire. No matter the source, within minutes whole streets were ablaze, fanned by a strong wind that raised the temperature high enough to buckle metal tramlines. Looters were out in force raiding shops and liquor stores and grabbing horses out of the shafts of fire engines to drag away their own wagons laden with ill-gotten gains. In their greed, and drunkenness, they took lethal risks and many were among the estimated 300 people killed, some of them shot by police.

The fire burned out of control for thirty hours with temperatures in the central firestorm estimated at 1800° C. A third of the city, some 17,000 houses and numerous offices, stores and factories were destroyed including the Custom House, Post Office, Chicago Rock Island & Pacific Railroad depot and the *Chicago Times*. Losses reached $200m.

1835 saw the Merchant's Exchange fire in New York that also consumed 500 additional buildings and in 1851 there was a huge fire in San Francisco which left only a quarter of the city undamaged. A Washington factory making fireworks for a Fourth of July display caught fire in 1864, causing an explosion in a cartridge laboratory alongside. Seventeen women were trapped and killed and many others injured, one of the earliest fires wherein the major loss of life was among young, female employees. Another firework factory detonation blasted most of Portland, Maine in 1866. Even Tombstone, Arizona, was not fireproof.

The obvious dangers of tall, narrow buildings packed with workers in New York's garment district were well known but, like the Fire Island horrors of London, they were usually criminally ignored by owners. Ironically the Triangle Shirtwaist factory fire in 1911 happened in a building deemed neither unsafe nor unlawful.

Though the top three storeys of the Asch Building in Washington Place, New York, were run as a sweatshop, there were fire hoses, buckets and an alarm system; it also had an iron escape ladder, even if it did stop well short of the ground. Few of these precautions were of much use when a small fire on the 8th floor grew to killer proportions within minutes as the flames fed on flimsy materials, paper patterns, wooden work tables and piles of tissue paper. Most girls on that floor escaped, but the fire engulfed the stairways above and licked upwards from window to window, cutting off all escape routes. Operators kept the elevators running for a while, saving many lives but, instead of discharging victims on the unthreatened fifth and sixth floors, wasted valuable time travelling to ground level and back up every trip. Those trapped on window ledges jumped to their deaths, burning like torches. Others plummeted straight through sheets and blanket stretched out to catch them. It was all over in quarter of an hour.

When firemen were able to enter the cooling ruins, they found bodies trapped between worktables, crushed behind locked doors, charred on stairways and several down the lift shafts having lost their frantic grip on oily cables. Out of the 635 working on an overtime rush order that Saturday afternoon, 147 were killed, most of them young women.

As elsewhere it took a tragedy to prompt official action. Tighter labour laws relating to safety at work were rushed through, prosecution of rogue employers made easier and a new bureau of Fire Prevention incorporated into the New York Fire Department.

Globally there was hardly a major fire that was not wholly or partially covered in London, often by re-insurance through overseas companies. International fire cover from reputable London insurers required steep premiums since the risk was high, and growing higher. More business was done by London companies with such countries as United States and the old dominions of Canada, South Africa, New Zealand and Australia, the latter prone to alarming bush fires that encroached on city limits, than with Europe. Among reasons for this reluctance to expand across the Channel were government regulations, commercial antagonism, national pride, political volatility, Balkan instability and *backward, social and economic conditions and the jealousy of native Offices*. Nonetheless, most companies had offices in European capitals, and in the Middle East, Far East and South America.

The high cost of adequate fire cover was a fatal reason why so many businesses were under-insured, or took out policies with what later proved worthless companies.

By this time not all firemarks were of metal, nor always fixed to urban buildings. In Australia, where arson and fraudulent claims proliferated in periods of slump, notices of linen were fixed to farm buildings, woolsheds and haystacks to warn off felons, and encourage informers. One reads: *Insured in the Norwich Union Fire Insurance Society, by whom £100 Reward will be Paid for Conviction of the Incendiary, if wilfully burnt.* These insurance notices were being attached to baled wool and fleeces for export right up to the Great War. Being perishable, and flammable, they are extremely rare and valuable collectorsí items.

The risks and losses entailed in overseas insurance escalated in the incandescent late 19th Century with one particularly horrific disaster in Paris in May 1887. By law all theatres were supposed to have a permanent fire guard, augmented by city firemen during every performance, though this had not prevented serious playhouse outbreaks. These legal requirements did not apply to public events in

Notable firemen

Spy cartoon of Massey Shaw

Captain Eyre Massey Shaw

Professional fireman.
Chief London Fire officer Brian Robinson

Edward VII keen amateur fireman

Whitbreads Company Fire Brigade

Wotton House. Once the home of Great Fire diarist John Evelyn.
Served as the fire service college 1947–86.

Fighting the Flames. American Scaling ladder

'Just Off' - Dulwich Fire Station

Practice rescue from 'blazing house'
Fire were a popular subject for post cards These are Edwardian examples

1924 Dennis Fire Engine. Note how little equipment was carried compared with a modern fire engine.

Recruits to the war time Auxiliary Fire Service

Helmet and gas mask issued to the war-time fire service

London Taxi 'doing its bit' as a blitz fire appliance

Fire dog Baron answers a call with the
Whitefriars LFB steamer

Fire dog Phoenix booted for action with his
handler.

LFEE's Fire dog Chance, by right the property of a weaver.

Shop Fire West Ealing London 1907

**GIs from US 805 Signal Service Company
clearing rubble from Selfridges after V2
rocket attack 1944**

London Multiple Occupancy Fire 1997 (Maida Vale) 1997

Arms of the Chartered Insurance Institute. With Salamander.

Modern Fire Engine 'Open day' at Westerham.

Blitz Memorial - LFCDA - HQ

**Memorial to George Ashford,
Highgate Cemetery**

Memorial Plaques 'Self Sacrifice' Postmans Park St. Martins le Grand

uncontrolled surroundings; all Europe was shocked at the mounting death toll of the fatally injured after fire broke out at a charity bazaar. The event was held in a temporary wooden structure, crammed with stalls and booths festooned with flags and bunting, and packed with eager Society patrons and guests. When celluloid film caught light during a cinematograph showing, the flames spread within seconds. There was a stampede for the few available exits but many could not escape, the *majority present [being] ladies whose clothes caught fire immediately when length of canvas velum and burning tar fell on them*. Hundreds of Parisians were badly injured, and among the 120 dead were many aristocrats headed by the sister of the illfated Empress Elizabeth of Austria.

Such a catastrophe, concluded one journalists's report, could not have happened in Britain since *Englishwomen are far more fearless in facing danger than their sisters of other nations owing to their constant association with the various forms of sport practised in this country...a panic of such dimensions would be impossible*. To his credit, the editor of the journal in which this appeared disagreed, noting that panic was inevitable in the face of such horror.

Chicago regained its unenviable reputation after this French challenge in December 1903. The *absolutely fireproof* Iroquois Theatre caught fire during a performance, the safety curtain failing to stop the swift spread of the flames. Many in the audience found the inward facing exit doors inoperable due to the crush of frantic people. The death toll constituted the worst theatrical fire in American history, with many of the 600 dead suffocated, crushed, trampled or killed when jumping from windows onto the cobbles far below. As in so many city fires, extending ladders were unable to be used effectively due to the narrowness of alleys round the back of buildings. In 1958, in spite of all the advances in fire fighting, most of the 95 victims of a school fire in Chicago died from smoke inhalation, all but three of them children.

The great early morning San Francisco earthquake was over in 48 seconds on 18 April 1906. Buildings of brick and wood collapsed into rubble or disappeared into spreading crevasses; however, it was the ensuing fire that caused most of the $300m damage, and over 700 deaths. Fractured gas mains ignited all over the shattered city which firemen were incapable of extinguishing since all the water mains were broken and it took time to draw water from San Francisco Bay. The firemen's problems were compounded by the cityís sprawling over several hills, the summits of which were barely attainable by labouring horses pulling heavy appliances. Like their London colleagues in Tooley Street, they lost their fire chief when a burning building collapsed on him.

By the time the flames were under control on Thursday night, more than 80% of the central area, 90% of it consisting of wooden buildings, had been destroyed and nearly 700 people killed. Many householders held fire policies but few had earthquake cover,leading to months of quibbling and prevaricating by the insurances companies involved over compensation due on any particular building. The exception was Lloyds of London whose chief cabled *pay all our policy holders in full, irrespective of the terms of their policies*. The goodwill generated in America by this one act lasted for decades, only to founder in disillusionment and law suits after the 1980s Lloyds debacle.

Between 1653-1760 there were five major fires in colonial Boston. The worst in 1711 killed a dozen people and destroyed over 100 buildings, and more would have been lost but for the fire pumps imported from England only a few years earlier. Another fire in 1872 damaged the wealthiest neighbourhood, with over 800 buildings lost or damaged.

Fire at sea presents victims with the deadly choice of burning or drowning, with disasters frequently occurring close to land, but far from rescue.

For example, an immigrant ship leaving Liverpool in 1848 caught fire while still in the Mersey and though many were saved the death toll topped 150. The tragedy of the '*Ocean Monarch*' prompted the *Times* to launch an appeal for those unfortunates whose dream of a new life in America had foundered before they were out of sight of their native land.

In the heyday of the Mississippi steamboats Ole Man River notched up an appalling toll of deaths: one account lists 2,500 deaths in the first half of the 19th Century alone. Many victims would have drowned after accidental collisions but man-made disasters were also frequent. Rival captains, urged on by avid gamblers, raced each other along the waterway, with sweating stokers shovelling coal into roaring furnaces and safety valves screwed down to raise boiler pressure far beyond safe limits. The inevitable explosions were spectacular, fiery and deadly, with the '*Moselle*' (1838) and the '*Montreal*' (1857) among the worst until 1865.

The Civil War was over in early April, the release of prisoners starting almost immediately. The steamboat '*Sultana*' embarked 2,300 passengers, over 2,000 of them Union soldiers, and, when she exploded near Memphis on 27 April, over 1700 people were blown to pieces, drowned or burned to death. It remains the worst passenger shipping disaster in American inland waters.

The '*General Slocum*', taking day trippers and a Sunday school group on a New York harbour cruise, caught fire in June 1904. Many of the 1000 bodies recovered from the sea and the wreckage were packed into temporary morgue coffins until claimed by relatives; the same coffins that would later hold the victims of the 1911 Triangle Shirtwaist factory.

When the French freighter '*SS Grandcamp*' unloading fertiliser blew up like a volcano in Texas City, near Galveston, in 1947 it killed over 580 people, including many firemen. Well aware of the obvious dangers, and with several hours warning of likely explosions, many of those who could have escaped were down on the dockside watching the billowing smoke and flames when the ship erupted. Many of the 3,500 badly injured were coated in corrosive petro-chemicals or burning oil and molasses.

In the history of the world the number of idle gazers who have perished in the pursuit of sensation must far exceed that of firefighters killed on duty.

The world's greatest showman, according to his own estimation, was also New York's worst fire insurance risk: no company wanted Phineas T Barnum, on its books. Between 1865 and 1872 his combined freak show and menagerie known as the Barnum Museum on Broadway, and its successors, drew thousands of non-paying spectators to several of New York's most melodramatic and costly fires. Confederate spies had attempted arson on the Broadway building in 1864, but crowds the following July got more excitement than they bargained for.

Although most of the caged birds and animals were set free uncharred by the firemen, a couple of prized exhibits were not so fortunate. A 30-foot python smouldering in a glass tank was despatched by an axe, not before the Bengal tiger had sprung out of a second floor window into the street. Spectators fled in panic as the *man-eater* rushed towards them, intent on devouring a victim and impervious to the flurry of shots from attendant police. It took Fireman Denham's close quarters attack with his axe to lay it low and then, in a further burst of Barnum-worthy heroism, he rushed back into the building to heave out both the Freak Albino and the Fat Lady, weighing in at 400lbs.

By September Barnum had re-opened his museum with the recaptured inmates and new additions but this too burned down in 1868, with the loss of a valuable performing bear. A third venture went the same way in 1872, at a cost of $300,000.

In late 1944 the Japanese launched their Windship Weapons, incendiaries that truly knew no frontiers. These bomb-bearing balloons were meant to drift 6,000 miles across the Pacific to ignite forest fires and create terror. Less than 300 of the 9,000 launched reached the coast between Canada and Mexico. One bedraggled object found in the woods was accidentally and fatally set off by children on a family picnic in Oregon. The site of the tragedy made it the *only place on the American continent where death resulted from enemy action during the Second World War.*

CHAPTER 18

TIME OF TRANSITION—THE GREAT WAR

Woman is apt to smoke in her boudoir where abound flimsy draperies
...more susceptible to ignition than where men usually do their smoking.

Under the autocratic rule of Captain Shaw, the Metropolitan Fire Brigade was equipped with sophisticated appliances from both Shand Mason and Merryweather. These two famous London manufacturers are to fire engines what Stephenson and Gresley are to locomotives.

Although the name changed through mergers and takeovers, Shand Mason's origins went back to 1774, and beyond that to the prototype 17ᵗʰ engines of Newsham. Their first steamer, drawn by three horses, appeared in 1858.

Merryweather's history can be traced to the fire engine works of Adam Nuttall in Long Acre. These passed to his widow and then to a Mr Hadley, under whose son Nathaniel the company became Hadley, Simpkin and Lott. In 1807 Moses Merryweather came down from Yorkshire as an apprentice to Lott, married into the family and eventually became sole owner of the firm. For reasons lost in the smoke, Henry Lott and Chief Officer Braidwood could not abide each other, to the extent that the fire engine maker quit his own factory when the chief of the LFEE called in Long Acre.

Owners of private fire brigades were addressed by James Compton Merryweather in a slim volume entitled *Fire Protection of Mansions 1884*. It was intended for the *owners and occupiers of large country seats, and for their principal servants*, with advice to guests to report smoke or the smell of fire to the butler or the housekeeper. Examples were given of the water supply, hydrants, hoses and Merryweather appliances ready for any outbreak at Blenheim Palace, Burghley House, Warwick Castle, Wilton, Hatfield and Hampton Court. In a description that must have had Bertie glowing, the Prince of Wales was asserted to be *no mean fireman himself, [and to have] taken care that nothing shall be wanting on his Norfolk estate...Sandringham*.

The same author intended *The Fire Brigade Handbook* for recruits, not established professionals, but it soon became an invaluable aid for all ranks of firefighters, as did Merryweather's specialist journal, *The Fireman*.

Charles Young published his definitive *Fires, Fire Engines and Fire Brigades* in 1866, the year of transition between the LFEE, and the Metropolitan Fire Brigade. Young was a mechanical engineer, who knew both Braidwood and Shaw, and this preface needlessly spells out that the *subject of steam fire engines, their construction, management and requirements* was his particular study. His book is a valuable contemporary account of the state of fire fighting, covering world-wide conflagrations from Nero's Rome 64AD to a Pimlico wheel works 1864. It also doubles as a practical manual on saving property and restoring breathing to persons overcome by smoke. Popular in its day, its 520 dense pages encapsulate far more information than even enthusiasts now wish to know.

In Britain rivalry was fierce to supply home markets and win export orders against manufacturers from the United States, Germany, France, Austria and Sweden as well as the Hungarians and Czechs. Daimler and Benz were as famous in Berlin as Delahaye in Paris, gaining their reputations in the early days of motoring, before branching out into fire appliances, as did the Dennis brothers.

Farm machinery first attracted the mechanical talents of John Dennis, but he left Devon to work for an ironmonger in Guildford, where he built his first bicycles. Later Speed Kings and Speed Queens sold so well that his brother Raymond joined him as a partner in his new Athletic Stores. A powered tricycle followed, with John being was prosecuted for driving this at a creditable but illegal 16mph up the hilly main street. 1901 saw the first Dennis car, at 8hp and 320 guineas a rich man's toy, and an exclusive one, with less than 500 motors on British roads at the time. At the 1903 Crystal Palace Motor Show, they took orders worth £30,000.

Dennis, but not all their rivals, quickly realised that motorised transport could mean more than private cars. One early success was a van for Harrods of Knightsbridge, followed by commercial buses, trucks and lorries. Their first fire engine went by sea to Glasgow in 1909, and next year began Dennis' long association with the London brigades. With fire engines shipped everywhere from Auckland to Zanzibar, Dennis soon boasted the A to Z of exports, and in 1913 ceased to manufacture cars at all.

In 1899 Merryweather marketed a weighty, steam-propelled *Fire King* appliance and in 1903 supplied the Tottenham brigade with the first motor fire engine. The first one seen in England was probably the Daimler-engined appliance, trailing yards of hose, which was exhibited at the 1895 Tunbridge Wells Show. Experimental machines driven by batteries or electricity proved unreliable so, until overtaken by diesel, petrol-engines reigned supreme. Dublin received a Leyland petrol fire engine in 1910, and in America the following year the Ahrens-Fox Fire Engine Co. produced petrol driven appliances for Cincinnati. Additional appliances included water tenders to augment the limited quantity carried in the engine's tank or for use where hydrants or the mains supply failed, as well as motorised scaling ladders, escape turntables and hose tenders.

Motorised appliances, like their horse-drawn predecessors, had to put safety before speed on the roads, even though lives were endangered by delay. Only since 1930 have fire appliances had the right to ignore speed limits in built-up areas, while still driving with due care and attention.

Though great camaraderie existed among all firemen, but international fire engine trials remained fiercely, if not always fairly, contested. Manufacturers, with orders at stake, took more than a sporting interest in challenges between horsedrawn and motorised engines, one spluttering, stinking, back-firing machine earning the nickname *Farting Annie*.

In 1904 brigades from Austria, Belgium, France, Holland, Italy, Scandinavia and Spain took part in the International Fire Exhibition at Earls Court. The Royal Berlin Fire Brigade, under the patronage of the Kaiser, arrived with so many bulky exhibits that they commandeered an entire hall. Among the innovative escape devices on show was a horsedrawn, telescopic turntable ladder activated by compressed air. Much applauded was the Pageant through the Centuries. This procession was headed by officers of the Roman Vigiles costumed as *aquarius, siphonarius, unicinarius et al.* Simulated rescues and fire fighting were enacted against a backcloth of blazing streets enlivened by shrieking damsels, flares, smoke and vast quantities of water. A very necessary programme note warned spectators not to be alarmed at shouts of *fire! fire!'*. (Incidentally,it remains a criminal offence to make a malicious, false cry of 'fire' in a public place).

By Act of Parliament, in 1904 the Metropolitan Fire Brigade became the London Fire Brigade (LFB), although the London County Council had controlled it since 1889. The LFB saw itself as a brigade apart, and for many years there was a distinct coldness, verging at times on feud, between it and the various county and provincial brigades, let alone volunteers. This extended to a lack of co-operation or enthusiasm for national links between the forces and great reluctance to accept outsiders into the London ranks. This isolation even led to ignoring the new Institution of Fire Engineers in Leicester, founded among others by the chief fire officers of both that city, Birmingham, Birkenhead and Edinburgh. This unhelpful attitude, mainly fuelled by the Londoners, did not finally wither away until the Second World War and nationalisation, in 1941.

Militancy was in the air at the turn of the century, caused not by the dangers or the hardship of the service but the long hours and stringent discipline which spilled over into what little there was of the men's private life. One day's leave in fourteen was granted in London with a single week's annual holiday, and firemen were not permitted to leave their stations unless on a call. There were increasing demands for the LCC to accept demands for trade union membership and, without prejudicing their fire fighting role, greater parity with the lives of the average working man. In 1902 an active, but nameless, fireman wrote that *an undercurrent of discontent pervades the whole brigade...a London fireman is practically bound hand and foot to the station where he belongs.* The tart editorial reply warned the men against agitation. Shorter hours meant lower wages; unlike many labourers they were fortunate not to rely on the cold charity of the Poor Laws to alleviate poverty in their old age.

Trade union representation for firemen did evolve. At one time it was divided between the Association of Professional Fire Brigade Officers, the National Union of Corporation Workers and the Municipal and General Workers Union.

Appliances and equipment continued to improve, but a satisfactory design of breathing apparatus (BA), was still not available, nor would it be for many years. To be of any use, BA, had to be portable, durable, efficient and not create greater hazards for the wearer than it purported to solve. The fireproof suit and breathing apparatus presented to Braidwood by the Paris fire chief had been far ahead of anything available at that time in Britain.

Primitive masks to filter out the worst of the smoke had been issued to some of the insurance company brigades. These facilitated breathing but could lead to a false sense of security, and death from inhaling toxic fumes or gas. Tackling a roaring blaze in dense smoke numbs and distorts all the senses. Fire consumes oxygen, and the closer to the heart of a fire a man approached, the less oxygen there was left to breathe. Firemen overcome deep in burning buildings were unable to escape before they suffocated because the brain, starved of oxygen, failed to function properly, distorting judgement and even inducing euphoria— all reasons why 'going it alone' is never permitted. Advances came with an elaborate apparatus attached to the fireman, forcing a regular supply of pure air into a special helmet from a pressure pipe originating outside the burning building. This contraption suffered from the same serious drawbacks as a diver's very similar equipment: it was cumbersome, the hose snagged on obstacles, it could be cut or crushed and the illusion of safety also led wearers into uncharted danger. It took much experimentation before a portable air cylinder with a double-valved face mask providing greater mobility and safety was made available.

City fires continued to claim lives and destroy property, few worse than the blaze in the General Electric's offices in Queen Victoria Street 1902. The company, which had its own brigade, permitted staff to work on the top storeys of a building accessible only by a spiral wooden staircase, and above workshops crammed with the usual flammable mix of materials, including chemicals and rubber. MFB ladders proved too short to reach the roof so, before a horrified, helpless crowd, eight girls and a youth were overcome by flames and smoke.

The inquest verdict damned all concerned, dismissing General Electric's plea that they were not in breach of the *Factories Act 1901* and *London Building Act 1894* since the premises pre-dated both. While praising the conduct of individuals, the MFB was condemned for its failure to save lives. Press and public accused Chief Officer Wells of sins ranging from hostility to innovation to falling morale among his men, and called for his resignation. Wells weathered the storm, but for once something was fairly speedily done to improve both the fireground practice and rescue equipment of the MFB.

An American craze caused bizarre nuisance to the long-suffering fire services. Drawn by clanging bells and the thunder of hooves, cyclists tried to overtake appliances in a mad race, causing both delay and accidents. This sport became so dangerous that police tried to intercept speeding cyclists or, failing that, stop them flinging machines to the ground and entangling and endangering firemen and their hoses.

An early motoring compensation case was that of a man suing the LCC in 1909 after being knocked down by a horsedrawn fire engine. Legal argument hinged on the duty of a brigade to respect public safety when responding to an alarm. The plaintiff countryman insisted he heard no warnings and that the loss of his arm and other injuries were due to the negligent and furious driving of the fire crew. Witnesses disputed the facts and the brigade was exonerated, with the judge hoping the LCC would offer the injured yokel something by way of charity.

Early motor engines were unreliable and dangerous. When they caught fire, dowsing with water could spread the flames on a river of petrol. The low flashpoint of petrol, unlike that of paraffin and lamp oil then in current use, made it very difficult to extinguish until new techniques using foam or the deadly poison gas of the trenches, phosgene, were developed. Petrol fires caused terrible injuries and many deaths, particularly in storage tank explosions. Not until 1926 was the *Victorian Act for the Safe Keeping of Petroleum* scrapped and new laws caught up with the motor age, imposing tight regulations on the storage of petrol and oil.

Equally serious, and more common, were fires and fatalities caused by cheap, household materials flooding the market, two of them causing more domestic tragedies than all the others put together. Cotton flannelette was flammable but cheap and widely used for children's clothes and nightwear. Celluloid was a chemical mix including alcohol and ether: as cellulose nitrate it formed gun-cotton, an explosive handled by military engineers only with extreme caution. In the home, however, it was widely used for trinkets, toys, men's collars and cuffs and personal ornaments. The popular bioscope halls contained numerous reels of celluloid film which frequently burst into flame when projectors overheated, as in the Paris bazaar tragedy.

The Edwardian Age was in its twilight when Lt Cdr Sampson Sladen succeeded Rear-Admiral De Courcy Hamilton as Chief Officer of the LFB in 1909. Despite the continuing modernisation of equipment and appliances, continued but horses were not yet ready to be put out to grass.

Brigade figures for 1913 show the Southwark HQ staffed by a chief officer, divisional officer and his assistant (South), 1 district and 8 station officers, 47 firemen, 17 coachmen and 3 pairs horses. There were 2 motor fire engines, 1 motor escape, 4 motor trailers, 1 hosecart and 1 horsed fire engine. In addition there were 9 horsed engines, 1 horsed escape and 1 manual engine for training and in reserve, and the main workshops and administrative offices of the brigade. In contrast Highbury had 10 firemen, 2 coachmen, 1 horsed engine, a hose cart, a horsed escape and 2 pairs horses. The even smaller station at Herne Hill had 7 firemen, a single motor escape and no fire engine.

Though the London insurance companies may have shifted responsibility for firefighting elsewhere, fire still devoured their profits. Losses were seldom less than 50-60% of premium income, and in bad years far higher.

Commercial Union (CU), had soon discovered that fire was the least profitable of their three branches of insurance, leading to no dividend being declared in 1866. Despite this, overseas expansion was mainly in fire risk cover with new agencies opening in Canada, and the United States. The latter started up within months of major fires in Chicago (1871) and Boston (1872), disasters which bankrupted many American companies, but fortunately not the newcomers.

By the 1890s fire insurance profits had improved and CU moved from Royal Exchange Avenue to Cornhill, stylish offices built by their old friends Cubitts. In 1927 these collapsed when adjacent construction work for Lloyds undermined the foundation, but, by 1929, CU was back in premises built by Holland, Hannen and Cubitts. In 1969 a 23-storey concrete and glass skyscraper in Great St Helen's became CU's head office, only to be shaken to its foundations and have its windows shattered by the IRA. The glazing was barely replaced before it was broken by a second bomb blast in 1994. For the CU risk, not charity, begins at home.

George Morant of Commercial Union was the first president of the Insurance Institute of London in 1907, which with the Federation of Insurance Institutes of Great Britain and Ireland was granted a royal charter in 1912 as the Chartered Insurance Institute. The former now has 13,000 members and the latter over 90 local and associated institutes. The Federation centenary in 1997 was marked by a memorable concert in Guildhall by the Insurance Orchestra and Lloyd's Choir.

The staircase walls of the Insurance Hall in Aldermanbury are decorated with historic firemarks from the Dawson Collection. These badges are links in the long chain that unites insurance and firefighting, a chain that is lengthened annually through the gifts of overseas visitors. There is also a small museum that is open to the public on application.

The Great War

Brigades depleted in numbers by the call of war...
and deficient in that all important matter of hose

At the height of the Napoleonic invasion scare a crusty admiral swore *I do not*

say the French cannot come, all I say is that they cannot come by sea.
A century later Blériot flew the Channel, demonstrating that Narrow Seas and 'wooden walls' were no longer a sure defence. Nonetheless, at the outbreak of war in August 1914 the government was confident that no armed Zeppelins could threaten Britain since experts had convinced them that there was no future in aerial warfare.

The Montgolfier brothers had risen above the Paris rooftops in 1783, sharing the wicker basket beneath the balloon with a cast-iron furnace fed by bales of chopped straw. It was the first lighter-than-air machine, and many successors burned up in flight or plummeted in flames. The grisly fate of Mlle Madeleine Blanchard, the first woman balloonist to perish, was illustrated in print in 1819. In 1937, seven years after the British R101 airship disaster, the zeppelin Hindenburg caught fire on landing in New Jersey, only 61 of her 97 passengers surviving the inferno. The use of volatile hydrogen was due to the American embargo on exports to Germany of safer helium. That civilian disaster killed off all commercial enterprises, but not before military airships and aeroplanes had confounded the experts by playing a minor role in the Great War.

The LFB was well below strength in late 1914, many reservists being recalled to the Royal Navy and regular firemen resigning to volunteer. Many smaller brigades also found themselves in the same position as the one *depleted by the call of war...and deficient in that all important matter of hose.*

In December 1914, German warships shelled Scarborough and on Christmas Eve an aeroplane bombed Dover. Further raids on Tyneside, Yarmouth, Colchester, Southend and Ipswich dismayed the government as much as they frightened the people who demanded answers to awkward questions. Why had they not been warned of the danger? Where were defences against such attacks? Where were the British planes? Where were the fire brigades to deal with the incendiaries dropped by the Germans?

Something would be done, the government hastily agreed, as air raids continued sporadically. But what? For a start there was propaganda, in its literal sense of propagating information. Give people the truth, if not exactly the whole truth, as did both sides, to the confusion of all concerned.

The War Office announced after one attack that nine zeppelins, unable to identify strategic targets, had bombed rural parts of Staffordshire and Lincolnshire, wantonly killing and injuring several people and damaging a picture theatre, parish room and dissenters' chapel. Berlin's account claimed that *England's industry lies in ruins. During the night there was a devastating air battle fought on a front of many miles, and it was won by German raiders.*

Sub-Lieutenant Rex Warneford, a naval airman, won the VC in 1915 after managing to fly immediately above an attacking zeppelin and dropping a bomb on it. It burst into flames and crashed near Ghent. The first one was brought down in England in September 1916, but whether anyone claimed the £1000 reward, offered by Mr Joseph Cowen, for such an exploit is unknown.

London suffered its worst aerial casualties in 1917 with 162 people killed in a raid on Liverpool St station, and 57 in another on the City. In January 1918 the last bombs hit an air raid shelter in Long Acre, long the head office of Merryweather, inflicting 41 casualties. Such civilian losses were unknown in previous wars and the final toll of Londoners killed during the Great War was 1400, with hundreds of homes and businesses destroyed by bombardment and fire.

The loss of experienced men to the Front proved so serious once the extent of aerial attacks became clear that the fire service demanded the recall of at least a proportion of their colleagues. In 1916 the government offered the unsatisfactory compromise of exempting existing firemen from conscription, only issuing the recall after the damaging raids of 1917. In the early days lack of co-ordination between fire crews and their equipment had badly hampered the efficient mobilisation of brigades from all over London. One vital improvement gradually incorporated was the universal adapter, a device that could unite with any of the twenty different hose couplings in common use.

Many country brigades were still manned by part-time volunteers and funded by inadequate subscriptions, some amounting to little under £22 per annum. Appeals to residents and commercial firms to contribute more generously were sweetened with the hint that it would lead to an *efficient and reliable fire service without coming upon the rates.*

Horses killed were in their thousands at the Front and replacements requisitioned from every available source back home. A 1916 report quotes a country brigade: *owing to the present dearth of horses it is no longer possible to horse the fire engine so the brigade will be unable to render aid in districts where there are no hydrants...but where there are hydrants of public water mains the brigade can render prompt and efficient aid by means of motor cars conveying men, hose and other fire appliances.* This was as unsatisfactory a way to fight a fire, as to fight a war. Towing the horseless engine behind a car was almost as inadequate, but did eventually lead to many brigades investing for the first time in a motorised appliance.

One sensible pre-War government measure had been a subsidy paid to owners of reliable, well-maintained lorries or trucks who would permit their later requisition in an emergency. Vehicles which passed the stiff tests were much in demand from other purchasers to the satisfaction of the manufacturers and their advertising; owners received £110 and the War Office acquired a reliable back-up transport facility. For once all sides were satisfied with Dennis, Leyland and Thorneycroft among the approved companies.

Munitions works of any kind, let alone temporary ones, were dangerous sites where serious fires and fatalities were common. One in Silvertown exploded in

January 1917 and, though the factory was almost empty in the evening, there were 69 civilian casualties. Two firemen were also killed and two children from the nearby fire station. Further explosions spread the fire, igniting 9m cubic feet of gas in an adjacent holder and blasting sparks across the river. The total loss exceeded £1m.

Another £1m fire was at Morecambe shell works, where ten more firemen lost their lives. Far worse was a series of munitions explosions in May 1916 at Faversham in Kent which killed 129 people, including several firefighters. Faversham had been noted for its powder mills for centuries, and was no stranger to fires. It was estimated, although censorship blurred the figures and loss of life, that over a thousand serious explosions occurred in British munitions works up to the end of 1916.

A consequence of these disasters led to a defeatist faction within the Ministry of Munitions recommending swift evacuation and abandonment of any blazing factory. This view was not shared by firefighters who countered with a list of valuable works saved by their efforts. What was not in dispute was the sad fact that much time, effort and bravery was too often wasted by lack of one man in overall control of a major incident as well as poor communications between brigades summoned to a fireground. These were faults that had been pointed out many times before and were only gradually being rectified.

Censorship in wartime is defensible in the cause of keeping up the morale of the civilian population and military forces abroad, and denying information or satisfaction to the enemy. For this reason details of several major disasters, including losses at sea, were suppressed.

One of the most terrible tragedies was a multiple crash involving five trains which occurred in May 1915 near the Quintinshill signal box on the Scottish border. A Southbound troop train carrying a battalion of the Royal Scots and the Northbound Scottish Express collided with a local train held on a wrong line, propelling wreckage across both tracks and two goods trains held on passing loops.

Many of the trapped and injured were incinerated when fire, caused by exploding high pressure cylinders and smashed gas lamps, raced through the splintered wooden carriages of the three passenger trains. Coal from the locomotives' tenders fuelled the blaze and, when the fire crews finally gained control twenty four hours later, 20 coaches and five goods trucks had been reduced to ash and charcoal.

Quintinshill remains Britain's worst ever railway disaster with 215 soldiers listed among the estimated 230 dead. The accident inquiry demanded swift replacement of wooden carriages with metal ones and an instant ban on gas lighting on trains. Implementation of both took several years, and more deaths, to come into effect.

As with the early locomotives, trains themselves caused fires from sparks and flying embers, and these often occurred in remote country, deep cuttings or in tunnels difficult to access. London, cross-hatched with railway lines and with half a dozen major terminuses, was acutely aware of the dangers, as were the major railway companies. Important junctions on mainline routes, Crewe and Derby, maintained fire trains that could leave for any emergency within fifteen minutes. Pulling power was no problem to a locomotive. Half a dozen red fire trucks would be coupled up, loaded with trained railway staff, pumps, ladders, hoses and axes and a 3,000 gallon water tank, a far greater capacity than any horsedrawn or motorised vehicle could transport. There were also water towers along the track.

Early fire boats were no more than wherries loaded with barrels of water towed to the scene by horses, or rowed by watermen who then operated hand squirts. Later primitive pumps were transported in this way. Effective waterborne firefighting arrived with steam, first to power pumps as at Tooley Street, and later to propel river craft. Steam driven tugs towed barges loaded with pumps, and were also able to push these shallow-drafted vessels close inshore. Fire boats, propelled by their own motors, formed the River Branch of the LFEE. Steam motors gave way to petrol, then diesel, now augmented by inshore rubber inflatables.

The greatest single loss of life of London firemen during the Great War was caused not by enemy action but a routine blaze. On a 1918 night of thick fog an outbreak in a storage building for animal feed in Battersea was not detected until it was well alight. When crews arrived, the roof had fallen in and they were hampered by smoke, fumes, blazing cattle cake and linseed oil and falling timber. Without warning the walls collapsed outwards, crushing and killing seven firemen. An enquiry failed to pinpoint the cause of the fire, although rats enticed by the linseed cake may have also chewed through electric cables and caused a short.

After hostilities ended there were several unexpected fires in the capital's food warehouses, still fully stocked. Rumour insisted these had been deliberately destroyed by enemy sympathisers, though why was never made clear.

Another mystery stemmed from a fire in a Shadwell rubber warehouse in 1920 where three firemen were killed, and two women found dead in a nearby house. An inquest showed the women had been poisoned in their sleep by carbon-monoxide gas seeping into the bedroom from the fire appliance pumps. Why had the noise, smell, heat and blazing light not wakened them in time?

On a terrifying night in August the same year, a blazing barge laden with petrol broke loose and drifted crewless at the whim of the tide. After hitting several tugs and barges the 'Dorcas' rammed a pier, setting them all ablaze, and then ran ashore alongside Woolwich Arsenal. Before the assembled fire engines could tackle her she exploded, spraying land and river with flaming petrol, smothering three appliances and setting warehouses and railway wagons alight.

In her death throes *Dorcas* provided ammunition for the LFB against the major oil companies. They were seeking permission from the Port of London Authority and LCC to build refineries and storage tanks much higher upriver. Permission was refused; as a result, when the Luftwaffe hit dozens of 2,000 gallon storage tanks at Thameshaven on 5th September 1940, the devastation was at least confined to a sparsely populated area below Tilbury.

The Armistice of November 1918 was greeted with weary relief, rather than prolonged jubilation. Huge problems faced the country with festering labour unrest, muted during the war, high on the list. Discontent came to a head in a series of confrontations and strikes, aggravated by the thousands of men returning to a *land fit for heroes* without hope of a job. Women, whose employment had been vital to the national effort were told their place was back in the home, not taking the bread out of working men's mouth—no matter that many were war widows with no male bread winner in the family.

The fire brigade, like the police, was forbidden to strike. However, as improved conditions of service had led to a better shift system, shorter hours (72 per week instead of 144), and abolition of the rule that all firemen, with the exception of senior officers, should live on station, there was no shortage of recruits, many of them ex-servicemen. Nonetheless, the service was overdue for reform and it caused outrage when the government ignored the recommendations on pay and conditions from the 1920 Middlebrook committee. Demands for a royal commission were led by Chief Officer Arthur Dyer, and this eventually began examining *Fire Brigades and Fire Prevention* in 1921. Expectations of real change were dampened by an ominous proviso in its terms that due regard should be *paid to consideration of economy.*

One of the most difficult issues was the dispute between proponents of a centralised national fire brigade and the die-hard local authorities unwilling to cede influence to any other body. In an attempt to boost brigade coffers, a side swipe was made at the insurers for not contributing to fire services which saved them money when buildings were prevented from burning down. The companies slyly agreed to consider this, but only if building insurance was made compulsory and they were given a voice in the running of local brigades. This unwelcome counter-attack effectively silenced the criticism.

When it appeared in 1923 the vast, verbose Royal Commission report boiled down to 142 recommendations, among which were: to resolve confusion of different laws affecting fire brigades by consolidation; that householders should not pay for attendance by a brigade at a fire; that local authorities should manage their own affairs and come under county control; more technical training; greater standardisation of equipment was necessary; motorised transport and conveyance of fuel to be effectively organised; pensions to firemen to be payable on retirement.

But, as always, there is more to it than simply bidding it be done. Deputations repeatedly trekked to the Home Office seeking belated implementation of various recommendations, some of which had been acted upon promptly, if not before time, like the Board of Trade's registration of the Institution of Fire Engineers. Among the aims of this professional association, first mooted in 1909, were improving standards through education and competitive examinations in a wide range of subjects including electricity and chemistry. Such qualifications would also raise the status of firemen alongside members of the older engineering institutions.

It took a further two years for a private member's bill to become the *Fire Brigades Pensions Act 1925*, granting half-pay for 25 years service rising to two thirds after thirty. This welcome news was shortly followed by the General Strike of 1926. Firemen themselves were still forbidden to strike under the Askwith Award (which had acknowledged the right to union representation for most lower grade firemen in 1918) and they had suffered a 2% pay cut imposed by the LCC, with worse to follow in the coming years of recession and soaring unemployment.

In full employment was the Fire King, terrorising the docks as if there had been no improvement in appliances and expertise since Braidwood's death. The toll of post-war destruction and loss mounted, as these examples illustrate: timber-yard 1921, £1m; tobacco warehouse 1923, £600,000; Wapping commodity warehouses 1930, £600,000; West India Dock bonded warehouse 1933, £500,000, Colonial Wharf commodities and wine 1935, £250,000.

A sideshow that drew thousands of idle gazers was the destruction of £200,000 of figures when Madame Tussaud's Waxworks went up in flames. One historic non-wax exhibit lost for ever was Napoleon's carriage with bullet-proof windows, captured after Waterloo and originally presented to the Prince Regent.

On a freezing March night in 1932 the Fire King returned to Tooley Street to ignite a multi-storey warehouse in Butler's Wharf stocked with a familiar, illegal, mix of flammable goods. Tea, coffee, sugar and rubber were well alight before the fireboats '*Alpha*' and '*Beta*' arrived but their efforts could not prevent the building being a total loss. The heat was intense, but so was the cold, with water freezing in the hoses and hanging in icicles from adjacent roofs. One fireman, caught in the spray, was frozen to a metal beam and had to be chipped loose by a colleague's axe.

> And the Fire King [still] laughed when he found he could tame
> The Fire Brigade with his funning.

CHAPTER 19

THE BLITZ—HEROES WITH GRIMY FACES

They were a grand lot and their work must never be forgotten. Churchill 1945

You almost ran out of tears. Blitz rescuer

The malicious, bloody flames of the Great Fire burned for four days. The aerial destruction unleashed in the fourth burning of London lasted for seventy six nights, between September and December 1940.

The London Fire Brigade's Chief Officer, Commander Sir Aylmer Firebrace, and his deputy, Major Frank 'Gentleman' Jackson, had long been aware how vulnerable the capital was to bombardment when, not if, war came again.

The government felt it had taken wise preventive measures in 1935 by sending an Air Raid Precaution notice confidentially to all local authorities. It then left it until 1937 before asking how such bodies would recruit, train and equip additional personnel, boosted by up to 75% of the cost paid by central grants. In 1938 an Act initiating an Auxiliary Fire Service (AFS), was passed, and by spring 1939 over 140,000 volunteers had stepped forward, many of them women. This was six months before the outbreak of war on 3 September 1939.

During these years progress had been made in co-ordinating all the autonomous fire brigades in England and Wales into one manageable whole. It was a formidable task since they numbered over 1600 and ranged from the professional brigades of Birmingham, Manchester and Cardiff to volunteer six-man parish crews. Estimates of 20,000 emergency fire pumps needed to combat massed aerial attacks contrasted with one small town brigade, producing a single Boer War rifle for the defence of the fire station.

Legislation in the form of two *Air Raid Precautions Acts* and a new *Fire Brigade Act*, coupled with endless administrative decisions, drew the threads together and implemented major innovations. Fire engines toured London, drumming up recruits with posters urging *Keep the Home Fires from Burning, Calling You—Apply at any Fire Station* and *Women! You are Needed in the National Fire Service* as full or part-time members. Fire boats carried the same messages on the Thames, with Commander Firebrace adding his own plea for women to volunteer during a BBC broadcast.

Along with several other public companies, John Lewis and Harrods invited recruiting fire officers to address their staff meetings, and were later grateful for lessons learned during these LFB lectures when the Oxford Street store and Harrods Depository took direct hits. The links between the brigade and John Lewis were close since the chairman, John Spedan Lewis, was a member of the appointments board of the fire service and Lord Woolton, then Minister of Food of pie fame, had been managing director when on the 1935 fire brigade review committee.

The government's aim was to raise 30,000 auxiliaries but, with the country still at peace, recruitment was slow and only picked up around the time of the 1938 Munich Crisis. Then, with Appeasement in the air, many recruits found themselves abused in the streets since, as was asserted, *it's people like you who cause wars*. Birmingham's Civil Defence leader, in biblical mode, urged *Ye have been entreated to join ARP and to train with them that are at the Stations of Auxiliary Fire and at the Posts of the Wardens of First Aid*. By the outbreak of war numbers nationally had reached 25,000.

Women were not trained as active firefighters but rather in the essential skills of control centre communications as well as despatch and driving vehicles and motorbikes. Their job could be a hazardous as any fireman's. Gillian Tanner, whose portrait is in the Fire Brigade Museum, drove a fuel vehicle through bombs and blazes to re-supply active appliances, insisting on deliveries being signed for, no matter how great the present danger. Though she was the only fire-woman to win the George Medal, Joan Hobson BEM was one of several others to be decorated.

The pre-war London Fire Brigade consisted of 2,500 firemen manning 57 stations in the metropolitan area. The sudden increase in personnel, new sites and unfamiliar equipment brought their own problems, as did the inevitable clashes between the experienced professionals and the hastily trained amateurs allocated to 360 new sub stations.

Along with Acts of God, outbreaks of war and civil disorder have never found favour with insurers, but they too did their bit in the emergency. The Commodities Insurance Scheme came under the *War Risks Insurance Act 1939*, and all the big companies, together with Lloyds of London, co-operated closely with government in administering its complexities.

The *Emergency Power (Defence) Bill 1939*, passed ten days before the outbreak of war, gave Parliament almost limitless authority. Notices were posted on wrecked buildings warning *Looting from premises which have been damaged by, or vacated by reason of, war operations is punishable by death or penal servitude for life*. Few quarrelled with that, *don't you know there's a war on*. It was the petty interference in all aspects of people's lives for their own good that caused chronic grumbling, and resentful incomprehension.

The most immediate impact came from the blackout, a necessary but depressing measure that continued in force well into 1945. Mass Observation found in survey after survey that the blackout topped the nation's hate list, far ahead of danger, rationing, evacuations, prices, inadequate transport or lack of entertainment. Neither did town and country differ in their loathing. As well as buildings, blackout applied to street lights and car headlamps, making accidents to pedestrians and drivers frequent. The whole undertaking became discredited during the uneventful months of the Phoney War, between September 1939 and May 1940.

The nation was urged to *Waste not, Want not, Make do and Mend* and save, collect or salvage absolutely anything from scrap metal, rags and bones to horse chestnuts and rosehips. Lists were published showing how all this helped the war effort: *1 saucepan = 1 bayonet; 2 kettles = 1 helmet; 2 flat irons = 6 hand grenades; 8lbs rubber = 1 Mae West life jacket; 1 ton assorted rags = 250 battle dress uniforms and 13 military tents.* The additional fact that a pound of boiled bones could produce several ounces of nitro-glycerine for high explosives must have resulted in stinking, lethal home experiments by small boys had not some key ingredient been wisely withheld.

I am a Firegirl was one in a poster series featuring women doing their bit for the war effort, and another called for women to train in the NFS as telephonists, despatch riders, drivers or canteen workers. A game on the lines of happy families involved collecting sets of fire brigade cards in different colours for badges, equipment and officers. Another party game based on pin the tail on the donkey was *Decorate Goering*, ridiculing the bemedalled Luftwaffe commander.

Practical leaflets were issued to all households. *Poison Gas, Remember your Gasmask, ABC of ARP, Masking your Windows for the Blackout, Air Raid First Aid* and *Home Storage for Food Supplies.* A poster of a blazing incendiary warned of aerial bombardment: *London Shall not Burn—Beat Firebomb Fritz— Britain's Fire Guard is Britain's Defence.*

A further spate of recruiting posters under the heading National Service demanded *Have you chosen your job, if not do it today. Volunteers urgently needed for ARP wardens, stretcher parties, ambulance drivers, auxiliary fire service, police war reserve ... .*

Despite shortages, paper was made available at Christmas so the public could respond to the posters encouraging them to *Do your Duty, send us a Greeting Card.* A series of cheerful cards covered most branches of the armed, national and volunteer services from soldiers, sailors and airmen to firemen, wardens and nurses. A special Civil Defence card included the police, wardens, rescuers, firemen, ambulance drivers and stretcher bearers. One shows a fireman weighed down with gear, struggling to pick up a hose above the caption *Oh, I do hope the war ends before I get all my equipment.*

There was no end in sight in 1941, and even the *end of the beginning* lay far ahead in late 1942 with the victory at El Alamein. The true beginning for Britain came in May 1940 when, backed by massive air power, German armies attacked France, Holland and Belgium, having already overrun Norway and Denmark. Churchill became Prime Minister and the long battle fought with *blood, sweat, toil and tears* became grim reality.

By June the remnants of the British Expeditionary Force had been driven back to the Belgian coast and rescue vessels were massing at the Channel ports. To safeguard these the Admiralty ordered the LFB's fireboat 'Massey Shaw' to proceed to Ramsgate, but next day she joined the motley armada of craft bound for the Dunkirk beaches, her crew armed with .303 rifles. She was not built for seagoing, but with a shallow draft could get close enough for men to scramble up climbing ropes and be ferried out to larger ships offshore. Under aerial and artillery bombardment she made three return trips from England during Operation Dynamo, taking on board over 700 of the 335,000 men rescued by the Little Ships from death or imprisonment. Every river station crew cheered her up the Thames on her voyage back to Blackfriars, her mission completed. Years later a bloodstained flag was returned to the fireboat by the family of a rescued soldier who had used it to staunch his wounds. This, with a model of 'Massey Shaw', is in the Museum.

The London Blitz is even more extensively recorded than the Great Fire, so this chapter presents only a selection of incidents from among thousands.

The aerial Battle of Britain began on 10 July 1940 although the AFS really had their baptism of fire on 24th August. That night German bombers attacked a fuel depot on the Essex shore and the West India Docks before dropping explosives on the City. A minor raid compared to what lay ahead, the devastation was far beyond anything experienced in training, compounded by the fractured water supplies, blazing gas mains and blocked roads. So many appliances were destroyed or temporarily put out of action that London taxis were commandeered as auxiliary fire vehicles to pull pumps, and continued to do so throughout the war.

The *Blitzkrieg*, or lightning war, hit London on 7 September and continued almost without a night's break until the New Year. Grumbling, complacency and sneers at the under-employed emergency fire services vanished overnight, and the only bonus of the night attacks was that crews could see their way through the blazing streets.

Adequate supplies of water were essential but, with hundreds of fires burning simultaneously, the demand was insatiable. Firemen's hoses melted or were crushed by falling masonry as high explosives cratered the streets and fractured even deep-laid water mains. Steel dams holding 5,000 gallons were hastily erected in some areas, capable of keeping just one pump operating for ten minutes. Larger emergency reservoirs were created from bomb site basements by raising and sealing the walls, and then fencing them for safety in the blackout. On winter nights firemen needed axes to break the ice while buildings flamed all around them.

Often appliances could not get through to fires or were hit themselves *in the thick of a raid with mines, bombs, incendiaries falling as if all hell had been let loose.* On many nights the blackout was a mockery, since nothing could alter the phases of the moon or the rhythm of the tides. The Luftwaffe calculated the nights when a full 'bombers' moon' lit up the estuary and guided formations to their targets up the silver ribbon of the Thames at its lowest ebb. LFB Orders not to use the telephone to call up appliances for fear of enemy eavesdropping were ignored. Huge fires far more easily and treacherously signalled to follow-up German raiders the presence of vulnerable fire crews.

The bombardment included high explosive bombs, incendiaries, and parachute mines that exploded just above ground. Only the superhuman efforts of the NFS and the other Civil Defence services, police, ambulance crews, volunteer fire watchers and the capital's citizens saved London from total destruction. Teams of firewatchers turned up after a day's work to patrol buildings and churches and took to exposed rooftops when the sirens wailed. Explosives falling close were smothered with sand or dampened by hand pumps, or calls made to brigades pinpointing fires too fierce or out of reach. Incendiaries falling through the roofs of empty, locked buildings caused fires impossible to quench, if fire crews could not quickly gain access.

Mr John Lewis had opened a small shop in Oxford St in 1864 which, by the 1930s, was rivalled in size and turnover only by Selfridges further along London's busiest shopping street. On 18th September an incendiary bomb fell on this West House, fire spread rapidly and by morning much of the store and the site of the original shop were gaunt ruins, three firemen having been killed by a secondary explosion. D H Evans and Bourne and Hollingsworth, also in Oxford St, were also badly damaged that night though *the basements of these great buildings afforded adequate shelter to many.*

Being always at the scene of greatest danger, fire personnel losses mounted. In the first week of the Blitz 22 firefighters were killed and, on 17 September, seven AFS personnel were killed by a direct hit near Oxford Street. In October 1940, high explosives destroyed the fire sub station in Plaistow, killing ten officers, but the worst single loss was in April 1941, when Bow fire station took a direct hit, killing 36 firefighters and staff, 21 one of them on standby duty from the Beckenham brigade. Physical and mental exhaustion took their toll as the raids went on, from weeks into months.

Mass Observation continued surveying and publishing, keeping to itself that 1% of the population believed the war would go on for ever. In the same defeatist spirit, the government initially tried to stop people sleeping in tube stations instead of rendering them orderly, warm and sanitary. Officials believed that being safe underground *would breed a shelter mentality and they wouldn't come up again in the morning and go to work.* Tube stations did proveto be the salvation of thousands, except for those luckless shelterers killed when bombs exploded down lift shafts, as at Bank station, or drowned after water mains or sewers shattered. West End stores opened their basements to householders, Dickins & Jones in Regent St being a favourite.

The National Government, admittedly beset on all sides by graver decisions, initially disallowed an appeal by the AFS for a second uniform on the grounds of cost. Weary firemen returning to their stations would strip off their sodden uniforms, drape them in front of fires and radiators and shiver in their underpants waiting for them to dry, often struggling back into the damp, steaming garments when another call came through.

The *Fire Services (Emergency Provisions) Act 1941* was passed in May . The following August the *National Fire Service* came into being under the wing of the Home Office, with England and Wales divided into 33 areas, Scotland into six. At its peak the NFS numbered 100,000. Commander Firebace was appointed to the combined roles of Chief of the Fire Staff and Inspector-in-Chief of Fire Services. London was divided into five areas under Major Jackson, and Mrs Betty Cuthbert, a pre-war AFS recruit, became Chief Woman Fire Officer at the Home Office. Provision for a fire service college, for the training of personnel and the standardisation of equipment, had been included in the 1938 Act, but postponed until late 1941. This finally opened in a requisitioned seaside hotel in Sussex.

A star based on the Maltese cross with the shield of the London County Council in the centre was adopted as the insignia of both the NFS and AFS. The eight points, or tenets, stood for the chivalrous virtues of gallantry, observation, tact, perseverance, sympathy, explicitness, dexterity and loyalty. It remains the badge of today's firefighting brigades.

Much of the credit for the smooth integration of fire services was due to the *National Fire Service Drill Book* which for the first time laid down universal procedures for all contingencies, including repairs and maintenance. This was followed several years later by the *Manual of Firemanship*, the fireman's bible, and in seven volumes was almost as long. Incompatible hoses and couplings imported from America gave rise to crude jokes over the rival merits of a good screw or flexible male and female connections, until adaptors and hose spanners put an end to this particular problem, if not the jokes.

The immense re-organisation and reduction of senior positions was not achieved without friction and dissent, particularly in the selection of chief regional fire officers and fire force commanders. Resistance to change and local grievances often swamped the national interest when popular officers were outranked by newcomers, or precious, new appliances transferred to 'undeserving' higher risk sections of the capital. Increased centralisation also led to over-administration, and at a time of shortage tons of paper directives, orders and memoranda were despatched in all directions.

Selfridges restaurant was hit by an incendiary in 1941, and the damage would have been worse but for the efforts of its firefighting team. In December 1944 the store was hit again, this time by a V2 rocket, and lost most of its hundreds of windows. General Eisenhower's HQ was on the opposite side of Oxford St; little did the Germans, or indeed almost anyone else, know that vital communications between Whitehall's Cabinet War Rooms and Washington passed through the sophisticated scrambler installed deep within Selfridges.

In November, a parachute mine exploded near the junction of Oxford St and Tottenham Court Rd, demolishing the Dominion Theatre and Lyons Corner House at a time when patrons were emerging from both, as well as many pubs and clubs. A fireman in the Soho Brigade had never seen so many dead bodies in his life, recalling with horror a roofless car with both occupants decapitated.

No target was larger or more conspicuous than St Paul's and while it miraculously remained unharmed, raid after raid, Londoners linked their own chances of survival with that of their cathedral. On 30th December, the night *Hitler meant to start the second Great Fire of London as the prelude to invasion* the whole City was ablaze—the Royal Exchange for the third time in its history, Guildhall, livery halls, Wren churches and thousands of houses, shops and office. The cathedral was surely doomed.

The photograph on every front page next morning was the most famous image of the Blitz. For those who had seen the reality, it crystallised their memories of the *night when London was burning and the dome seemed to ride the sea of fire like a great ship lifting above the smoke and flame.* Another witness could hardly believe Wren's masterpiece still stood *in a desolation comparable to Ypres.*

It was largely thanks to the nightly vigilance and bravery of firewatchers roaming the roof that prevented fallen bombs and incendiaries from doing grave damage. Though the north portico was damaged, and the Victorian high altar destroyed on separate occasions, one delayed-action bomb failed to explode. When removed by a UXB disposal team, it blew a 100ft wide crater in Hackney Marshes.

By New Year's Day 1941 nearly 14,000 people had been killed in the Blitz.

The fashionable Café de Paris in Leicester Square was considered the *safest place to dance in town.* On 8th March a stick of bombs fell on the Rialto Cinema and penetrated the basement night-club. On a bad night for the West End it took over an hour for ambulances to get through the flaming street. Among the 34 dead in the Café was the band leader, and the incident made banner headlines. Few then, or now, remember the 17 people killed on the same night in a Soho restaurant, or the 48 killed in a nearby tenement block a few weeks later.

Throughout the Blitz it was the East End, the docks and the City that bore the brunt of the nightly attacks, the few heavy raids on the West End were accorded news coverage quite out of proportion to the suffering endured elsewhere. Though visits by the King and Queen to these poorer, devastated neighbourhoods after a raid were appreciated, the press bias against reporting their plight caused lasting resentment. When bombs fell on Buckingham Palace, it was treated as a welcome *we are all in this together* propaganda coup by government, though unintended by Hitler.

Each night brought its own horrors and heroism. On 19 March 1941 over 1800 fires were started in a 500 bomber raid which killed 750 people. Even worse was 16 April when hundreds of fires blazed and over a thousand died.

During brief respites in London, firemen went to the aid of other stricken cities: Coventry, Birmingham, Portsmouth, and as far as Liverpool. Commander Firebrace was inspecting the Liverpool fire services on the worst night of the May bombing, an occasion when yet again the incompatibility of hose couplings between brigades hampered fire fighting. By the end of the week's onslaught, the Mersey docks were in ruins and 76,000 Liverpudlians homeless. The death toll caused by bombs, blast, fires and explosions was put at 1700, increased later to a more probable 4,000. Other cities badly hit, and with fire services rendered almost helpless, ranged from Belfast, Glasgow and Hull to Bristol, Southampton and Plymouth.

The cheerful stoicism of Londoners under fire has been exaggerated, but the fatalistic belief that *if your number's on it, your time's up* helped people endure the unendurable as did a leavening of humour from a cockney who had just moved house, so *Hitler didn't know his new number.* When it was all over, those who lived through the Blitz mourned those who had died, and were grateful but numbed by their own survival. Most acknowledged that on two nights it had seemed certain that neither London nor its people would see the dawn. The first was 30/31 December 1940, and the second 10/11 May 1941.

Though no-one knew it at the time, the May raid was to be the last of the Blitz; however, the impending attack was not unexpected thanks to the code-breakers working on 'Enigma'. All fire service leave was cancelled, over 2,5000 appliances were at the ready and fire watchers scanned the skies from every rooftop. From 10,000' formations of bombers followed the Thames westward, hitting their targets—the docks, the railway stations and the bridges, and making a blazing pyre of the British Museum. Scarred buildings that had survived the past six months were destroyed, the fires ran into hundreds and by daylight nearly 1500 civilians were dead.

A London alderman, Leonard Styles, condemned the Luftwaffe's *deliberate attempt to create terror by fire* when over 2,000 were burning out of control by midnight. Nine fires were classified as conflagrations, 20 as major, 37 as serious and 210 medium. Firefighters came close to despair. Surrounded by five acres of flaming buildings around Elephant and Castle, the hoses severed by falling buildings and with paint blistering off the engines, one felt *for the first time in thirty two years a fire was beating me and there was nothing I could do about it.* Another, contradicting Lord Mayor Bludworth's comment on the Great Fire, reckoned his efforts were as futile as peeing on a bonfire.

As in 1834, the House of Commons blazed and flames encroached on both the Abbey and Westminster Hall. Firemen had no key to unlock the ancient Hall to drag their hoses inside. While they hesitated, a veteran MP seized a fireman's axe and attacked the solid oak doorwith the magnificent war cry, *as a Privy Councillor I have the authority to do it myself.* It took fifty pumps and half the night to get the fire under control, not helped by struggling thigh deep in water while being bombarded by falling of debris and loosened chunks off Big Ben. Meanwhile, downstream at Beckton the largest gasworks in the world blew up in deafening fireball, seen and heard miles out to sea.

As at the height of the Great Fire the wind played tricks with memory, and so it was in the Blitz. Some recalled it as brisk and warm, others as hot and swirling and later as a sinister tempest; records actually showed that the light breeze of the evening had died away by midnight. Again the truth was that while individual fire storms formed their own searing vacuums, a few streets away all was calm. The chief of RAF Bomber Command had watched the great fire raid of 30 December 1940 from the Air Ministry roof and was to see that Churchill's prophetic words that the Nazis *had sewn the wind, let them reap the whirlwind* were fulfilled in 1945 over the cities of the Reich.

One telling historical statistic emerged from the ruins: 700 acres of London were destroyed, one and a half times that of 1666, although not all in one compact area.

By 1943 the NFB was working well as a co-ordinated force, honed by experience, with Chief Officer Frederick Delve taking over as Chief Regional Officer for the whole London area. Naturally the public grumbled that it had taken too long and had only come to peak efficiency after the Blitz was over. Surely the chances of further bomber raids were now highly unlikely. Massed ranks of Junkers were not seen over London after May 1941, although sporadic raids occurred in 1944 on provincial cities. Of these Baedeker raids, the worst set the heart of Exeter ablaze.

Operation Overlord, the Normandy Landings of June 1944, was the best kept secret in history. During the long months of build-up, Operation Colour Scheme was prepared along with other secret projects such as the Mulberry floating harbours and Pluto fuel pipe line. The job of the firefighters in Colour Scheme was to combat any fires caused by enemy action or allied accident in the vast stockpiles of oil, petrol and ammunition stored in south coast ports waiting to be transported across the Channel.

Volunteers had been selected from the NFS to accompany the invasion force, crewing ten fireboats and forming four columns of an 'overseas contingent', and offered the legal inducement of being treated as POWs if captured. Though they were specially trained and kitted out with unique shoulder flashes and para-chutist-style blue berets, at the last minute the top brass recruited instead an Army Fire Service from the Pioneer Corps to sail to France. Only one of the four disappointed NFS columns saw action, having been seconded to the US Army in January 1945, advancing with them through France into Germany.

Alerted by their codebreakers and spies, the government knew the Germans were poised to retaliate with new weapons, but with no knowledge of what form these would take. What was unleashed on Britain, within days of the Normandy Landings, was the first of Hitler's rumoured 'V' secret weapons, fired across the North Sea from impregnable bunkers.

'V' stood for *Vergeltung*, vengeance; high explosive, flying bombs. Droning V1s, mocked by the war-weary population as doodlebugs, cut out before falling, to give those on the ground a slight chance of escape. There was no defence against their sinister and silent cousins that struck in September 1944, rocket-pro-pelled V2s, which detonated a one ton explosive warhead on impact. On 18 June the Guards Chapel close to Buckingham Palace took a direct hit from a V1 dur-ing Sunday service. A young soldier, *whose eyes stared unseeingly at the sky,* was one of 120 people killed, most of them from the services. Coming so soon after the jubilation of D-Day, the government sought to minimise the tragedy's effect on morale by asking newspapers to spread obituary notices over several weeks.

While the raids continued on England Paris was liberated but meanwhile Holland, Norway and Denmark were occupied until the end, Panzer divisions were massing west of the Rhine and the Allies fighting their way north of Rome. Dresden was bombed in mid-February 1945. V2 rockets terrorised southern England until six weeks before VE Day, 8 May. In all, 2381 V1s and 511 V2s killed nearly 3000 in the London area, causing widespread destruction by explo-sion and fire.

Firemen, police, wardens, ambulance crews, medical staff and passers by had been in the front line for nearly six years, coping daily with situations unimagin-able in their peacetime lives: pulling the dead and injured from unstable rubble or flaming wreckage; retrieving dismembered bodies and severed limbs; restrain-ing parents plunging into burning houses to save their children; transporting sur-vivors to hospital through streets choked with ruins and exploding gas mains and, worst of all, being beaten back while hearing the cries of trapped victims cut short as the fire reached them. To add to the horror, incinerated, dehydrated adult bodies recovered from intense fires were reduced to the size of blackened chil-dren.

Many who lived through the Blitz find their fortitude discounted, and their patience sorely tried, by the 'stress, counselling and compensation' culture of the 1990s. A retired naval surgeon, then newly qualified Dr Aidan Long at the London Hospital, recalls his first emergency call of the Blitz. In addition to medical supplies he was given quantities of bromides, the tranquilliser of the day, to calm the expected hordes suffering from shock and hysteria. Neither that night, nor in the months to come, did he find anyone needing such palliatives in the devastated, grieving East End. If *London could take it*, so could the Londoners, from doctors, nurses, police and firemen to shopkeepers, bus conductors, typists, pensioners and children. Notices in front windows advised firemen how many people lived in a house, and space was left for the location of pets' sleeping baskets. Smokey and Rover were also catered for by Bob Martin's *Fit and Hysteria Pills for Pets*, guaranteed safe and effective for cats and dogs when the sirens sounded.

It occurred to few mothers to give a child so much as an aspirin. *Mummy, Mummy, what's that horrid noise? Bombs, darling, now go back to sleep again.*

Compensation for firefighters injured on duty was meagre, as were pensions for the families of those killed. Colleagues and the public made collections to help individuals worst hit and from this voluntary effort grew the National Fire Service Benevolent Fund.

By VE-Day, the London Region Fire Brigade numbered 42,000 members controlling 10,000 assorted fire fighting vehicles. During the war it had answered in excess of 50,000 calls and, with the other emergency services, saved the lives of thousands of Londoners but at a price. On the Home Front, 80,000 civilians died through enemy action and a similar number had been seriously injured. 793 firemen and 25 firewomen had been killed in England and Wales, and over 7000 injured.

London firefighters accounted for 327 of the dead, with over 3000 injured. All are commemorated by 'Blitz', a striking memorial to all the firefighters of the Second World War, unveiled by the Queen Mother in May 1991 in St Paul's Churchyard. It is based on the artist's original version in the hall of the LFCDA in Lambeth, which faces the London Fire Brigade roll of honour.

While the Fire Court argued in the aftermath of the Great Fire, John Aubrey had admired Nature's regeneration among the ruins. So it did again after the War, with many bomb sites summer bright for decades with purple sprays of rosebay willowherb, the 'fireweed' of the Blitz.

CHAPTER 20

THE FLAMING FUTURE

Kevlar, Nomex and the LFCDA

Fire—that most unpredictable of hazards

London slowly rose again from the devastation inflicted by the Blitz, and its V1 doodlebugs and V2 rockets. One of the last bombsites, on Ludgate Hill below St Paul's, was not redeveloped until the 1990s, by which time many hasty post-War buildings had already been demolished.

After the material destruction and social turmoil of six years of war, nothing could be the same again, though some tried to put back the clock. Conflicting reactions surfaced over the future of the fire service. One group wanted a swift return to 'normal', while the other sought to build on the critical lessons experienced 'under fire'. Since the National Fire Service had proved itself under the extreme conditions of war, they argued, why not retain it in peace?

The outcome was a compromise. The new Labour government honoured its predecessor's wartime promise and returned fire brigade control to local authorities. As a sop to advocates of maintaining central control, it limited these to 140, not the twelvefold pre-war figure. Old legislation was repealed and the Fire Services Act became law in July 1947, with the London County Council again responsible for the capital, an area that today extends over Greater London.

Europe at the time, and for decades after, trod a tightrope between fragile peace and cold war. Wartime alliances fractured; in 1947 tension was heightened when the Russians blockaded land routes into the German capital, an illegal act that was by-passed by the months-long allied Berlin Airlift of food and fuel.

For war-weary civilians these were anxious times under the threat of atomic attack from the East. The regrouped Auxiliary Fire Service and Civil Defence Corps called for volunteers to 'do their bit' again on the Home Front. The public were soothed by helpful leaflets, advising stockpiling food under the stairs and pasting brown paper over windows to deflect radiation. London boroughs were reminded of their legal duty to maintain high levels of Civil Defence, an order listlessly obeyed by some and ignored by others, the latter dismissing any preventive measures as futile against looming annihilation. Some local authorities would later defiantly declare themselves nuclear free zones, a message not clearly understood in the Kremlin.

In 1968 the danger was reckoned to have receded far enough for the AFS and

CDC to be quietly disbanded again.

Planes overflying Britain loaded with low-level nuclear waste for reprocessing are 20th Century radiation scares but similar fears came to a head after the 1874 Grand Union Canal explosion. The *Illustrated London News* raged against citizens being exposed to appalling dangers with gunpowder and nitro-glycerine transported as trade goods under such loose regulation that it was surprising not that such accidents happened, but that they happened so rarely.

Just as after the Great Fire, many fine City buildings, wrecked churches and familiar alleys were swept away for ever. The area between Moorgate and Whitbread's Brewery was totally flattened and eventually the controversial, new Barbican development rose above the old, street plan. Of the City's two fire stations, one is at Dowgate and the other, under threat of closure, at Barbican.

Uniforms have gradually become uniform throughout England and Wales. All firefighters now wear yellow overtrousers, rubber boots and dark blue tunics and trousers of manmade, fire resistant Nomex III. Visibility is highlighted by fluorescent strips and helmets made of non-conductive Kevlar, to withstand electric shock and heavy blows. For additional safety the new, lighter Drager PA94 breathing apparatus incorporates an automatic distress signal, activated if the user remains immobile for more than 20 seconds.

Shouts of Hi! Hi! went out with the horses and bells later gave way to sirens. Fire engines have three levels of urgency to warn traffic to pull aside: a two-tone blast, a wail and the final imperative yelp.

Special Services responding to '999' calls can face floods, building collapses, rail crashes, airline disasters, motorway pile-ups, crushed bodies, trapped passengers and injured children. Crews of four-person Fire Rescue Units are equipped with protective clothing, heavy cutting and lifting gear and power generators for emergency lighting at night or underground.

The complexity of cargoes carried by rail or road can mean spillages of sugar, flour or fertilizer, leaking oil, oxygen or treacle. The danger of explosion and fire is ever present from ruptured gas pipelines, tankers of liquefied natural gas or fallen pylons. Added to these are a poisonous cocktail of hazardous chemicals, HazChems, whose warning icons range from oxidising, irritant, environmentally dangerous to explosive, corrosive, very toxic. Back at base, any one of 50,000 entries on the computerised Chemical Information Retrieval and Updating System, CIRUS, can be accessed and relayed to the fireground.

New industries and new technology have spawned fresh hazards to add to the heat, smoke and stench familiar to the bucket-wielding, squirt-handling 18th Century firemen. Despite high pressure hoses, chemical foam and aerial ladder platforms, fires still have to be fought in perilous proximity to the flames, enervating humidity and the added horror of darkness when power supplies suddenly fail.

The cavernous halls of London's wholesale meat market are supported by cast-iron pillars; however, Smithfield is a fearsome place underground. In January 1958 fire broke out in its labyrinth of railway lines, passages, stairways, ventilation shafts and cold storage cellars. It became a choking, blinding fog when leaking acid and gas thickened the smoke, the stench augmented by burning cork, asbestos and roasting meat. Nearly 400 appliances and 1700 firemen took two days to contain the fire but not before two firemen wearing breathing apparatus were overcome and buried beneath frozen carcasses. Tally boards keep track of all those issued with apparatus during an incident; though both men were alive when found, neither survived after being rushed to Bart's Hospital.

Ashore and afloat inert gases build up in empty fuel and chemical tanks. In July 1969 fire broke out in an empty turpentine tank at Dudgeon's Wharf, Millwall. After several hours it was thought to be out and an acetylene torch was used to cut free a base cover while five firemen were still on top of the tank. The inrush of air triggered an explosion that blew off the roof and killed them all.

In November 1984 fire raged through the tube network beneath Oxford Circus station. Damage was extensive, though mercifully only a few of the thousands of passengers evacuated were injured and no lives lost. It was a terrible warning of what could happen on the London Underground, what fire brigades repeatedly warned would happen, and what did happen three years later. By then smoking had been forbidden on trains—but not on platforms, escalators or in booking halls.

Five lines converge in subterranean layers at King's Cross and around 19.30, on 18 November 1987, smoke and sparks were noticed below the Piccadilly Line 'up' escalator. At 19.36 a '999' call was logged at Wembley Fire Control. The nearest fire station was two minutes away at Euston but, by ill chance, that crew was already out on a call. It took the Soho appliance eight minutes to get through the traffic and in the light of the night's tragedy those lost minutes were deadly, even though no time was lost in tackling the emergency.

Other brigades were converging on King's Cross from all over London as the incident was constantly upgraded from the original 'Pumps Four' by Station Officer Colin Townsley. By then passengers were already trapped by the flames while firemen, struggling to contain the fire and penetrate to its source, were at the same time urging luckier dazed and choking passengers to the surface, and safety. The incandescent flash-over that burst through the concourse claimed many lives. The final toll was over thirty dead, with hundreds severely burned or suffering internal injury and agony through inhaling smoke and toxic fumes.

Random and terrifying, flash-over is an explosion of super-heated gases acting like rocket propellant on surrounding flame and smoke, enveloping, suffocating or incinerating anyone in its path. One killed was Colin Townsley, who had turned back from a clear exit to try and rescue an unconscious woman.

On 27 November Londoners and firefighters from all over Britain lined the streets for Townsley's funeral. When the flower-decked fire appliance bearing the coffin passed the blackened buildings of King's Cross, it was saluted by a thousand strong guard of honour. An empty seat was conspicuous in the following fire engine and officers of his own Soho Red Watch acted as pall bearers. Townsley was posthumously awarded the George Medal and also honoured, with so many others over more than a century, in the Firemen's Corner of Highgate Cemetery. As with Braidwood, he was remembered in verse:

> No need to ask them questions, their faces tell it all,
> They came back riding four, they were five before the call.
> ...And each will write an epitaph, to the Guv'nor they knew
> Who gave his life in a job he loved, a fireman through and through.

The enquiry attributed the outbreak to a discarded match or cigarette igniting fluff and grease beneath an ill-maintained, wooden escalator. Minor fires involving such escalators had happened several times before and London Regional Transport, who admitted that safety standards were not what they should have been, was harshly criticised for not seeing them as potential sources of danger. Equally at fault was LRT's assumption that fires were inevitable [and failing] to recognize the unpredictability of fires...that most unpredictable of all hazards.

King's Cross was yet another enquiry to add to the sorry list of inquests, investigations, commissions, surveys, studies and reports that over the centuries have tried to interpret the causes of past fires, and prevent future ones. These good intentions have consistently been thwarted by cumbersome legislation, dilatory authorities, perfunctory compliance and negligent employers. Even when the law has proved effective, there is little sanction against careless workers, thoughtless householders and malicious vandals. Audible through the confusion, and refusing to be silenced, is the voice of folk memory still whispering that fatalistic belief that fires are inevitable.

The 1980s and 1990s were a shocking sequence of fires, explosions and terrorist attacks throughout the UK, with nothing immune from destruction save that mythical marble temple under water. The white heat of technology that makes deep sea oil platforms and jet airliners possible still cannot ensure they are any less vulnerable than London hospitals and theatres, dating from the days of Braidwood and Shaw:

1983 Charing Cross Hospital, Strand, two killed; 1983 Amoco Oil Refinery, Milford Haven, explosion and fire, £10m loss; 1985 Bradford City Football ground, 56 spectators died in one wooden stand, fire probably ignited by a thrown cigarette as a King's Cross; 1988 Piper Alpha oil rig exploded in a fireball, killing 167 men; 1988 Lockerbie, Pan American airliner exploded killing all on board, suspected, but unproven, terrorism; 1990 Savoy Theatre, Strand, burned out;

1991 Downing St, Whitehall, IRA mortar attack; 1996 freight train fire led to five month closure of the Channel Tunnel.

No matter which brigades are called out to major incidents, the lessons learned are shared throughout the fire service, and techniques refined to cope with the next disaster.

Fire is a great leveller in more senses than one, with castles as vulnerable as cottages. In 1992 flames burst through the roof of St George's Hall and enveloped Windsor Castle, a sight comparable to an erupting volcano to airline pilots approaching Heathrow. Next morning the Queen inspected the smoking ruins, looking as desolate as any other owner who has seen their home ravaged by fire.

The fiery history of St Paul's shows that though lightning can strike twice in the same place, more often multiple fires have sinister causes. As in the 18th Century, companies are wary of insuring the property of anyone who has once suffered from fire. Figures taken at ten year intervals from the reports of the Association of British Insurers show the increase in genuine UK claims from £261m in 1977, to £638m in 1987 and £707m in 1996. One powerful deterrent to fraud, jointly initiated by the Home Office and the ABI in 1991, is the Arson Prevention Bureau. As well as insurers, firefighters and other experts comprise its practitioners' arm, the Forum of Arson Investigators, based at the Fire Protection Association in Hertfordshire.

The Fire Service College had moved in 1947 from its 'temporary wartime' home near Brighton to Wotton House near Dorking, owned by a Mr John Evelyn; a house surely haunted by his ancestral namesake the diarist who had witnessed the puny attempts of untrained firefighters against the whole Citty in dreadfull flames.

The Institution of Fire Engineers remains in Leicester where it was founded, but in 1986 the Fire Service Staff College left Wotton House to join the established Fire Service Technical College at Moreton-in-Marsh. This is now the Fire Service College, under Commandant Terry Glossop, where over 6000 firefighters annually, from all ranks and many countries attend training courses or refreshers.

Fainthearts need not apply since challenges include: 4-storey hot fire simulator; multi-storey building with crawling galleries, lifts and humidity chamber; floating 4000 ton concrete ship, dock and warehouse; high-rise block for collapsed building rescues, complete with sewer; 3-storey domestic house; fish and chip shop; chemical cracking plant; oil storage tank; high voltage demonstration electricity grid; rail network and six-lane motorway.

All 32 London boroughs, and the City, are represented on the London Fire and Civil Defence Authority, LFCDA. The Authority's formidable responsibility includes 113 fire stations and extends over 620 square miles, protecting a population swollen to 10m during the working week. The sole river station is at Albert

Embankment where the Dunkirk veteran 'Massey Shaw' can sometimes be seen moored alongside the 'London Phoenix', or its successor, the new 'Firehawk'.

Recruits start with the yellow helmet of Firefighter and can rise through Leading Firefighter to Sub-Officer and then to command as a Station Officer, with white helmet and thin, black band. Higher up the ladder come Assistant, then Senior Divisional Officers, Assistant and Deputy Chief Officers and finally Chief Officer, with white helmet and thick, black band. Each station has four Watches—Red, White, Blue, Green—working two consecutive days of nine hours, then two consecutive nights of fifteen hours followed by four days leave. Controllers play key roles at fire station and HQ where '999' calls are logged, priorities assessed and appliances allocated on a sliding scale from Pumps Two up to every vehicle within range. Press officers' telephones never stop ringing since the information at their fingertips is invaluable to all brigades, the police, journalists, broadcasters, politicians—and authors.

In 1996 the London Fire Brigade logged 280,000 calls and attended 188,000 incidents: 51,000 fires, 64,000 special services and 71,000 false alarms, over 16,000 of them malicious. (The coastguard answered 251 hoax calls out of 11,000, roughly the same ratio (1:5) as the LFB). Five London firefighters were killed between 1987-1996 and over 1000 members of the public, shocking statistics only slightly redeemed by the 10,000 rescued. At a major outbreak, apart from the fire engine, correctly called a pump ladder appliance, there will be a command support vehicle, aerial ladder platforms, turntable ladders, fire hose layers, pump foam units and fire rescue units.

Brian Robinson CBE joined the fire service in 1968 and was a graduate and later course director of the Fire Service College. He was appointed Chief Officer in 1991 in succession to Gerald Clarkson, and additionally Chief Executive in 1996. As chairman of the Federation of British Fire Organisations, his responsibilities include representing Britain in Europe, and internationally. A modernist, he oversaw the computerisation of the '999' service when deputy chief, and in the same fast forward mode set out his strategic plans in *Toward the Next Century*.

Many women have followed Susan Batten, the LFB's first woman recruit in 1982, although by 1880 Girton College Cambridge had sported a fire fighting force of lady students trained by Captain Shaw and adept at both hose and ladder work. In 1996 a Bristol store blaze, later proved arson, killed Fleur Lombard, the first woman officer to die on duty. (Women killed in the wartime AFS were not, officially, front line firefighters.) As a newcomer to the force, Fleur's Watch had treated her warily, but not for long, and her chief, Andrew Walters, said how fortunate his Avon brigade had been to recruit her. In a warm tribute he emphasised that Fleur was there to do the job she loved, not to make a point.

The public's love of being in at a good fire is now brought into the home by television and never have idle gazers had such choice of entertainment. Brian

Clark, seconded from the LFB, was for many years adviser on ITV's 'London's Burning', where the actual fire station of Dockhead SE1 doubles for the series' location, Blackwall. The BBC cameras countered with real life action with the Merseyside brigade in 'Firefighters', while Channel 4 filmed the challenges faced by the Baltimore Fire Department. The American city has a population of 600,000, similar to Leeds, but operates from 46 stations compared with six in Leeds.

The British TV programmes featured false alarms, a growing menace to all brigades. Many such calls are genuine mistakes made in good faith, others are caused by faults sounding off fire alarms or triggered by burning toast, but the rest are malicious. The fire brigade must answer all calls, so appliances despatched on wild goose chases are often unavailable to respond to real emergencies. Too many crews are lured by vandals to burning roadside bins, skips or derelict buildings only to be ambushed with abuse, bricks and bottles, and even flaming Molotov cocktails.

Fire brigades can enforce safety measures on hotels, hospitals, offices and factories, but only advise local authorities on the regulation of schools and hospitals since the fire service is not the enforcing body. They also advise local authorities, who have powers to grant licences to clubs and cinemas; over 60,000 premises were inspected in London in 1996. If the owner of a building that admits the public consistently fails to meet safety standards it can be closed down until such work has been done and approved.

Private houses, the majority with children, the elderly or infirm, are exempt from any regulations. A Home Office report shows most burned, occupied buildings lacked fire or smoke alarms because the perceived personal risk and general risk of fire as a cause of death and injury is low, especially amongst older age groups who are more resistant to owning an alarm. One smoke alarm above a stair well or outside the bedroom and one in the kitchen are recommended, as are portable extinguishers and fire blankets that can prevent domestic accidents from turning within seconds into fatal disasters. It is small comfort that most people recognise the chip pan as being the main cause of kitchen fires since not all are aware that smothering is the only safe way to deal with the flames. In one year in Kent, over-heated oil (chip pans) resulted in most fires from a single cause; 335 in homes against only five in commercial premises. Workmen's blowtorches maintained their dastardly reputation by causing 23 fires.

In 1997 a new Euro Standard EN3 & BS 5423 came into effect relating to portable fire extinguishers. Fire Protection Services plc explain the new directive in *Seeing Red*: a minimum of 95% of the canister must be red and only 5% of the new code zone be used to identify contents, so out go the clear-cut British colour codes of red/water, black/CO2 (carbon dioxide), cream/foam, blue/powder. Deep in the small print of this deluge of Euro-advice lies the warning that simply repainting existing extinguishers will not give compliance with EN3.

In Thorn Security's armoury are ThornNet and computer-controlled Minerva, which can evaluate 80 zones of fire detection in a building from a single control panel. Looking back over a century of fire protection systems, Thorn reckons that a high proportion of businesses are damaged beyond recovery by a serious fire and even among those that do, no insurance company however generous can ever compensate for everything lost.

Prevention is better than Fire.

Learn not to Burn is linked to the National Curriculum, with officers talking to schools and pupils, visiting local fire stations to hear from those in the front line what it means to be a firefighter. Younger children have a Play with Care book and pictorial chart showing the quickest and safest escape routes from a burning house.

In the 1990s two LFB officers, Steve Chasty and Peter Woodman of the Schools Liaison team, launched a fire safety programme in Russia supported by the charity Friends of Russian Children, FoRC, and British fire brigades. One aim, with the backing of Colonel Alexander Koryukhin of the Moscow Fire department, was to place a Russian edition of the LFB's Junior Citizens ABC Life Safety Manual in every city school, and then throughout the Russian Federation. It hardly needed the two officers' visit to a children's hospital burns unit to emphasise the need for greater fire safety and awareness.

Fire brigades help the public help themselves to safety, with all stations offering free advice and a wide range of leaflets. These cover the obvious like Keep Matches Safe, Never Smoke in Bed, Don't Overload Sockets and Smoke Kills in Seconds, the practical Know your Home Escape Plan, Get a Fire Blanket and Test Electric Blankets and also the essential *Fire Survival Guide.*

Ironically, the titles show how Londoners have often only exchanged the hazards faced by their ancestors for modern ones. Candles no longer ignite bed curtains, clay pipes seldom set fire to thatched roofs and few muskets are fired to put out blazing chimneys. But neither Lord Mayor Bludworth on his night time foray to Pudding Lane nor Lord George Gordon leading his rabble left wives and children at home to the perils of matches, smouldering cigarette stubs, frayed cables, chipped sockets, faulty televisions, gas leaks and the plumber's blowtorch.

In an issue harking back to the 18th Century fire office brigades, the LFCDA feels the Home Office places too much emphasis on risks to property rather than risk to people. The authority is also concerned that assessments fail to reflect the complexity of the diverse London area, the movement of people throughout any 24 hours and the nature of complex and dangerous industrial processes carried out in many buildings.

Another worry is the increase in legal actions brought against the fire service. One officer ordered a sprinkler system turned off in a burning building since the steam generated was hampering his men's efforts. He was later accused by the business's owner of causing the destruction of his premises. In another incident, not a fire but a fatal accident on a building site, a fire officer's authority to supervise a rescue attempt was challenged in the courts. He had arrived at the accident scene to find an operator using a mechanical digger to try and free his workmate from a collapsed trench, stopped this and insisted on manual digging efforts. Unfortunately the trapped man died, and his widow sued for compensation.

Money, as ever, is at the root of present, and past, problems. In November 1977 the old issues of low wages, long hours and, in this instance, perceived broken government pay promises resulted in nationwide industrial action. This led to the first official withdrawal of labour in the LFB's history, although it joined the strike action mainly in solidarity with other more militant brigades. (The 'Winter of Discontent' started at the end of the following year during which most public service unions went on strike over similar issues).

With fire stations closed and picketed throughout the capital, the disused tram tunnel beneath Kingsway, normally London's flood control point, became the LFB's key centre, manned by senior officers co-ordinating responses to all emergencies. The public was largely sympathetic, while many firefighters discreetly lent their expertise to the army and the police at major outbreaks but lives were still lost that might have been saved under normal conditions. Londoners' lasting memory of the dispute is of army appliances dragooned into action as fire engines. Many were crewed by troopers of the Household Cavalry, which did little to justify the seductive name of Green Goddesses for these cumbersome vehicles.

The strike started on 15 November—the day fire ravaged part of the old Charing Cross Hospital—and lasted until February 1978. By then attitudes had hardened and the LFB only reluctantly accepted the nationwide settlement. The insurance companies breathed freely again and the Green Goddesses returned to barracks, where they remain on shrouded standby for future emergencies.

Funds from central government have always been tight but the most recent budget cuts have pared resources to the bone, resources already stretched by the increasing number of officers entitled to retirement pensions and higher compensation claims.

Twenty years on from the strike, the Fire Brigade Union to which over 90% of firefighters belong is deeply concerned at planned job losses and station closures. The Department of the Environment was lobbied by firefighters in November 1997 and warned that if London's firefighters are out on strike and troops are brought on to the capital's streets, the government will have to address the issue of fire service underfunding. By January 1998 there were calls for a strike ballot after plans were announced to cut £10m from the brigade's budget.

The London Fire Brigade moved from Southwark Bridge Road to Albert Embankment in 1937, now the HQ of the LFCDA. Winchester House, once home of Captain Shaw, is now the Fire Brigade Museum with the main staircase lined with the portraits of chief officers from Braidwood to the present day. The last impressive beard belonged to the equally impressively named Sir Lionel de Latour Wells, in 1903.

Exhibits range from lead fire marks and wooden water pipes to a parish engine and a mosaic badge made from fragments of blitzed shop fronts. The Museum is, in the Chief Officer's words, *the social history of London...onwards through two world wars up to the present times when dangers to life and property come from different directions but are nonetheless threatening.* The Overseas Room is running out of shelves to display its international collection of helmets donated by visiting firemen. Firemen themselves collect memorabilia as the range of 'wants' in Collector's Piece in *London Fire Fighter* shows. Anyone swap a set of cigarette cards for a gooseneck swivel or brass elbow?

Winchester House is haunted. Not by Shaw in his silver helmet, but paupers from St Saviour's burial ground. When construction work in the 1980s turned up bones and skulls these nameless phantoms took revenge. Objects fell off shelves, helmets flew across rooms, pictures tilted askew and, most mysterious of all, a clapperless ship's bell rang out. Only when a priest blessed the reburied bones and exorcised the site did they quieten down again, or did they? Unexplained noises are still heard, certain rooms suddenly turn chill and a musty smell sweeps through them.

Believers in ghosts and believers in God must all hope the Lord harkens to the official prayer...for all who serve in the London Fire Brigade, grant to each one courage, an alert mind and sound judgment so that they may be kept safe in the midst of danger.

In 1990 the Insurers became the 91st City of London Company, the Fuellers 94th and Lightmongers 95th, all with links to the hazards of fire. Finally, over three hundred years since the Great Fire, came the Company of Firefighters to promote the development and advancement of the science, art and practice of firefighting, fire prevention and life safety...[and] good professional behaviour. Somebody with a sense of history was quick to appropriate for the new Company the London telephone number of 0171 600 1666.

The risks of terrorist or criminal attack now rival those of fire in the Square Mile with well over 500 banks and 170 security houses from 75 different countries. The 1996 Collection Fund received council tax and business rates amounting to £567m, of which the City Corporation kept only £7m. The rest was paid into the national rates pool, which supports local government and contributes towards the £276m precept of the London Fire and Civil Defence Authority. In

1997/98 only £25 of each London household's council tax was allocated to run the fire brigade—roughly 50p per week, less than the cost of a packet of firelighters.

The public pays nothing for calling out the brigade to a fire, but charges are now imposed for breaking into houses when owners forget their keys or drop them down drains, for pumping out flooded commercial premises and other non-fire mishaps. Passengers trapped in lifts are set free, free, but cats are left up trees. A fireman with years of experience insists that any moggie'll come down of its own accord when it's dark, cold, wet and hungry enough.

Of the four historic fires detailed in previous chapters, only one might strike again at any time. The odds are against any flame-haired pagan queens, revolting peasants or demented, noblemen threatening London either side of the Millennium but accidental outbreaks, like the source of the Great Fire, are as real a threat as ever.

Fire remains an insidious, ubiquitous enemy claiming lives and destroying property as it has always done, with only a thin, blue line standing between us and its fury. Firefighters combat the Fire King in the spirit that failure is not an option; the fire protection industry reckons that 50% of businesses hit by serious fire never recover; insurance companies survey the ruins in the knowledge that the price of fire is always too high.

Early recorded fires

Fires shown in italics are not London fires but are included to give an historic perspective. Also listed are several major tragedies, which while not strictly fires, involved the fire service.

AD61	Boadicea's Icenii torched Londinium
125	Hadriatic fire—accidental
1086	Aldgate to St Pauls'
1091	*Crowland Abbey*
1102	*Winchester*
1113	*Worcester, Crowland Abbey*
1116	*Bath*
1116	*Peterborough (9 days)*
1123	*Lincoln*
1130	*Colchester*
1137	*York (cathedral +39 churches)*
1140	*Nottingham*
1174	*Canterbury*
1184	*Glastonbury*
1189	*Carlisle*
1212	Southwark. Priory St Mary Overie, both ends London Bridge
1251	*Carlisle*
1272	*Norwich*
1381	Peasants' Revolt—Southwark, Savoy Palace, etc.

Fires from 1600

1666	Great Fire of London
1676	Southwark, 624 houses + town hall
1682	Wapping, 1000 houses
1691	Whitehall Palace + 150 houses
1697	Whitehall Palace—12 killed
1716	Wapping—150 houses
1718	Custom House, Thames St
1725	Wapping—70 houses (1783 & 1800)
1748	Cornhill—wigmakers, 100 houses, taverns inc. George & Vulture, coffee houses inc. Garroways, Jonathons, Jerusalem—lives lost
1765	Cornhill and adjacent streets
1761	Fishmongers Hall by London Bridge
1780	Gordon Riots—Newgate Gaol, Langdale's Distillery etc.
1791	Albion Mills, Blackfriars
1791	Rotherhithe, Cherry Garden stairs—£500,000

1791	Wellclose Sq. sugar warehouse burned 10 days—£150,000 loss
1794	Ratcliffe Cross—650 houses, East India Company warehouses worst 18th century fire with £1.1m losses, tents for homeless
1799	The Temple, Kings Bench Walk
1800	Lower Thames St—3 East India Company warehouses—loss £300,000
1814	Custom House, Thames St—loss £200,000
1814	Bankside Mustard Mills—loss £150,000
1815	The Royal Mint
1820	Rotherhithe—60 houses, many ships—loss £200,000
1821	Mile End sugar refinery—loss £200,000
1834	Palace of Westminster, Houses of Parliament
1838	The Royal Exchange (2nd fire)
1841	Tower Armoury—280,000 stands of historic armour
1844	Toppings Wharf, Tooley St, Southwark
1861	Tooley St warehouses—Braidwood killed
1882	Alhambra Theatre, Leicester Square
1886	Hampton Court Palace—£20,000 loss
1897	Great Cripplegate fire, Fire Island
1902	Queen Victoria St office building—10 workers killed
1903	*Coney Hatch, Herts Asylum—51 killed*
1909	Arding & Hobbs department store, Clapham—9 killed
1912	Barkers of Kensington, department store—5 killed
1915	*Quintinshill, Scotland—worst rail disaster—235 killed*
1914-18	The Great War—zeppelin raids
1918	Battersea, cattle feed warehouse—7 firemen killed
1921	East London timberyard—loss £1m
1923	Tobacco warehouse, docks—loss £800,000
1925	Madame Tussaud's Waxworks, Baker St—loss £200,000
1935	Colonial Wharf, Wapping—warehouses, loss £.5m loss
1940-45	Second World War—Blitz, VIs & V2s
1946	*Savernake Forest, Wiltshire—ammunition train explosion*
1951	British Rail goods storage—3 firemen killed
1958	Smithfield Central Markets—2 firemen killed
1965	Grocers Hall, Cheapside
1969	Dudgeon's Wharf, Millwall—5 firemen killed
1971	Tooley St, Southwark, warehouses
1973	Central Criminal Court, Old Bailey—IRA bombing
1974	*Flixborough Chemical works, Humberside—28 dead, loss £30m*
1978	Midland Railway warehouses, Camden Town—1 fireman killed
1980	Alexandra Palace—loss £30m
1983	St. Thomas's Hospital, Lambeth
1983	Donnington, Salop, military stores—loss £150m.
1983	Charing Cross Hospital, Strand 2 killed
1983	*Milford Haven, Amoco Oil Refinery*
1984	*York Mister Struck by lightening*

1985	Bradford City Football stadium—56 dead
1986	Hampton Court Palace—1 killed
1987	King's Cross station—31 killed, inc. 1 fireman
1988	*2nd fire Donnington military stores*
1988	*Piper Alpha oil rig, North Sea—167 killed*
1988	*Lockerbie, Scotland—Pan American airliner explosion—all killed*
1989	*M1 Motorway Leicestershire, British Midland Boeing 737—47 killed*
1990	Savoy Theatre, Strand—burned out
1991	Downing St, Whitehall—IRA mortar attack
1992	Windsor Castle, St George's Hall—restored Nov 1997
1992	Baltic Exchange, St Mary Axe, City IRA bombing
1993	Bishopsgate, St. Ethelbridga's City—IRA bombing
1996	Docklands, Canary Wharf—IRA bombing
1996	*Channel Tunnel, freight train*
1997	Heathrow Airport, Terminal 1—burger bar

The London Fire Brigades

A Fireman…must always carry his appliances with him as without them he is of no use.' Captain Shaw

Chief Officers
London Fire Engine Establishment

1833-1961	James Braidwood
1861-1865	Captain Sir Eyre Massey Shaw

Metropolitan Fire Brigade

1866-1891	Captain Sir Eyre Massey Shaw
1891-1896	James Sexton Simonds
1896-1903	Captain Sir Lionel de Lautour Wells

London Fire Brigade (LCC)

1903-1909	Rear-Admiral James de Courcy Hamilton
1909-1918	Lt.Commander Sampson Sladen
1918-1933	Arthur Reginald Dyer
1933-1938	Major Cyril Clark Boville Morris
1938/9-1938	Commander Sir Aylmer Firebrace
1938-1941	Major Frank Jackson (dep.Chf.Off LFB)

National Fire Service

1948-1962	Sir Frederick William Delve
1962-1965	Leslie William Thomas Leete

London Fire Brigade—GLC

1965-1970	Leslie William Thomas Leete
1970-1976	Joseph Milner
1977-1980	Sir Peter Howard Darby
1981-1986	Ronald Alfred Bullers

London Fire Brigade—LFCDA
London Fire & Civil Defence Authority

1986-1987	Ronald Alfred Bullers
1987-1991	Gerald Dawson Clarkson
1991	Brian Gordon Robinson
1833-66	London Fire Engine Establishment
1866-04	Metropolitan Fire Brigade

The London Fire Brigades

1904-1941	London Fire Brigade (LCC)
1941-1948	National Fire Service (NFS)
1948-1965	London Fire Brigade (LCC)
1965-1986	London Fire Brigade (GLC)
1986-	London Fire Brigade (LFCDA)

1904-1941	London Fire Brigade (LCC)
1941-1948	National Fire Service (NFS)
1948-1965	London Fire Brigade (LCC)
1965-1986	London Fire Brigade (GLC)
1986-	London Fire Brigade (LFCDA)

Further Information

London Fire Brigade Museum

Winchester House, Southwark Bridge Road SE1 — Over two centuries of fire-fighting exhibits in the old HQ of the Metropolitan Fire Brigade — visits by prior appointment only. 0171 587 2894.

London Fire & Civil Defence Authority, LFCDA HQ

8 Albert Embankment, Lambeth SE1 7SD — Fire boats sometimes moored at pier opposite

Guildhall Library

Aldermanbury, EC2 — Reference only — open to the public. 0171 606 3030

Museum of London

Barbican EC2 — Comprehensive, chronological history of London. Early fire fighting equipment. 0171 600 3699

Chartered Insurance Institute

20 Aldermanbury EC2V 7HY — 1889 Dawson Collection of fire marks and additions. Display of insurance and fire fighting items. — visits by prior appointment only. 0171 606 3835

Norwich Union Museum of Insurance and Fire Fighting Items

Surrey St, Norwich NR1 3NG — visits by prior appointment only. 01603 683343

ILLUSTRATIONS

Grateful acknowledgement is made to those who supplied photographs or prints, as well as to those who kindly permitted photography on their premises.

Cigarette cards—**Imperial Tobacco Company.** Thames waterman—**Company of Watermen and Lightermen.** Hand in Hand fireman—**Commercial Union.** Fireman Robbins; Norwich Union Firemen—**Norwich Union.** Arms—**Guild of Firefighters.** 1861 Tooley Street fire—**Sir David Burnett.** 1711 Sun firemark—**Royal & Sun Alliance.** 1748 Cornhill fire—**Guildhall Library.** Model 18th Century fireman and appliance; Model 19th Century escape ladder—**LFB Museum.** LCC fire engine—**Merryweather.** Fire helmet and gasmask—**Westerham Fire Brigade.** 1924 fire engine—**Dennis Fire.** Company fire brigade—**Whitbread Archive Collection.** Wotton House—**Fire Service College.** 1780 Newgate in the Gordon Riots—**Museum of London.** 1944 V2 rocket attack—**Selfridges Archive.** Phoenix—**Northumberland Fire Brigade.** Chance; Arms; Braidwood's funeral procession and portrait; Imperial Grenade Extinguisher; London taxi in Blitz; Women AFS recruits; Captain Shaw; Spy cartoon; Chief Officer Brian Robinson; 1997 15 pump fire—**London Fire Brigade;** Firemark collection; Arms with salamander—**Chartered Insurance Institute/Anna Milford.** 1660 London panorama G F Watts plaques in Postman's Park; 'Blitz' memorial LFCDA HQ and Firemen's Roll of Honour; Highgate cemetery; Memorial wall and Fireman Ashford's grave; Pudding Lane plaque; Monument—**Anna Milford**

Bibliography – chronological order

1603	John Stow; (1945 *Survey of London*) – Everyman Library
1641-1705	John Evelyn; *Memoirs* (publ. 1818) – Frederick Warne
1657	James Howell; *Londonopolis* – pamphlet
1660-69	Samuel Pepys; *Diary (edition 1865)* – Bell & Daldy
1666	John Crouch; *Londons Bitter-Sweet Cup of Tears* – pamphlet
(1666)	William Taswell; *Autobiography and Anecdotes* (ed. publ. 1853)
1667	*The Countries Sense of London's Suffering* – pamplet
1668	Samuel Rolle; *The Burning of London in the Year 1666* – pamphlet
	London's Tears mingl'd with her Ashes – pamphlet
1667	Samuel Wiseman; *London's Fatal Fire with its Diurnal and Nocturnal Progression*– pamphlet
1668	*An Act for the Preventing of Fires* – pamphlet
1670	Thomas Vincent; *God's Terrible Voice in the City* – pamphlet
1679	Captain Bedloe; *The Popish Plot & the Burning of London* – pamphlet
	Act in Favour of Catholics and Relief of Papists
1780	William Vincent; *Plain and Succinct Narrative of the Late {Gordon} Riots* – pamphlet
1848	William Hosking; *Guide to the Proper Regulation of Buildings in Towns* – John Murray
1851	*Crystal Palace construction Technical papers* – Inst. of Civil Engineers
1866	Charles Young; *Fire, Fire Engines & Fire Brigades* – Lockwood
1876	Eyre Massey Shaw; *Fire Protection, Complete Manual*
1884	James Compton; *Merryweather Fire Protection of Mansions*
1897	Edwin O Sachs; *Fire and Public Entertainments, 1100 Notable Fires* – Layton
1912	George Clinch; *London* – Methuen
1920	George Clinch; *Story of London's Great Fire* – Bodley Head
1926	Arthur Hardwick; *Memorable Fires in London Past & Present* – Post Magazine
1927	Bertram Williams; *Fire Marks and Insurance Office Fire Brigades* – Charles and Edwin Layton
1930s	Robert J Blackham; *London's Livery Companies* – Sampson Low
1931	Jack While; *50 Years Fire Fighting in London* – Hutchinson
1931	Sidney Gamble; *Outbreaks of Fire* – Griffin
1933	C Whittaker-Wilson; *Two Thousand Years of London* – Methuen
1942	Sydney R Jones; *London Triumphant* – Studio Publications
1942	*NFS Anthology Fire and Water* – Lindsay Drummond
1944	Jack While; *Fire! Fire! Fire Fighting in Peace and War* – Frederick Muller
1948	Robert Bignold; *Five Generations of the Bignold Family (Norwich Union)* – Batsford
1949	Cdr. Sir Aylmer Firebrace; *Fire Service Memories* – Melrose
1952	Eric Bennett; *Worshipful Company of Carmen of London* – Simpkin Marshall

210 Bibliography

1952	Aytoun Ellis; *The Hay's Wharf Story 1651-1951* – Bodley Head
1954	R F Hazell; *River Thames Wharf Directory* – Gaselee & Son Ltd
1957	G R Blackstone; *History of British Fire Service* – Routledge
1960	P G M Dickson; *Sun Insurance Office 1710-1960* – OUP
1960	John Bromley; *Armorial Bearings of the Guilds of London* – Frederick Warne
1962	Elizabeth Burton; *The Jacobeans at Home* – Secker & Warburg
1964	Bernard Ash; *The Golden City* – Phoenix House
1966	W Eric Jackson; *London's Fire Brigades* – Longman
1969	Christopher Hibbert; *London, Biography of a City* – Penguin
1970	Harold Clunn; *The Face of London* – Spring Books
1971	Patrick Beard; *The Crystal Palace*
1974	A F Scott; *Everyone a Witness, Stuart Age* – White Lion
1976	Peter Beresford Ellis; *The Great Fire of London* – New English Library
1978	Simon Goodenough; *The Story of the Fire Engine* – Orbis Publishing
1978	Anna Milford; *Ring the Bells of London Town* – Terence Dalton
1979	Gilbert Torry; *The Book of Queenhithe* – Barracuda Books
1980	Alex Forshaw; *Smithfield Past and Present* – Heinemann
1981	Neil Wallington; *Firemen at War* – David & Charles
1983	Ben Weinreb & Christopher Hibbert; *The London Encyclopaedia* – Book Club Assoc.
1984	Ronald Cox; *Oh, Captain Shaw* – Victor Green Publishing
1995	Stewart J Brown; *Dennis (Fire Engines), 100 Years of Innovation* – Ian Allan Publishing
1986	Charles whiting; *London Under Fire* – Guild Publishing
1986	George Robbins; *Tilling in London* – Capital Transport Publishing
1987	Muriel Nissel; *People Count* – History Gen. Registry Office – HMSO
1989	Brian Henham & Brian Sharp; *Badges of Extinction 18/19thC Insurance Badges* – Quiller Press (Spons. Ellis & Buckle)
1989	Norbert Ohler; *The Medieval Traveller* – Boydell Press
1989	Neil Wallington; *Images of Fire* – David & Charles
1989	*City and River* Museum of London Exhibition booklet
1992	Sally Holloway; *Courage High* – HMSO
1992	Martin Lloyd-Elliott; City Ablaze – Bloomsbury
1992	M H & R M Hazen; *Keepers of the Flame* (USA)
1990s	*History of the New River* Thames Water
1993	Illustrated London News; *Victorian Science & Engineering* – Science Museum
1996	*Corporation of London Annual Report*
1996-97	*London Firefighter* LFCDA quarterly magazine
1997	*Fire Facts London Fire Brigade* LFCDA

• • • • • • • • • • • •

Newspaper archives on tape – Guildhall Library
Library - London Transport Museum
Library – LFCDA, Southwark
Guide – London Fire Brigade Museum